THE KENNEDY WHITE HOUSE

Family Life and Pictures, 1961–1963

CARL SFERRAZZA ANTHONY

A LISA DREW BOOK / A TOUCHSTONE BOOK

PUBLISHED BY SIMON & SCHUSTER

NEW YORK   LONDON   TORONTO   SYDNEY   SINGAPORE

TOUCHSTONE
Rockefeller Center
1230 Avenue of the Americas
New York, NY 10020

For information regarding special discounts for bulk purchases,
please contact Simon & Schuster Special Sales:
1-800-456-6798 or business@simonandschuster.com

Designed by Diane Hobbing of Snap-Haus Graphics

Manufactured in the United States of America

10   9   8   7   6   5   4   3   2   1

Library of Congress Cataloging-in-Publication Data
Anthony, Carl Sferrazza.
    The Kennedy White House : family life and pictures, 1961–1963 / Carl Sferrazza Anthony.
        p.   cm.
    "A Lisa Drew book."
    "A Touchstone book."
    Includes bibliographical references and index.
    1. Kennedy, John F. (John Fitzgerald), 1917–1963–Family–Pictorial works.   2. Kennedy, John F.
(John Fitzgerald), 1917–1963–Pictorial works.   3. Presidents–United States–Family relationships–
Pictorial works.   4. White House (Washington, D.C.)–Pictorial works.   5. Washington (D.C)–
Social life and customs–1951–Pictorial works.   I. Title.
E843.A58   2001
973.922'092–dc21   2001034769

ISBN 0-7432-2221-0

Unless otherwise noted, all photos courtesy of the John F. Kennedy Library.

Page 4: *Jack, Jackie, and their children, just below the spot where Jackie threw her bouquet on their wedding day. Newport, 1961.*

CONTENTS

To Rich, Bill, Kitty, and all of the Sullivans

1

A FAMILY AFFAIR

The Inauguration, January 20, 1961

> *This is what I've been looking forward to for a long time. It's a great day.*
> —AMBASSADOR JOSEPH P. KENNEDY

> *President Kennedy swears to uphold the Constitution. From now on, no Kennedy will serve more than two terms, waiting his turn until his older brother is through.*
> —WASHINGTON STAR POLITICAL HUMOR COLUMN, "POTOMAC FEVER," JANUARY 20, 1961

The elderly woman who unobtrusively slipped into Holy Trinity Catholic Church in Georgetown later recalled that she was "bundled up with a lot of funny-looking scarves." She had reason to be. The night before, a freak storm had covered Washington, thick white flakes falling slowly but constantly. The morning sun glazed the virgin banks of snow all over the capital city, as if it were indeed some flawlessly tailored movie set staged by the heavens—or at least by old Joe Kennedy. Despite the outward physical beauty, it was still a biting twenty degrees, and the temperature would not rise through the day.

Once in church, the woman was stunned to see her eldest son come in. "I hadn't urged him to go. I would have except that I thought he was so severely overwrought with work and with responsibilities," she said. "But the fact that he did go on his own, and did think it was important to start his new administration out with mass in the morning, gave me a wonderfully happy feeling." As mass ended, she made her way outside and smilingly stopped a Secret Service agent as he and his colleagues hustled to their backup cars and the president-elect's limousine. "I'm the president's mother. Will you please have someone come with a car, and pick me up and take me to my house?" He looked at the old woman bundled in babushka and galoshes and said "Sure." The car never came. "Evidently he thought I was either an imposter or demented. . . ."

Rose Kennedy had rigid and absolute ideas on the central role that Catholicism played in her life, and she hoped and urged that it would be just as vital to her children. She didn't manipulate them emotionally to do what she wanted—she just expected them to. Not letting her son know she was at the church was typical of her. She could be physically remote from her eldest son when it came to motherly affection, despite the fact that she was wrapped up in her children's well-being and success. Her parental instincts were, however, no match for those of her husband. Joseph Patrick Kennedy not only told his children—especially his sons—what to do and how to do it, but he expected them to do it flawlessly, at least to all outward appearance. He demanded nothing less—and rewarded them richly with laughter, material comfort, and unconditional love. His bark, however, was often worse than his bite, and his now-adult children were as comfortable ribbing and teasing him as he had always been with them.

The night before, Rose had permitted herself a rare public display of affection as she held Joe's hand while drinking in the glamour of the 1961 Inaugural Gala. It was a moment of personal triumph for her, she who had raised the man about to become president. "I wanted power," Joe Kennedy bluntly admitted later that year. "I thought money would give me power, so I made money only to discover that it was politics that really gave a man power. So I went into politics."

Rose had endured forty-six years in a marriage to this odd character—the ruthless and utterly independent seventy-two-year-old former ambassador to Great Britain, movie mogul, investment banker, real estate entrepreneur, and multimillionaire grandson of poor Irish Catholic immigrants. He loved to shower her with gifts, but he had also tested her loyalty with his frequent pursuit of other women. Like most wives of her era, Rose believed that her children were her most tangible achieve-

ments, and watching her son live to be feted by the world was in itself a feat. Her eldest son, Joe, had died at twenty-nine in a 1944 plane crash as a navy pilot during World War II. Their second eldest daughter, Kathleen, had also died in a plane crash, at age twenty-eight in 1948. The eldest daughter, Rosemary, now forty-two years old, was living in an extended care home in Wisconsin; she was mentally retarded, and her condition had been worsened by a then-experimental operation intended to limit her unpredictable behavior.

The world did not yet know much about Rosemary or her condition, but there were more than enough Kennedys to keep the world distracted at the 1961 inaugural events. Besides the president-elect, John Fitzgerald ("Jack"), there were his brother Robert Francis ("Bobby") and his wife, Ethel; brother Edward Moore ("Teddy") and his wife, Joan; sister Eunice ("Eunie," as she was sometimes called) and her husband, Sargent Shriver; sister Patricia ("Pat") and her movie star husband, Peter Lawford; and sister Jean and her husband, Stephen ("Steve") Smith. What made the Kennedys radically different from previous First Families was that the public already knew their names and faces. Not only were there many of them, but they had all been repeatedly photographed and seen on television during the 1960 campaign.

If the family had already faced early death and illness, it was also blessed with longevity. Kennedy would be the only president of the United States who was to have a grandparent alive to witness his swearing-in. Unfortunately, ninety-five-year-old Josie Fitzgerald was too frail to leave the home she shared with her son Tom and his wife, but she was

THE PRESIDENT'S PARENTS

JOSEPH PATRICK KENNEDY,
    BORN SEPTEMBER 6, 1888

ROSE ELIZABETH FITZGERALD,
    BORN JULY 21, 1890

MARRIED OCTOBER 7, 1914

there in spirit. Days before, Tom had found the family Bible in their attic, a Catholic Bible, wrapped it in a shopping bag, and turned it over to Secret Service agents. It was the Bible upon which Kennedy would place his right hand and repeat the presidential oath. In her extraordinarily simple, old-fashioned living room in Dorchester, a suburb of Boston, Josie Fitzgerald, like millions of other Americans that day, turned on her television set to watch the Kennedys.

The daughter of Irish immigrants, Josie had known poverty and tragedy. A sister had drowned, a brother lost his leg in a train accident, two siblings died as babies, and two others were alcoholics. She married her second cousin John Fitzgerald. It was obvious to relatives that she was loved by him, but by the time he became mayor of Boston in 1906, "Honey Fitz," as he would be called, also confessed to the *Boston Post*, "Me for the pretty girls . . ."

As she raised her three sons and three daughters, Josephine never acknowledged emotionally unpleasant matters or problems. This might now be termed "dysfunctional," but her response represented the survival and social mechanisms of all women of that era. The idea of divorce was not even mentioned. If her husband was unfaithful, it was something to be accepted—for he also loved Josie and the children, and remained devoted to their well-being. Her social life was anchored to the Catholic world of Irish Boston. Her primary devotion was to the Church and its leaders. "To my mother," said her eldest daughter, Rose, "the Church was a pervading and abiding presence." She held a "conviction that children need firm discipline. . . . She brought us up quite strictly. . . . She made it clear we were to behave ourselves . . . be punctual, neat, and mannerly." All of this had been part of Rose's inculcation—along with the bright

Just before his death, former Boston mayor John "Honey Fitz" Fitzgerald told his grandson and namesake, John Fitzgerald Kennedy, "You are the one to carry on our family name. And mark my word, you will walk on a far larger canvas than I." Yet he also reminded his grandson "how fleeting our small political battles are compared with the enduring legacy of family." 1948.

lights of fame and enjoyment of reflected glory she experienced as the mayor's daughter.

Josephine Fitzgerald boasted quite a roster of descendants. Through her sons Tom, Fred, and John, and her daughter Agnes, were born about a dozen great-grandchildren, but it was through Rose that Josie had the largest legacy. Although none of the toddlers and young adolescents (the eldest was nine years old) would be seen during any of the inaugural, their sheer number was already newsworthy. Along with the president-elect's own two children, Joe and Rose had sixteen other grandchildren. The Robert Kennedys had three daughters and four sons, the Edward

President Kennedy with his grandmother Josephine Fitzgerald. BOSTON HERALD

Kennedys had one daughter, the Shrivers had two sons and one daughter, the Lawfords had two daughters and one son, and the Smiths had two sons. By the time the administration ended, there would be three more grandchildren. Nor had her most famous progeny forgotten Josie. The Sunday after the November election, on his way back from church, the president-elect stopped off at a modest house on an undistinguished road not far from the family's rambling "compound" of summer homes in Hyannis Port on Cape Cod. The delicate Josie lived here for most of the summer and fall in a tiny house bought for her by her son-in-law Joe. She came out on the porch to welcome the president-elect, but was uncertain how to behave in front of

the dozens of photographers taking their picture and shouting questions at her. He protectively told her, "Just look at me, Grandma." He held her hand. She patted his arm. "You're the next president!"

The family had begun flocking to the capital three days before the inauguration. On Tuesday morning, January 17, Joe and Rose Kennedy arrived from Palm Beach in rough weather. Already in Washington were the Smiths, who had a home in Georgetown, and the Robert Kennedys, who had a home in suburban Virginia. Ted and Joan Kennedy, and Joe and Rose stayed together in a rented Georgetown home, while the Shrivers stayed with the Smiths. The Shrivers would soon enough become permanent residents of the capital city, relocating from their home in Chicago to a rented estate in the Maryland suburbs, a large house called Timberlawn. Also in Washington, working against the clock, was Peter Lawford. With his close friend Frank Sinatra, Lawford was organizing the Inaugural Gala, a showcase of dance, music, comedy, singing, and dramatic readings by famous performers.

Staying at the downtown Statler Hilton with Sinatra, Lawford was caught up in the frenzy of rehearsals while his wife, the president-elect's sister Pat, stayed with the Robert Kennedys in suburban Virginia. Lawford had arrived in Hollywood in the 1940s, befriending young stars like Nancy Davis, the wife of actor Ronald Reagan; Shelley Winters; Montgomery Clift; Liz Taylor; Debbie Reynolds; and Marilyn Monroe. The teen idol of his day, however, was the man Lawford seemed most to emulate, the great Sinatra. They had first become friends while working together on the 1947 film *It Happened in Brooklyn*. Lawford was now part of Sinatra's inner circle of show business buddies, often performing together as an emblem of youthful cool in dinner jackets as the "Rat Pack." The group was made cooler by its absolute integration: African American Sammy Davis Jr., Jewish Joey Bishop, and Italian American Dean Martin. A lot of negative things would later be connected to Lawford—his substance abuse, his womanizing—and some consider him Jack's family connection to a darker side of underworld businessmen, molls, and showgirls. What would never be said of Lawford was that he had any racial bigotry, a rare attribute among wealthy white American circles in 1961.

The president-elect flew in to the capital from Palm Beach several hours after his parents. He immediately headed to his home in Georgetown, where—with his wife and children still in Florida—he held meetings among the packing boxes. That night, he and his parents went to his sister Jean's house, where she and her husband, Steve, held an early evening party for over a hundred guests including both family, old friends, and the stars who had been imported from Broadway and Hollywood to perform at the Thursday night gala. Jean was the youngest of the four living sisters and, in many ways, the most traditional, wife and mother of two little boys. Steve was the grandson of an Irish immigrant who became wealthy in the New York tugboat industry; the other grandfather had been a congressman. He had worked as coordinator of Jack's campaign schedule and as a general manager. Now Steve and Jean would live in Washington while he worked for Jack's State Department. All around the lawn were large white heated tents. Rose made her appearance in a dazzling Givenchy gown. Jack wore an equally dazzling tuxedo and smile.

Jack left directly for New York—dressed in black tie—where he stayed through part of Wednesday for a round of further meetings, including one with the governor of Puerto Rico on Latin American affairs. There was also some personal business: visits to the dentist and to the tailor for his inaugural suit. The tailor let it slip that Kennedy had gained some weight and the suit had to be altered, a public revelation that irritated the incoming president, who was extraordinarily conscious of his image.

In the week preceding the inaugural, Kennedy declared that the headgear for his event would be the traditional top hat, as opposed to the homburg, which had been worn at Eisenhower's inaugural. He hated any sort of hat, and usually he went without one. But the occasion called for it. He returned to Washington that Wednesday night. On Thursday he conferred with President Eisenhower at the White House, then with the Chairman of the Joint Chiefs of Staff and his designated heads of the FAA and the Labor Department. As he made his way to an AFL-CIO meeting, Kennedy carried a fedora he had been given by the milliner's union. It was, in fact, a serious matter. By going bareheaded in winter so frequently, Kennedy was setting a dangerous example for the extinction of the American men's hat—or so the union believed when it looked at its suddenly sinking sales report. As he emerged from the meeting, the union proudly boasted that the president-elect had ordered another hat. Nevertheless, they probably saw the writing on the wall: the fact that he wore the fedora briefly as he emerged from the building and headed to his car had less to do with his sudden embrace of hat wearing than with the rapidly accumulating heavy snowflakes that had begun falling that morning. Six inches were expected, and the city went into a panic.

Despite the snow, the president-elect and his wife made it over to Constitution Hall for a concert of classical music. Getting from there to the armory for the gala was managed only because paths were cleared and streets with less accumulation were used. As the limousine zigzagged through some residential neighborhoods, Jack piped up, "Turn on the lights so they can see Jackie!" The gala was a fund-raiser intended to bring in over a million dollars to pay off the campaign debt. The Kennedys managed to get to the armory through the blinding snowstorm now quietly blanketing the usually bustling capital in a cape of gleaming white. The Inaugural Gala was hopelessly delayed, most of the seats in the cavernous old building empty, its intended revelers stuck in Cadillacs stalled in snowbanks along the way. At one hundred dollars a seat and ten thousand dollars a box, about twenty thousand people had been expected. When Jack and Jackie finally got there at ten-thirty, only some eight thousand people had managed to get through

the drifts to the armory. Nevertheless, the show went on ten minutes later.

This gala was an intended moment of glory not only for producers Sinatra and Lawford, but also for the latter's wife—the president-elect's sister Pat. Strains in the Lawford marriage were apparent but not beyond repair. Since the days she had dated the English actor, Pat's father had saucily—and sarcastically—denigrated Lawford, as if supporting his daughter by acting was less manly than politics or business. "I raise them to be active in public service," said Joe Kennedy, "and everyone is. Every one of my sons-in-law, too. All except Peter Lawford."

During the Inaugural Gala, the president-elect had seated Pat proudly and prominently at his left side throughout the show, and later publicly thanked Sinatra and "my sister Pat's husband" for it. Seated near his father because they both smoked cigars, Kennedy took in every act—Harry Belafonte, Ethel Merman, Bette Davis, Jimmy Durante, Milton Berle, Sidney Poitier, Tony Curtis, Janet Leigh, Gene Kelly, Nat King Cole, Shirley MacLaine, Angie Dickinson, Ella Fitzgerald, Laurence Olivier, Leonard Bernstein, Fredric March, Louis Prima and Keely Smith, and Helen Traubel. Jack's neighbor in Georgetown, artist Bill Walton, watched the president-elect and recalled, "He saw the whole thing and adored it—sat in the front of the box, with a big cigar, and you knew this was one of his great moments; you could tell, because it was all aimed at him. Here was the reigning prince, and he was loving it."

The princess, though, was not loving it. Managing to sit through it all was a physically and emotionally spent Jacqueline Kennedy in a white gown. She was on the verge of collapse. At one o'clock, she slipped out and into her car, hoping to get a good night's sleep. An hour later, the moment the gala was over, a caravan of Kennedy cars left for Paul Young's, a Washington restaurant that had been rented out by Joe for a private party. It didn't get going until 2 A.M. As one of the new president's best friends, Paul "Red" Fay, made his way in, escorting the starlet Angie Dickinson, Joe Kennedy barked at him, "Wait until I tell your wife how you are conducting yourself!" Joe then turned to Angie and snapped, "Why are you wasting your time with a bum like this fellow?" They all laughed, and Joe waved them in as he greeted more of his arriving guests.

Jack arrived soon after. When he spotted Dave Powers and Kenny O'Donnell, his two aides at the core of what would be called his Irish Mafia (or, as Jackie called them, "the Murphia"), he couldn't resist a swipe in a tone similar to his father's gruff humor: "You two are living like presidents. I suppose you'll be laughing it up here for another three hours after I go home and get into bed with my inaugural address." Jack then found Red, one of the few individuals the president-elect genuinely confided in. He pulled him into the restaurant pantry and excitedly asked, "Have you ever seen so many attractive people in one room? I'll tell you, Dad knows how to give a party." Jack stayed for an hour and a half, indulging in the lobster and champagne dinner.

The next morning, after church at Holy Trinity, Kennedy briefly stopped to unveil a plaque at a small ceremony across the street from his home. Noticing that many of the reporters had on homburg hats, Kennedy quipped, "Didn't you get the word? It's top hat time." As he began dressing in his cutaway coat, light pearl waistcoat, and gray striped trousers for the ceremonies, he found that he didn't have the right type of collar. In such a frantic moment, Jack turned to the person he always sought out in a crisis—his father. Joe Kennedy sent over one of his wing collars. This

time, however, even Joe couldn't help. Jack had gained too much weight; the collar wouldn't close. This set off a hunt for other collars. Finally, a large one was found in a pile in the back of the president-elect's sock bureau.

With eight inches of snow on the ground, Inauguration Day began. While Jack and Jackie headed a motorcade over to the White House for coffee with the Eisenhowers, outgoing Vice President and Mrs. Nixon, and incoming Vice President and Mrs. Lyndon B. Johnson, the new extended First Family began taking their places on the inaugural stand.

Capturing much of the day's activity around the new president was a photographer named Cecil Stoughton. An army lieutenant, he was an aide to the army's General Chester "Ted" Clifton, who served as the new president's military aide. Clifton had suggested that Stoughton come to take pictures that day. Eventually he became the family's most intimate chronicler, traveling with the president not only to official events but also to family parties, holidays, and vacations, and photographing their everyday lives. Stoughton, National Park Service photographer Abbie Rowe, and naval photographer Robert Knudsen would create a magnificent archive of tens of thousands of photographs, the first thorough pictorial chronicle of a First Family. It was only coincidence that it was the first First Family to engender such international fascination.

Clifton witnessed an incredibly private incident—one neither Kennedy's most cynical enemies nor his most adulatory friends would have anticipated. In the moments before he was to take the oath of office, the soon-to-be Commander in Chief sheepishly asked his subordinate, "Could you arrange it so that Mrs. Kennedy and I can have a private word?" A room was cleared, and the couple went in and closed the door for a few minutes.

Left to right, first row: Pat Nixon, Mamie Eisenhower, Lady Bird Johnson, Jackie Kennedy; left to right, second row: Pat Lawford, Bobby Kennedy (head turned), Eunice Shriver, Edith Wilson. January 20, 1961.

Whatever he said to her was never disclosed by either, but undetected by even some of those who knew him longest was Jack's growing dependence on his wife's love and support.

Photographers set off a blinding series of white flashes that bounced off the glazed snow on the Capitol Building when Jackie Kennedy, in beige hat and beige coat, which was trimmed with light brown-colored sable, descended to the platform. Jackie sat on the right side in seat 1, row A. On her right were Lady Bird Johnson in green, Mamie Eisenhower in red, Pat Nixon in blue, and two rows behind Mamie, in violet, Edith Wilson—who managed to crane herself into most photographs. Near these First Ladies were the rest of the Kennedys.

Next to Mrs. Nixon sat Joe Kennedy, then Rose Kennedy, and, at the end of the row, Ann Gargan, Rose's niece, who had become a companion to her uncle Joe. Behind Mamie, in row B, sat the Shrivers, the Lawfords, Ethel Kennedy, and the

Smiths. In row C, behind Joe, Rose, and Ann, sat Teddy and Joan Kennedy, and the president's best friend—the only non–blood relative almost always included in family events—Lemoyne "Lem" Billings. In the last row, row E, behind Ted and Joan, sat Janet and Hugh Auchincloss, Jackie's mother and stepfather. Robert Kennedy was seated in row D, with the cabinet.

In the most unprecedented example of presidential nepotism, the new president's brother would be the attorney general. Bobby had not wanted the job, and spoke out consistently against taking it. Jack was especially resistant to the idea. "I don't know what's wrong with him. Jack needs all the good men he can get around him down there," Joe complained. "There's none better than Bobby." Other ideas had floated right after the election: couldn't Bobby take over JFK's soon-to-be-vacated Senate seat, run for governor of Massachusetts, or work in the White House as a chief of staff? However, Joe wanted Bobby to be attorney general, and even two of his adult sons combined could not overcome his will.

Despite the fact that Jack was about to become president of the United States, he was still the son of Joseph P. Kennedy. During Christmas, at the family's Palm Beach home, Jack coaxed his friend and Senate colleague George Smathers of Florida to casually approach Joe at the other end of the pool and try to persuade him out of his ambition to have Bobby head the Justice Department. Joe not only exploded at him but jumped up and marched right over to the president-elect. "Goddamn it, Jack, I want to tell you once and for all," he yelled at his son. "Bobby spilt his blood for you. He's worked for you. And goddamn it . . . I want him to be attorney general, and that's it."

The president-elect reverted to role. "Yes sir," he replied, dutifully subdued. In the end, Jack explained, "Ah, hell, you can't fight the old man." Now onboard with his father, Jack determined to make the appointment—although he still cringed at the inevitable criticism he would soon get in what should otherwise have been a delightful "honeymoon" with the press. "I'll open the front door of the Georgetown house some morning about two A.M.," he joked, resigned to making the announcement, "look up and down the street, and if there's no one there, I'll whisper, 'It's Bobby.'"

Still, Bobby refused the entreaties of all his siblings and parents. Jack called him to meet over breakfast at his house, explaining, "I need the help of my brother, more than I need anyone else." It was a done deal. The next day, Jack had him return to his Georgetown house where they would stand together on the steps and announce the appointment to the press. As they reached for the door, Jack suddenly stopped and looked sternly at his younger brother. "Comb your hair," he told him. "And don't smile too much or they'll think we're happy about the appointment." As the expected editorial attacks began, Jack tried to joke again, "I see no harm in giving my brother a little legal experience before he goes out to practice law."

Bobby—now his brother's closest confidant—could be harsh and demanding; some used the word *ruthless* to describe him, too, as they did his father. But he never expressed dismay at being seated with the Cabinet, so far away from his brother at this historic moment. Rose Kennedy, however, was quite flustered. "That day I was going to suggest that they put the father and mother nearer to their son," she later smilingly complained. "We were way at the end of the row, and in a lot of pictures you couldn't see us at all." It was said with as much pride and frustration as a mother in a bad seat at her son's high school graduation.

Rose, however, had only wanted a picture with

Rose and Joe Kennedy watching their son's inaugural—from behind a pillar. 1961.

TIME-LIFE

her son to remember that day. She was more hurt that Joe was not taking center stage. "As Jack's mother, I am confident Jack will win because his father says so, and through the years I have seen his predictions and judgments vindicated almost without exception," she had written in her diary that previous June. Whatever bruises she might have suffered as a result of her husband's dalliances, Rose kept her feelings locked within herself and never spoke about them—emulating her own mother. Her wifeliness, however, was no act. She believed in and loved her husband—and she wanted him to get his due. "I doubt," she wrote in her diary, "[Joe] will ever get credit for the constant, unremitting labor he has devoted to making his son President."

Jack, however, had done his part to credit his father. The day after the election, when the family gathered in victory at the Hyannis armory, sister Pat recalled that her father, who "never wanted even to imply any credit to himself for Jack's successes," decided to "stay at home out of the range of photographers and reporters. Jack suddenly realized what was happening. He went out of the car, went back up to the porch, and told Dad to come along. . . . Jack insisted on it. And finally he talked Daddy into getting into our car."

The Roman Catholic cardinal of Boston, His Eminence Richard Cardinal Cushing, had long served unofficially as the Kennedy's family priest, and it was he who delivered the invocation. As he droned on a bit, Jackie was seen gently smiling. The events leading up to this moment had been triumphant for the star of the moment, Jack, with his broad white smile, his golden tan, and his thick auburn hair, the youngest man to be elected president. It was not hyperbole to say he looked like a movie star and enjoyed every moment of it, his renowned charisma shining forth. The anticipation of seeing Jackie, however, was all the more intense because she had briefly been spotted only once, like the bride before the wedding.

On Wednesday, January 18, she had arrived from Palm Beach on the *Caroline,* Joe Kennedy's private twin-engine Convair plane, later purchased and owned jointly by Jack and his siblings. Held behind a steel lattice fence on the tarmac at National Airport, "women's page" reporters frantically tried to soak up details of her clothes—red beret and plaid tweed suit—as photographers snapped in a frenzy. She stood there somewhat dumbfounded for about fifteen seconds, palpably self-conscious, uncertain whether to move close to the fence and shake hands or even acknowledge the crowd. She gave a quick little wave, barely raising her arm, feeling the attention was silly. While

Jack and Jackie Kennedy at the christening of their son John. 1960.

the Kennedys partied and friends and family flew in from all over the world, Jackie withdrew even further. Part of her apprehension was undoubtedly from the anxiety about, as she said, "losing your anonymity at thirty years old."

She also had serious health concerns. On November 25, Jackie had given birth to her son John. He was premature by five weeks and was placed in an incubator for a lung development condition. Jackie had undergone problematic cesarean surgery and remained hospitalized for fourteen days. Her obstetrician, John Walsh, announced that she would likely require six full months of recovery time. Unfortunately, this all occurred during the transition period, and there were heavy demands on her as her family prepared to move into the White House. Jackie was given permission by her doctors to tour the private quarters of the White House with Mrs. Eisenhower only on the condition that she do so in a wheelchair. No such chair was provided, and she had to walk up and down stairs for several hours. She was breaking up her Georgetown home and also planning for another move, into a rented weekend home in Virginia.

The plan to have her recuperate in her in-laws' Palm Beach home was an unmitigated disaster. There was constant disruption: transition staff and her husband's advisers, reporters and photographers coming in and out of the house, details and decisions she needed to address quickly. On top of this she worried about her delicate infant. She had already lost one baby in miscarriage and another as a stillborn. Overriding all of this was the fact that she was an intensely private person, which made her extremely shy and demure. She also likely suffered some separation anxiety at leaving the baby and her three-year-old daughter, Caroline, in the midst of all the life changes, with their nanny in Florida. The end result of this was not only a continuance of weak physical health but also overwhelming waves of fear. While she was successful at masking her deep anxieties to some degree, they inevitably emerged, usually in what she intended to be sharp wit but which often came out as cruel sarcasm, followed by delayed mortification for what she had said. Her one real confidante, her sister, Lee, was herself recovering from the difficult premature cesarean delivery of her daughter Tina and living in London, and was unable to attend the inaugural. So Jackie forced herself to put on an act, as if everything were swell. Young, trim, tanned, Jackie and Jack were the picture of health to the public. It would have been hard to convince people otherwise—had the Kennedys even wanted to.

They had already learned that much of the public did not always want reality from a First Family.

Jackie herself recalled the days preceding the inaugural: "I had been in my room for days, not getting out of bed. All the details were getting too much. . . . I was just in physical and nervous exhaustion because the month after the baby's birth had been the opposite of recuperation. I missed all the gala things. . . . I always wished I could have participated more in those first shining hours with him, but at least I thought I had given him the son he longed for. . . . The period was not the happy time in my life that it looks like in all the pictures. . . ."

Jack Kennedy had his own health problems, but his Addison's disease was something that could be concealed. It could eventually kill him, depleting his body's natural ability to fight off infection. For now, cortisone shots helped keep it at bay. The only visible sign of the disease was a slight golden glow to his skin—Kennedy's perpetual tan. Hiding the constant low-grade pain in his lower back and shooting nerve pains down his leg, caused by a ruptured disk, forced him to be an actor about physical agony. Under the care of Dr. Janet Travell, he received shots to reduce the tissue swelling and relax the muscles. On Inauguration Day, he appeared perfectly fine. Underneath his formal morning suit, however—and the public did not know this—he had to wear a tight brace corset for the pain. In the hypermasculinized mid–twentieth century, Jack Kennedy made himself into the virtual national role model for the tough, stoic, man's man who above all refused to express weakness or pain in any form. The fact that he immediately shed his coat and hat in the bitter cold as he approached the inaugural stand was a move calculated to bolster that image.

As she watched Jack place his hand on her

mother's Bible, where her own birth and christening were recorded, Rose Kennedy was overcome with religious feelings. "Thanksgiving to almighty God that I, out of all the millions of mothers in the world, on this day I was the mother of the president-elect," she later described her thoughts, "the humble gratitude of a mother to her God for endowing her son with the courage, determination, dedication which made it possible for him to be elected to that great office."

As the new president delivered his eloquent inaugural speech, in which he famously beseeched his fellow citizens, "Ask not what your country can do for you—ask what you can do for your country," his wife watched him intensely, her eyes never wandering from his face. With strong and specific ideas about the dignity required for and about everything having to do with the presidency, Jacqueline Kennedy anticipated her husband's inaugural speech as the most important moment of the day—not the dreaded balls and the hordes crammed into them.

As the ceremony ended and distinguished guests and the family ascended the steep stairs, it was Jackie who this time requested a moment with *him*. In the rush of it all, the best she got was his brief attention in the Rotunda of the Capitol, where he stopped to look into her eyes. "There was so much I wanted to say!" she later recalled. "But I could scarcely embrace him in front of all those people. So, I remember I just put my hand on his cheek and said, 'Jack, you were so wonderful.' " It was a move quite typical of the couple. If other people were around, they were tentative, almost deeply embarrassed by any display of emotion. This was not so much Jackie's natural reaction—for she was more likely to impulsively hug and kiss her husband. She might have begun their life together with a romanticized version of him, but he was cer-

tainly still (and would remain) the great love of her life. She, however, had learned to react more as he would, and at least try to be more like him. He became antsy and squeamish about anything even suggestive of romantic emotion. He ordered photographers never to snap him kissing or hugging his wife.

While Jack did not want his macho public image compromised, his relationship with his wife was not as absolute as they both tried to convey. Jackie knew Jack like a book, and he used her sensibilities often to guide his own thinking on matters of performance. Of his speech itself, the often humorously archaic Jackie compared it to "Pericles' funeral oration." She had actually heard a good many pieces of the speech. While she and Jack rather conspiratorially kept from the public the fact that they discussed political affairs such as personnel, speechwriting, scheduling, and, generally, the influence of personality on domestic and foreign policy, she was constantly educating herself about her husband's work—whether it was silently taking in the discussions and debates he had with some of his advisers in their home or gently including herself in a political discussion with him and an ambassador or a cabinet member who happened also to be a close friend to both of them. Among the bonds that kept them cemented were their discussions about the fickle, quicksilver nature of human behavior.

As the ceremony broke up, President and Mrs. Kennedy and the new attorney general and his wife headed to a private luncheon in the Capitol Building. Meanwhile, at the Mayflower Hotel, buses marked FAMILY were dropping off dozens of Kennedys and Fitzgeralds along with Jackie's paternal relatives, the Bouviers; her maternal relatives, the Lees; and her stepfather's relatives, the Auchinclosses. The crowd included people of every

Jackie and Jack Kennedy moments after his inaugural. 1961. WIDE WORLD

The inaugural luncheon for the new president (far left). Between Jackie Kennedy and Lady Bird Johnson sits Chief Justice Earl Warren. Bess Truman is second from right.

imaginable age, socioeconomic sphere, and political persuasion—from Park Avenue society matron Maude Davis, the paternal aunt of the First Lady, in pearls and mink, to one-year-old Kerry Kennedy, who crawled and haltingly walked about with her bottle; from the president's Fitzgerald first cousins, who drove all the way down from Boston, caravan-style, never having been to Washington before, to the First Lady's wealthy Lee first cousins, who jetted in from their home in South America.

The crowd quickly assembled into five tribes after circling each other at the buffet tables, sitting at round tables in corners of the room. "Just who are these freeloaders?" Joe Kennedy blasted to the new White House social secretary, Tish Baldrige. "Your family, Mr. Ambassador," she replied. Joe

Kennedy had a signature way of speaking. He could strike terror in many a millionaire's heart with his acerbic, biting, and harsh declarations—but they were often lined with a sarcastic wit and smart humor. He walked up to some of the lunching strangers and flatly asked their names. He returned to Baldrige, "his eyes twinkling," as she recalled. "This is going to cost me a lot of money," he roared, then smiled. "But you're right. They are all family. And it's the last time we get 'em all together, too, if I have anything to say about it."

Once both luncheons were over, all branches of the families began making their way toward Pennsylvania Avenue. President and Mrs. Kennedy headed the motorcade down the avenue in an open car, waving to the tens of thousands of freezing but enthusiastic citizens in hats, gloves, scarves, furs, and cloth coats. As the cavalcade turned up Fifteenth Street, Jackie gave her husband a persistent nudge and whispered to him. He turned suddenly to look up at a specific window of the Treasury Building. Gathered there and waving to him were his Kennedy nieces and nephews. Their parents and grandparents were making their way at that moment to the parade reviewing stand, just around the corner, built in front of the White House.

Joe and Rose were already sitting in the front row of the reviewing stand when the car carrying the new president and First Lady passed. In a gesture later heralded as an important one, Jack rose in his open car and tipped his hat to his father. However, when Jack entered the reviewing stand and Joe stood up for *him*, Rose recognized the more amazing turning point in their relationship. "There are no accidents in politics," Joe quipped about his high visibility that day. "I can appear with him anytime I want to now."

Joe's sitting alongside his son on the inaugural stand was the most public moment the president and his father were to have together. During the campaign, Joe stayed out of sight, knowing there was great speculation about him—rumors of rum-running, allegations of anti-Semitism and pro-Nazism during the war, his friendship with Senator Joseph McCarthy, the use of his millions to underwrite the campaign. Rose said Joe continued to be instrumental to the campaign, but "in his own way." As she rather bluntly added at the time, "[It] seems better for Jack at this time that his father stay out of things." Behind the scenes, in the days before the inaugural, Joe had been his usual self—hoping Jack would use portions of his remarkable speech made just days before to the Massachusetts legislature. "Yes, Dad, I will . . ." "Well, I hope you're working on a good one, because it should be good—it should be your best." Jack repeated flatly, as if by rote, "Yes, Dad."

Still, when the question of youthful inexperience arose, Jack smiled off suggestions of available sages. "If I need somebody older, there's no need to go out of the family. I can always get my father. . . . The great thing about Dad is his optimism and his enthusiasm and how he's always for you. He might not always agree with what I do, just as I don't always agree with him, but as soon as I do anything, there's Dad saying: 'Smartest move you ever made . . . '" Father and son were both purposefully remote as they stood before each other on the inaugural stand, trying their best never to reveal weakness, but they loved each other intensely. When attorney general designate Robert Kennedy and his wife passed them in an open car in the parade, it provided a good reason to focus outward again, with no chance of the moment sliding into sentimentality.

Meanwhile, friends, family, and cabinet designees were invited by Jack to come sit with him for a bit and watch the parade. When he called down Red Fay, it seemed like the moment would result in just another photograph with the new president. It was more than that. In typical Jack style, he introduced Fay to the new vice president, Lyndon Johnson, as "the new under secretary of the navy." A touched Red was shaken back to reality when Jack rapidly quipped—never permitting a moment of sentiment to spill over him—"If he gets by the FBI."

Jackie stayed on the stand only for a little while and then retreated to the warmth of the house and the necessity of bed rest. She remained there for several hours before dressing for the Inaugural Ball that night. As friends, colleagues, and officials were brought up to sit with him on the stand, Jack would ask, "When the parade is over, won't you

Attorney General and Mrs. Robert Kennedy in the Inaugural Parade. January 20, 1961.

join us in the house?" As darkness began rapidly to descend and the wind became bitter cold, he told his military aide, "I'll stay if it takes all night!" and reviewed the parade to the last contingent with the Johnsons, the Dillons—Dillon was the Treasury secretary designate—and a handful of friends. The only family members left with Jack were Bobby and Ethel Kennedy. "He was exalted," recalled his new special counsel and speechwriter, Ted Sorenson, of the endless parade of lights that now passed in the black-and-white world of a winter night. "It was no secret that he wanted the presidency. He had won it in a bitter contest. Like most men, he was ambitious in his profession, and now he was at the pinnacle."

The others had gone inside the white mansion behind them, the tall windows of its rooms glowing a warm gold on the iced lawn. Sprinkled heavily throughout the East, Green, Blue, and Red Rooms, packed with officials, were the disparate members of the five clans. They tended to cluster around the gargantuan punch bowl of Russian caviar—courtesy of Soviet leader Nikita Khrushchev—and other delicacies on the buffet. Jackie was not seen. She was resting in the Queen's Bedroom upstairs.

"Aren't you going to join us?" her mother, the

infamously willful Janet Auchincloss, who had swept into the bedroom unannounced, pointedly asked the new First Lady. Jackie said that she didn't have the strength. Janet stormed out, telling her, Jackie later recalled, "There is nothing more terrible than disappointing other people." She expected her daughter downstairs shortly.

Meanwhile, the new First Lady's iconoclastic cousin Edie Beale tried to warm things up downstairs, while everyone waited for Jackie. Edie had rarely left Gray Gardens, her home in East Hampton, New York, which she shared with her mother, but her aunt Maude had insisted that attendance at the inaugural was de rigueur and she was doing what she called her "Bouvier duty." She had taken the train down from New York and bought a beautiful new gown, but she was nervous. She approached Joe Kennedy, trying to make light conversation, and recalled several dates she had had with his namesake eldest son. "Had he not died and had we married, I would be First Lady today—but Jackie is going to be a wonderful First Lady." She said Joe seemed in a trance, looking around "somewhat stunned" by the meaning of this day. Another Bouvier cousin tried to slip upstairs to see Jackie but was politely and firmly told that Jackie had given orders that no one was to disturb her.

The determined mother of the First Lady went upstairs to see her daughter again, this time insisting that Jackie at least make an appearance at the foot of the staircase and address the crowd of cousins. She reminded her daughter that some cousins had come from Europe and others from South America. "It is your obligation, your duty to greet them," Jackie later recalled her mother "absolutely insisting." For perhaps the first time in her life, Jackie openly disobeyed her mother. It was a small act of defiance on the face of it, but rather an important turning point. Jackie had so often found herself manipulated by those she loved—who had strict ideas about what they thought she should be doing, rather than respecting what she wanted to do. When it was clear that Jackie had learned willful defiance well from Janet, her mother began criticizing her hair as it was being styled. It would be a common Janet complaint in the years to come, but Jackie kept her hair the way she liked it. "She's up in the Queen's Room, trying to relax," a defeated Janet finally explained to the relatives downstairs. "I don't know if she'll be down."

Seemingly oblivious to the crowd's disappointment about Jackie, Eunice Shriver was excitedly taking in the history of the rooms she explored. Eunice was rather an armchair historian herself, conscious of the history-in-the-making moments unfolding for her family. She had recorded the parade with her home movie camera. Now warmed inside her brother's new home, she managed to steal away with Lem Billings, who had become another brother to her ever since he and Jack were in prep school together. Together they somehow got upstairs and found the Lincoln Bedroom, bounced a bit on the old bed, and then used Eunice's camera to take pictures of each other. The new president's sister said it reminded her of the scene from *Gone with the Wind* when the plantation house has been abandoned during the war by the white aristocracy and those who had once been just "the help" suddenly found themselves in possession of it. "We're rich now!" she paraphrased jokingly from the movie.

That was Eunice: never afraid to express her exuberance. Unlike her brother Jack, it was easy to tell when she was joking, happy, upset, or angry. She had a gusto that was rare not only for women of the day but for men, too. Her loyalty to her fam-

Eunice Shriver recording the Inaugural Parade with her super 8 movie camera. 1961.

ily was unwavering, but she always was realistic about them. She knew how the men in her family operated, and she often called their bluff. "We'll make Bobby attorney general so he can throw all the people Dad doesn't like into jail," she cracked. "And that means we'll have to build a lot more prisons." She had a wicked sense of humor—coming to one of Jack's Halloween parties as a pregnant nun. She had been a serious and excellent student, graduating from Stanford. After working in the trenches of social work in Harlem, the millionaire's daughter then found employment in Washington, D.C., where she shared a house with Jack, then a congressman. Her passion was helping those often neglected by society: first it was in the State Department, helping to resolve the problems encountered by American prisoners of war who had been held by the Third Reich; then it was as an executive secretary for a Justice Department commission on juvenile delinquency. She sought, found, and married a man who was the mirror image of herself—uncompromising morally, an equal unthreatened by her intelligence and activ-

ism. In her enthusiasm for the inauguration and the receptions and parties around it, she had severely sprained her ankle running through the airport. It didn't prevent her from enjoying all of it.

Eunice's love and pride in her family—and her insistence that they listen to her—was not only evident at moments like the inaugural. She was the one person in the family who consistently visited their sister Rosemary in the special care home at St. Coletta's in Wisconsin, where the mentally retarded sister of the president lived. To her, the issue of mental retardation was not one with which her own family should deal privately in shame, but a public issue affecting all different kinds of families around the world. Although her then-congressman brother Jack made himself scarce in those days when she would bring home not only at-risk and troubled children but retarded children for suppers of fried chicken made by their cook, he never dared belittle her intense commitment. Comparisons are odious and particularly unfair among siblings. Still, all things being equal in terms of what the Kennedys were taught about service to the less fortunate, Eunice Kennedy Shriver was the most compassionate of all of them. She didn't just write checks but held, hugged, and gave human dimension in helping those sorts of people her class seldom would have touched. Eunice, her husband said proudly, "really loves the people who have least."

After campaigning nonstop across the country for Jack, Eunice had to be hospitalized for nervous exhaustion. While she was recuperating at home she read about a mental health congressional study. It failed to mention an issue she knew quite a bit about—retardation. She spoke with her father, insisting that more needed to be done on the issue than the work she had already begun through the Joseph P. Kennedy Jr. Foundation. With his agreement, she went to Jack and urged him to create a presidential commission on the problem. "That's a good idea," he warily replied. That he hadn't said no was all Eunice would need. So, to her, the inauguration was more than the start of Jack's presidency. Not only would Sarge have a substantive role in the administration after completing his transition work researching potential executive branch appointees, she would too.

The media—and later history—would recall this night as one of the most glorious of Jackie Kennedy's life. "As though trapped in some fright-

ening nightmare," her mother's friend Molly Thayer wrote after speaking with Jackie about it, "she was conscious but unable to move." Dr. Travell prescribed her a harmless Dexedrine pill to help rally some energy. As Jackie recalled, "When it was time to get ready for dinner—I couldn't get out of bed. I just didn't have one bit of strength left and felt absolutely panicked." She hadn't eaten since lunch, her legs had cramped—and her hairdresser and makeup stylist were trying to finish their work. And then it was time to be dressed in the inaugural gown she had helped to design.

The music stopped downstairs at around seven. A few minutes before, John F. Kennedy entered the White House for the first time as the new pres-

Jack enters the White House for the first time as president. 1961.

ident of the United States, wearing his top hat. He gleefully tipped the hat to the butlers who greeted him at the North Portico. Then he stepped through the door—and never put on another top hat in his life.

As Jack entered, Janet stopped apologizing to relatives for Jackie's absence and flung her arms around her son-in-law, worried that he was cold. Jack shook hands, had a drink, and greeted the guests around the room. He excused himself to go upstairs and change. He was upstairs briefly—joining Jackie in a conversation with her godfather and favorite cousin, whom she had always seen as an older brother, Michel "Meash" Bouvier. They telephoned Lee and Stas Radziwill. Jack genuinely liked his sister-in-law and her husband, and wished they could have been there to share everything he now summarized for them in the transatlantic call. Soon after, he slipped out briefly to attend a supper given by his designated Federal Aviation Administrator, George Wheeler, and his wife, Jane. It was also a chance to catch up with some of his siblings, who had run over to the Wheelers' from the White House.

Jack got back to the White House at about nine P.M. The Kennedys were helped to dress by George Thomas, an African American, and Providencia "Provie" Parades, an immigrant from the Dominican Republic, the president's valet and the First Lady's personal maid. With his bad back, Jack had to be helped into the layers of the formal white tie and tails he had worn to the Wheelers'. In the interim, "Provie" helped the wan First Lady into her white gown and cape. Some of their other staff would be at the balls that night—like Jackie's secretary, Mary Gallagher—but the manager of the White House, Chief Usher J. B. West, oversaw the further preparations of the family rooms while the Kennedys were out. Soon he would become the most indispensable aide in running the private lives of the new First Family—and a friend to the First Lady as well.

The Lyndon Johnsons arrived at the White House and waited in the Red Room, where Jack soon joined them. "I have never seen you look lovelier," the president remarked when his wife joined them minutes later. "This calls for a champagne toast!" When an aide gently reminded him that they were running behind schedule, Jack snapped, "We shall take ten minutes to drink a toast to my wife!"

At the Mayflower Hotel, the crowds crushed in dangerously, everyone shoving and craning to get a good look at the new president and his wife. At the next ball, in the armory, the official party was seated in a box on a tier about thirty feet above the crowds. Here they seemed to relax a bit more, listening to the Meyer Davis "society" orchestra's music being played. Soon came the official promenade down a center aisle right below the presidential box. Couple by couple, out came the cabinet. A roar went up when Bobby and Ethel, the new attorney general and his wife, appeared. In the presidential box came a brief but audible cheer from Joe Kennedy. Seated directly behind Jack, however, was the third son, Teddy.

As Jack made his way to another Inaugural Ball, there was an uncomfortable moment when he suddenly crossed paths with Phyllis MacDonald. She was the wife of Torbert "Torb" MacDonald, a Massachusetts congressman who also happened to be a close Harvard friend of Jack's. "When I'm president," Jack had asked Torb some weeks before the election, "what is it you want me to do?" Torb said he wanted to fill the Senate seat Jack was about to leave. Jack agreed, and Torb even turned down a chance to run for the governorship of Massachusetts. It was not to be, recalled Phyllis, because "Mr. [Joe] Kennedy put his foot down." At

Jack Kennedy beams back at his mother, Rose, at the Washington Armory Inaugural Ball, Jackie beside him. His doctor, Janet Travell (far left), carefully watches him. His sister-in-law Joan and brother Ted stand next to Travell.

the Inaugural Ball, Jack saw Phyllis and immediately said, "I'm sorry about the Senate seat." Phyllis admitted, "It was painful."

Instead, Jack arranged with Massachusetts governor Foster Furcolo to appoint the mayor of Gloucester to the post. The mayor was one Ben Smith, Jack's Harvard roommate. Smith, however, was only a placeholder, keeping the seat warm for an as-yet-undeclared candidate. That candidate was to be Jack's brother Teddy.

Jack had served only two years of his second six-year Senate term. Law required a senator to be thirty. Voters were to elect their own substitute senator in 1962. Teddy would be thirty then, and Ben Smith had no interest in challenging the brother of his old pal the president. "Listen, this thing is up for grabs," Ted correctly assessed. "The guy who gets it is the one who scrambles for it, and I think I can scramble for it harder than the next guy." The youngest son, Teddy, was exuberant and jolly, a man not only of confidence but of great humor. As the baby of the family, he was especially close to his mother—but he loved to make everyone laugh and had the ability to get a smile out of his stern father.

During the holidays, in his Senate office, the president-elect had talked with Ted about the Senate idea. Teddy suggested that maybe he could have a State Department post. The president-elect wisely said no—Ted needed to work all of Massachusetts. "Don't lose a day, Teddy, you ought to get out and get around." So Teddy could show the state some mettle, Jack phoned a staff member of the Senate Foreign Relations Committee and arranged for his brother to join a departing delegation to Africa. Ted doubted he could go that day, not having even discussed it with his wife. "Well, I'd go," said Jack. Joining two Democratic senators, Ted toured nine countries in fifteen days. He was hailed as a sort of prince—this young brother of the mag-

netic new American president. In the Ivory Coast, in the visitors' honor, a seven-course dinner was served on gold plates. As Ted traveled through Africa in the weeks before the inaugural, Jack floated the idea of his 1962 candidacy as an anonymous tip to a friendly *Boston Globe* reporter while they sat poolside in Palm Beach.

Still, Jack and also Bobby were said to have a lingering ambivalence about the *third* brother being thrust into national office: there would be even harsher accusations of nepotism that could damage the image of the Kennedy administration. "You boys have what you want now, and everybody else helped you work to get it," Joe yelled at his two eldest sons. "Now it's Ted's turn. Whatever he wants, I'm going to see he gets it." And that was that.

As the party left the armory and headed for the third of what would be a total of five Inaugural Balls, Jackie began to collapse, and she stumbled. An aide immediately rushed her to the car. No photographers were around at the moment, and she was at least thankful for that: "I simply crumbled. All my strength was finally gone! So I went home and Jack went on with the others."

The heat of the adoring crowds, however, only energized Jack Kennedy. By the third, fourth, and then final ball, he loosened up considerably, cracking witticisms and jokes to the masses. To break up some of the discomfort of having thousands of people simply cluster around and stare at him in his box, he quipped, "I . . . still have one unfulfilled ambition—and that is to see someone dance!"

As always, this man could use humor in all its forms—from sarcasm to understatement—to avoid anything suggesting sentiment. But it would be incorrect to write him off as absolutely remote or purely analytical. While he detested overt emotion, he was intensely sensitive about himself, others'

Jack and Teddy Kennedy at the Inaugural Ball. That night, Teddy began talking about his ambition to be elected to the United States Senate. Their wives, Jackie and Joan, sit beside them.

perceptions of him, and what might be termed the touchstones of his psychological development. For him, recollection and often sad memories were outlets for his natural human feelings—but indulged only in private to his wife or brother Bobby. Even with his parents, he always managed to wall off any suggestion of emotion, which he equated with weakness. Despite the fact that he worked hard at building an image of himself as one who only looked ahead to the future, the new president not only studied world history but often stewed in his own personal history. As he was leaving for his limousine from the last ball, the president spotted an old Boston friend, Joe Leahy, who

had met him during his first campaign, for Congress in 1946. Kennedy rolled down his car window and shouted, "Joe, how about giving us a few bars of 'Danny Boy'?" And in his crisp Irish tenor, Leahy obliged, singing the sad old song that the Kennedys and many Irish American families loved to hear.

Kennedy, however, did not return to the now-darkened, solemn White House in such a reflective mood. Instead, he had heard that an old neighbor and acquaintance, columnist Joe Alsop, was having an after-ball cocktail party. Kennedy shocked Alsop and delighted the guests by unexpectedly coming to the party at two in the morning. He was famished. Alsop had no real dinner food. He did have some frozen terrapin that could be cooked. Despite the richness of such a meal at so late an hour, Jack eagerly gorged on the food while charming, bewitching, flirting with, and regaling—*seducing*, really—the old friends, beautiful young women, and off-duty journalists who crowded around the charismatic new leader of the free world. He finally left at 3:32 A.M.

As the time neared four A.M. John F. Kennedy walked into the White House, went upstairs, and entered the Lincoln Bedroom, where he spent his first night in the White House. Across the hall, in the Queen's Suite, the new First Lady was long in a deep slumber—despite the smell of paint wafting through the private family rooms. These two guest suites were temporary quarters for them. The family's bedrooms, "den," "living room," dining room, and kitchen were in a state of havoc, renovation on them having just begun that afternoon.

"When we first moved into the White House on Inauguration Day, everything we had came in little boxes," Jackie recalled. "It was so confused. They were painting the second story, and they had moved us way down to the other end. The smell of paint was overpowering, and we tried to open the windows in the rooms and we couldn't. They hadn't been opened for years. Later, when we tried the fireplaces, they smoked because they hadn't been used. Sometimes I used to stop and think about it all. I wondered, 'How are we going to live as a family in this enormous place?' "

Kennedy had to be up early the next morning for the swearing-in of his cabinet. It was a rather unprecedented ceremony for Jack, and Jackie had insisted that the new team bring along their children. After solemn oaths and formal, unsmiling pictures had been taken, the scene erupted with fresh crew cuts and ponytails as dozens of teenagers, little girls in ankle socks and white gloves, little boys in knee socks and short pants, and babies barely out of diapers ran or waddled up to their parents and excitedly jumped up and down as they waited to shake the president's hand. The group would include most of Jack's nieces and nephews. The new attorney general stole the day, however—by sliding down the banister of the Grand Staircase.

The president's own two children, infant John and three-year-old Caroline, had been left at the ambassador's Palm Beach home with Maude Shaw, their English nanny (the Kennedys always spoke of her in the old-fashioned British form—"nurse"). Rose would oversee their care until they arrived on February 4. That day, as Jackie carried in her baby son, and after Jack walked Caroline over to a snowman her mother had asked a household staff member to build for her, the four of them came together for the first time under the canopy of the arched entrance to the oval Diplomatic Reception Room on the ground floor. The new First Family was home.

On the first day Caroline and John Kennedy came to live in the White House, a snowman built by one of the gardeners greeted the former. February 4, 1961.

Jack, Jackie, and all of the Kennedys were turned into Jet Age popular culture material, including Jack-and-Jackie bottle stoppers, silver spoon heads, stick pins, Marx Toys' miniature statues, a Jack Kennedy salt-and-pepper shaker (he was the pepper shaker; the rocking chair was the salt shaker), a Jackie head planter, a Jack-and-John injection mould plastic statue, and a "First Family" charm bracelet with links of the faces of the President and Mrs. Kennedy and their two children.

The Jet Age

I believe that the times demand invention, innovation,

imagination, decision. . . . My call is to the young in heart,

regardless of age.
—JOHN F. KENNEDY, ACCEPTANCE SPEECH, DEMOCRATIC NATIONAL CONVENTION,
1960

For those who think young.
—1961 PEPSI COLA ADVERTISEMENT SLOGAN

America at the time Kennedy was president was radically different from the way it is today. There were no E-mails, cell phones, ATMs, or fax machines. There wasn't even a photocopying machine in the White House. Jack's and Jackie's secretaries were still typing on typewriters using enough colored carbon paper to make triplicate copies. Staff memos were "mimeographed." International telephone calls were still often unreliable, and telegrams ticked out by transatlantic wire services were more certain. *People* didn't have computers—only large companies had the monster machines that took up entire rooms. There were no panty hose, light beers, or pushbutton phones. Sports clubs were called gymnasiums and were used only by "health nuts." The most popular board game to sweep the country in 1961 was the Game of Life, the objective of which was to get rich, get married, and have as many kids as possible. Beef ruled on the charcoal grill, asbestos in the classroom. Anxiety over crime was rare. Howard Johnson's orange roof was more familiar than McDonald's golden arches. People didn't have to look up Zone Improvement Codes before sending out a letter. Coca-Cola came in green glass bottles. There was no nutritional information on food or warnings on cigarettes. Citizens and the media blindly trusted government. Citizens blindly trusted the media.

People thought that the future *had* already arrived.

It was not yet the Age of Aquarius, with its acid trips, but the leisurely train travel of the Fabulous Fifties had faded. It was, in fact, "the Jet Age," the new and fast jet plane having been inaugurated for widespread public travel in 1959. In the commercial and popular imagination of the American people, Space Age Martians had been replaced with Jet Age astronauts. Indeed, as Jack Kennedy promised, America would send a man to the moon before the decade was finished. Jets got people moving—just what the new president said

THE NEW LOOK

YESTERDAY

THE KENNEDY WAVE

TODAY

'YOU DON'T TELL ME HOW IT WENT WITH YOU TODAY
AND I WON'T TELL YOU HOW IT WENT WITH ME'

"BUT YOU AREN'T JACKIE AND I'M NOT THE
PRESIDENT AND THIS AIN'T THE WHITE HOUSE!"

"I've got a crush on Jacqueline Kennedy."

Jokes about the Kennedy family were ubiquitous in Jet Age America. This grouping of six cartoons touches on different elements and individuals: Jack Kennedy's thick head of hair compared to Harry Truman's balding head; the job of attorney general being filled by the president's brother Bobby; Caroline Kennedy and family dog Charlie in a crack about the minimum wage being raised; the popularity among mothers of the "John-John" haircut, Jackie's favorite haircut for her son John; a reference to the attractive and popular First Lady, Jackie Kennedy; the international popularity of Jack and Jackie, as if they were two halves of a sun.

he would do for the country. He and Jackie were part of a new global "high society," a wealthy, powerful postwar class that appeared in all the right places during all the right seasons—thanks to the speed of jet travel. The Kennedys were the first example most Americans had of the "Jet Set."

More than any other president, Jack Kennedy was utterly integrated into the national consciousness, as if he were selling ideas like "vigor" and "Peace Corps" as the character logo for "U.S. government," just like the captain selling Cap'n Crunch cereal. This was the first generation of young people hit with color television cross-marketing: Saturday morning cartoon characters sold toys from Hasbro or Marx on cereal boxes from Post or General Mills; characters on the *Beverly Hillbillies* drove Cadillac and Mercury cars. Although not entirely unwittingly, Jack and Jackie launched themselves straight into the eye of Jet Age pop culture. Two decades earlier, there had been Roosevelt jokes on the radio, mostly about the president and his wife, occasionally about their sons, grandchildren, and pets. But there had never been an extended family in the White House that set off the kind of reaction the Kennedys did in 1961. Since they so aggressively sought widespread publicity about themselves (not only in print but most importantly in photographs and television) as they helped Jack win the presidency, seemingly every mood and move of the individual members of this unusually large, wealthy, attractive family became part of the mainstream media and, through it, the public imagination. Quickly, the nation came to know their idiosyncrasies and stories—Caroline's dead hamster, "John-John's" love of helicopters, Jack's back problem, Bobby's fifty-mile hike, the London parties of "Princess Lee," Teddy's law school exam, Ethel's swimming pool antics, Rose's daily attendance at sunrise mass.

One of the era's hottest commodities was a comedy album about them all. Vaughan Meader's *The First Family* (and subsequently, *The First Family II* and *That Other First Family*—about the Khrushchevs) spoofed the clan and their activities. On one of the hit comedy albums of the era, *My Son, the Folk Singer*, by Allan Sherman, Sherman sings of discount dresses ("Pick a Dress of Cotton," to the tune of "Pick a Bale of Cotton") with the lyrics, "See how this one fits on me? Just like Jackie Kennedy!" Sherman's album inspired a spoof of the spoof, a record that had a Rose Kennedy character singing folk songs about *My Son, the President*.

Endless kitschy products featured Jack in his rocking chair: for teenage boys there was a plastic model kit from Aurora, a company that usually made monster and airplane models, that even featured an Oval Office fireplace backdrop; a plastic-and-rubber toy president for smaller children; and a ceramic Jack as a pepper shaker and his removable rocking chair as a salt shaker for the family kitchen. There were pairs of "Jack-and-Jackie" heads on teaspoons and bottle stoppers. Matching "Jack & Jackie" wall plaques replaced the Elvis-on-velvet pictures popular in homes in the fifties. For little girls, there were Madame Alexander Caroline dolls complete with pink plastic Mary Jane shoes, and Magic Wand cut-out dress dolls of Jackie and Caroline together. A "First Family" charm bracelet had charms of the faces of different Kennedys, including little John and Caroline. Satirical "coloring books" for adults were published with political rhymes about different family members. For teenage girls, Ponytail made black vinyl wig and hat boxes, and small suitcases with pictures of Jackie dashing around the globe. A plaster flower vase produced by Inarco came in the shape of Jackie's head and face, suspiciously reminiscent of the Madonna figure in the Pietà. A full set of Kennedy cards enclosed in bubblegum packs could be collected and traded. "The Exciting, New Game of The Kennedys" was a board game divided into sections such as "Social Standing" and "Personal Image." It had play money with a picture of Joe Kennedy on the bills, and the winner was to accumulate the most "states." There was even a comic book with cartoon frames tracing President Kennedy's life story and that of "Caroline's mommy."

The most popular subgenre of the Kennedy craze was the near obsession with the shockingly young and radically chic First Lady as a symbol of "style." Lookalike models, store mannequins, and knock-off fashions all copied her look. Also in 1961, on the animated cartoon series *The Flintstones* (which was often watched by adults), the two consumerized housewives Wilma Flintstone and Betty Rubble are on a wild shopping spree using their new "charge plates" when they pass a mannequin in the department store. "There!" shouts Wilma, pointing to a pillbox hat and beige suit on the dummy, "it's the Jackie Kennelrock look!" a tagline informed by both the First Lady's popular style and her famous spending habits on clothes. On the sitcom *The Dick Van Dyke Show*, about a suburban couple, actress Mary Tyler Moore emulated the Jackie look, wearing her hair in a bouffant with flip curls, appearing in A-line sleeveless dresses or capri pants and bulky turtleneck sweaters. When asked her greatest ambition, Miss America 1962 said, "To be more like Jackie."

THE FIRST FAMILY

JOHN FITZGERALD KENNEDY,
BORN MAY 29, 1917

JACQUELINE LEE BOUVIER,
BORN JULY 28, 1929

MARRIED SEPTEMBER 12, 1953

CHILDREN:

ARABELLA KENNEDY,
STILLBORN AUGUST 23, 1956

CAROLINE BOUVIER KENNEDY,
BORN NOVEMBER 27, 1957

JOHN FITZGERALD KENNEDY JR.,
BORN NOVEMBER 25, 1960

PATRICK BOUVIER KENNEDY,
BORN AUGUST 7, 1963;
DIED AUGUST 9, 1963

• • •

To remember the Jet Age only as a time of powder blue pop culture and laugh track sitcoms, however, is to dismiss the terrifying crises the nation faced and to belittle entire segments of the population who were not having such a good time.

It also reduces the Kennedy administration—with its uncertain movement toward civil rights, buildup in Vietnam, and nuclear war games with the Soviet Union—into the cloying "Camelot," an ill-considered metaphor forgivable only because it was concocted by the traumatized president's widow.

To be "Negro" in America in 1961, even if one moved within a wealthy, well-educated, and liberal circle of white Americans, meant, at best, to find discomfort in the most routine aspects of life: finding a roadside motel or a fancy hotel room; eating in a fine restaurant or at a Woolworth luncheon counter; going to public schools—or private ones, state colleges, or Ivy League universities; trying on clothes in a department store or being allowed into a haute couture house; swimming in a public pool or joining a private club. Kennedy offered the hope of changing all of this, a chance at equal opportunity regardless of race.

In the beginning of his term he was slow to deliver. As Jack and Jackie were preparing for their regal visit to Paris, Vienna, and London in the spring of 1961, nonviolent racial integration activists—the Freedom Riders—on their way to New

The president, in his trademark two-button jacket and Wayfarer sunglasses, reviews troops at White Sands military base. June 5, 1963.

Orleans in buses were attacked by natives of Anniston and Birmingham, Alabama. Television probably was the most important factor in emotionally moving America toward integration. When Birmingham police commissioner Eugene "Bull" Connor ordered police to use violence to repel civil rights marchers in the city, it was all instantly captured on the relatively new media of videotape and shown on that night's evening news. Seeing human beings being chased and bitten by trained dogs or thrown onto streets and into buildings by the burning pressure of fire hoses stunned the nation at large. Perhaps for the first time the fight for desegregation in the South was no longer merely an issue of Negroes marching for civil rights but one of human beings demanding the dignity of equal rights. Certainly, it changed Jackie Kennedy.

Like her husband, Jackie encountered African-Americans in situations largely confined to their work as dressmakers, maids, clerks, and other service industry workers. When she saw the TV coverage of hoses being turned on people in Alabama in the summer of 1963, she was shocked. But she had by then already done more than simply react. When Bobby Kennedy resigned from the Metropolitan Club because it barred African-Americans from membership and with like-thinking former members formed the integrated Federal City Club, Jackie urged them to use the top floor of the White House as their headquarters before they secured a clubhouse. She sharply rebutted racist criticism from Americans while she toured India, a land of nonwhite people. In carefully considering the classmates to be placed in her daughter's White

House kindergarten class, Jackie included young Avery Hatcher, the son of the black assistant press secretary to the president—and he was frequently photographed playing with the First Daughter.

Even when she was asked by the president himself to manipulate things a bit for public relations purposes, she refused on principle. During the historic 1962 Lincoln Day reception for the largest gathering to that time of African-Americans in the White House, the president and his advisers were skittish about negative backlash that might arise from too much publicity about the event. Jackie sat with her husband, the Johnsons, Ethel Kennedy, and various black leaders that evening for a picture—but she refused Jack's request that she distract the white wife of black performer Sammy Davis Jr. and keep her from being photographed with him in a picture to be publicly released. Her husband saw things more pragmatically. He felt he had to: he did not yet have the power as president to get civil rights legislation passed in Congress, and if he tried anything beyond symbolic support he would alienate and insult southern Democrats whose support he needed to pass education, medical care, and other domestic legislation. It was still an America where a newspaper snapshot of a friendly wedding kiss for a groom—who happened to be Sammy Davis—from a friend who happened to be the president's sister Pat could scandalize the Louisiana legislature.

The balance of power in the Kennedy marriage mirrored that of most American couples of the era. He was the breadwinner and the boss; she was the dutiful and devoted wife. Despite the fact that Jackie had genuine talent as a writer and an excellent education, when she said, the night before her wedding, that she hoped to continue working as a writer, published author Jack shot her down: "Well, Jackie, one writer in the family is enough!" She acquiesced to her husband, as she had to her mother earlier in turning down an opportunity to work as a junior magazine editor in Paris after graduation. Those women who needed to work had it worse off. Not until Kennedy signed the Equal Pay Act in June 1963 was there a legal basis for a woman to earn the same salary as a man performing the same job. Some 30 percent of the workforce was women. Even professional women were still largely viewed by society as attachments to their fathers or husbands. The First Lady was never addressed formally (nor referred to herself) as Jacqueline Kennedy. It was, at least initially, "Mrs. John F. Kennedy."

Thus, like millions of women, Jackie became a traditional wife and mother—in her case, of course, one who had a full staff to do the actual day-to-day work. Still, there was an expectation that she conform utterly. She was not encouraged to ask her husband about his work, although in a short time, they would confer on politics. Basically, however, her job was to make sure the cooking, cleaning, and parenting were done well. Maybe this was why so many upwardly mobile mothers, whose junior executive husbands wanted them to do the same things, related to a woman who was materially so unlike them. Women went nuts for Jackie. They copied everything about her—hair, clothes, voice, activities, even the brand of cigarettes she was said to smoke. Whenever she appeared, or whenever she was rumored to be appearing, hordes of women waited for hours just to glimpse her. If Mamie Eisenhower was the way most American women were in reality, Jackie Kennedy was the way most of them wanted to be. With members of the emerging and permanent middle class finding themselves with disposable income for the first time in their lives, she became a fixed role model. Jackie headed a preservation committee, liked

French food, and had a flair for design. Wives who could afford "help" a day or two a week took charge of local Civic Association committees or "improved their minds" by taking classes in French cooking, watercolor, and fashion design.

Like Jackie, American women were also largely judged by their appearance. "Blondes have more fun" and "Only her hairdresser knows for sure" were the popular tag lines of hair dye companies that urged them to do all they could to "improve" their look. A lack of intelligence combined with sexual appeal was often considered irresistible in the female. "You're stupid," ran the punch line of one 1961 *New Yorker* cartoon of a man looking at a smiling, buxom dame on the sofa next to him; "I like that in a woman." Hugh Hefner's Playboy Clubs opened in 1962 with women dressed in bunny ears and body suits serving as cocktail waitresses.

The shock of the 1963 scandal involving the British government's war minister, John Profumo, was not so much that he was having an adulterous affair with model Christine Keeler; it was the fact that she was having a simultaneous affair with a Soviet agent. It was a chilling warning to politicians

Astronaut John Glenn shows some of the president's nephews and the president the direction in which he orbited the globe. February 26, 1962.

The president's son John plays with computer machine knobs in the film room. October 9, 1963.

all over the world. Just a year before, President Kennedy had cut off a relationship with a woman who was also seeing an organized crime leader—immediately after he learned that the FBI was following her. In this age of the popularized "swinger," if a married man had an affair, a wife usually divorced him or acquiesced. Jackie Kennedy deeply loved her husband, so she simply removed herself from being in a place where she learned too much. In this way, she acquiesced.

Jack was as macho as his favorite fictional character who starred in novels and films during the

Kennedy presidency—James Bond, Secret Agent 007. People expected this. Presidents did not yet shed public tears or admit that they had vulnerable moments. The one exception was in Kennedy's role as father. He was to be uninhibitedly affectionate to his children—unlike most fathers of the era. This was no act for Jack Kennedy. Perhaps more than for anyone else in his entire life—even his wife—the president had absolute, unconditional love for his daughter and son. The public also managed to relate to them: they cut their little boys' hair in the bowl-shaped "John-John" style

Tourist security at the White House. Tourists only had to show their cameras and handbags to Secret Service agents in a temporary trailer set up near the East Wing. October 23, 1962.

and had their daughters wear little white gloves like Caroline. These were not trends set by the Kennedy kids, but rather a reflection of how other little children looked at the time and were thus a validation of what most parents were doing. When Daddy came home, the kids waved finger paintings in his face for approval. This is exactly what Caroline and John did, and when the delighted president made it known to the media, the public was charmed.

While, rationally speaking, parenthood had nothing to do with policy (in fact, it did with Kennedy), Jack's role as father only increased his popularity. Though he was elected by a razor-thin margin, Kennedy had amazingly high approval

numbers in polls throughout his administration. While he was certainly not universally beloved, JFK's youth, stirring exhortations for citizen participation in public service, and telegenic qualities made him a hero for many young people, particularly college students.

Like the president, the heroes of the age were those who never lost their cool: astronaut John Glenn, who orbited Earth; New York Yankee Roger Maris, who challenged the single-season record of sixty home runs set by Babe Ruth; Jack Nicklaus, who was unbeatable on the links. It was a man's world and would remain so, unquestioned by society at large until the "women's lib" movement got going toward the end of the decade. By then, the nation would be inflamed with even larger questions of life and death and the meaning of war. When Jack Kennedy became president, there were 16,000 American military "advisers" in Vietnam. In December 1961 some 4,000 Americans, the first two military companies, were sent from the United States to South Vietnam to help prevent the Communist North Vietnamese from taking over the south. They were told not to fire unless they were fired upon. During the entire Kennedy administration, 75 Americans died in Vietnam. In October 1963, Kennedy approved military recommendations for an initial withdrawal of 1,000 U.S. military personnel from Vietnam by the end of the year. Six weeks later, he was dead. Within five years the American military presence in Vietnam would rise from 16,300 to more than 500,000.

The Communist threat in Southeast Asia was nothing compared to its perceived threat in America. There was serious concern about a potential nuclear attack by the Soviet Union, rather than political infiltration, as had been the fear a generation earlier. In Kennedy's first year as president, the Berlin Wall was

The First Lady greets her frantic lady fans. May 5, 1962.

built by Communist East Germany, dividing the city in half. In his second year, the Soviets were found to be building missile sites in nearby Cuba and the world came very close to war. With the peaceful resolution of the Cuban Missile Crisis, however, the terror seemed to abate somewhat. Kennedy even initiated secret talks with Cuba aimed at rapprochement in June 1963. That same month he delivered his famous American University speech, which publicly urged peace with the Soviet Union and avoidance of any use of nuclear weaponry. Jackie considered it his most important speech, and it led to what she considered his most important act as president—the signing of the Nuclear Test Ban treaty four months later. All through the Kennedy years, however, the "space race" continued. Three weeks after the Russians sent the first human to orbit the earth in a spaceship, navy commander Alan Shepard, in the Project Mercury capsule called *Freedom Seven*, made a suborbital flight. Authentically or not, space, jets, action—these concepts became synonymous with President Kennedy and his years in the White House.

If a television network had introduced a new series called *First Family* in its spring 1961 lineup, it could have cast the Kennedys. Demographically, the new president and his family came right out of Central Casting: the pert wife who looked after the kids, dieted, and got into hot water with her husband because she spent too much on clothes; the darling little blond daughter who played with dolls and shot out funny witticisms as if she were an adult; the brown-haired little brother, always getting into trouble; the dad who had the last word but a soft touch. There were dictatorial in-laws, competitive brothers, kinetic sisters, and a flock of cousins. They were the first to be called "First Family."

Presidential families, like royal families, had sometimes been elevated to the levels of demigods—and they certainly did all they could to keep that perception alive. Yet no matter how privileged they were, with the Kennedys there was a greater sense of human connection. Americans always found their idealized president to be a del-

The president and Mrs. Kennedy, the vice president and Mrs. Johnson, and Ethel Kennedy, the president's sister-in-law, at a Lincoln Day reception for leading "Negro" Americans, the first such event in presidential history and the largest gathering of African-Americans up to that time in the White House. February 12, 1963.

The First Family on the flagstone path leading to the Oval Office from the South Lawn. 1961.

icate balance between king and commoner. Adams was too kingly, Jackson too common, Jefferson just right. There was enough of yachts, European vacations, Parisian gowns, Harvard educations, chums in British aristocracy, and Newport and Palm Beach in the Kennedy lifestyle to satisfy the nation's need for a slightly royal touch. Simultaneously, however, their stories were common ones.

Despite the fact that the Kennedys were millionaires with multiple homes and household staffs, the public would soon come to know that they also suffered from serious, dramatic, and scarring emotional and physical troubles. Material comfort did not shield them from such universal experiences. Many blue-collar and middle-class families found the Kennedys all the more attractive because theirs was the tale of the American Dream: in four generations, they had gone from poor Irish immigrants to the White House. That they were Catholics—members of a faith that made them outsiders—brought its own appeal. Not only Irish, but also Italian, Polish, French, Slavic, Hispanic, and German Catholics saw Kennedy as one of their own. First- and second- and third-generation immigrant families somehow related to them. Jews, blacks, and Asians felt that with

Even Caroline Kennedy had a "Jack" mask, as she is held by the real one. 1962.

Kennedy's inauguration as president, the doors were being opened to them, too, for the first time.

What most helped to make the Kennedy family so accessible to the public were the thousands of pictures that illustrated their saga. Photographs of the Roosevelts, Eisenhowers, and Trumans never appeared as frequently. Having had a business career in the film industry, Joe Kennedy knew the manipulative power of a good picture. He crafted the visual image of the Kennedys and, beginning in the early 1950s, managed to place beautiful picture essays about the family in *Life, Time, Look,* and other magazines owned by his media mogul friends like Henry Luce and Gardner Cowles. At the very least, these photographs introduced the senator and his expanding clan to the American public in an era when the American family reigned supreme as an ideal. Once the Kennedys were in the White House, the magazines let the nation behave like nosy neighbors peeking over the fence to cheer on a kid's birthday party, listen to a dad's jokes, and glimpse the unusual lady of the house go about her business in sunglasses and head scarf.

Having learned from his own father the political value of a good picture, Jack would often clash with Jackie about cooperating with photographers eager for access to their children (it would not be until the Clintons strictly banned press coverage of their daughter in the early years of their tenure that the potential damage of press coverage on young lives of politicians' children was fully realized). Except for a preinaugural photo session with art photographer Richard Avedon and an immediate postinaugural session with Mark Shaw, the children were not posed for any more "official" portraits for public distribution. Jackie even tried to discourage the White House from sending out pictures of her children requested by the public. During her frequent trips away, of course, the president opened the doors and let the magazine photographers in. Still, always with the larger sense of history in mind, Jackie knew that these years should be chronicled for the public record. Relying on the gentle and subtle presence of White House photographers, she permitted them to record real family moments—whether they were everyday life or special occasions. These official White House pictures could never be publicly released unless Jackie approved. Most were never released.

Military or government photographers had been around since World War II to snap official presidential activities. With the Kennedys, however, the age of the official White House photographer was really born. Cecil Stoughton and Robert Knudsen (Abbie Rowe being the third most prolific) did most of the work. As government photographers, they knew they'd be snapping official and military-related events; they never

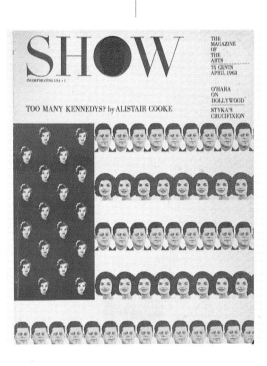

"Too Many Kennedys?" this Show *magazine article by Alastair Cooke asked after Ted Kennedy had become a U.S. senator. "Since the 35th president and his wife are about the most physically attractive couple to have lived in the White House, the urge of the publicists, magazines, networks and photographers to fuse two American dreams and reveal the White House as the ultimate movie set is irresistible. To put it mildly, the president has yielded to this urge and has manipulated it . . ."*

FROM THE WAY WE WERE, BY ROBERT MCNEIL

The president's nephews, sons of Robert Kennedy–Joseph II, Robert Jr., and David–holding model space rockets at NASA.

planned on capturing the shirtless president in his swim trunks, or his proper mother-in-law downing chowder on a sailboat, or the First Lady barefoot and smoking a cigarette. Jackie knew the world of photography, not only as a newspaper "camera girl" but from having come to appreciate it as an art. After a time she began to relax around these photographers and trust their discretion. She began to work with Stoughton and Knudsen, giving them access to genuinely private moments and offering friendly ideas on composition. Thus the Kennedys became the first White House family to have their every day chronicled in pictures.

Unlike the often staged and well-lit portrait and studio pictures of the First Family privately commissioned to photographers like Avedon and Shaw, and the work of photojournalist Jacques Lowe, the White House photographs were sometimes off-center, haphazard, and spontaneous. They were natural and real. Some of the pictures were so intimate that Jackie Kennedy later restricted public

access to them once they became part of the National Archives collection of the John F. Kennedy Presidential Library.

The pictures show that Jack and Jackie were human beings long before they became icons. In many ways, the photos now seem more honest and timeless than the innocent and rigidly discreet books and articles that were published at the time about the First Family. Consistently, the one truth that seems to emerge is that mother and father loved and cherished their daughter and son above all else. One also sees their marital relationship growing. For example, the president was famous for banning any pictures showing him being physically affectionate to his wife. In some of the 1961 and 1962 pictures, one sees Jackie slipping her arms into her husband's or hugging him around the neck. However discreet the photographers were, of course, he and she always knew when they were around. By 1963, Jack is no longer averse to displaying affection toward his wife. One picture shows them giving each other a full-body embrace. Of course, with the perspective hindsight allows, this photographic record takes on an element of poignancy by our knowing how the story of their time ended.

This is not to whitewash the corners of the marriage. Certainly, conflicts were part of it, as they are in any union, and his relationships with other women ultimately shaped and formed the dynamic between him and his wife. Behaving not at all unlike his own father and father-in-law, President Kennedy wandered frequently, continuing his behavior of thirty-five years of bachelorhood (and women–whether friends or strangers–made themselves easily available to him). To a degree, his wife was aware of these relationships yet never felt that the marriage would be terminated as a result of them. This might also have been because they

See the nice man?
He is my other uncle.
Doesn't he look like Daddy?
Color him the same.
He is next in line for Daddy's job.
Now he is learning the business.
He will start at the bottom.
He will be in Congress.

See the pretty lady?
She is my Aunt.
She is mommy's sister.
She says she's a Princess.
Where is her crown?
Where is her magic wand?
Is she really a Princess?
Do you think it's only a Fairy Tale?

enjoyed a healthy intimacy. They argued, they worried and looked after each other, they spent time alone together, they teased each other, and they eventually learned to express their love for each other. But, again, the White House pictures make one thing absolutely clear—their children were their most passionately shared common denominator. So, despite what the president might have done when his wife and children were away, or when he was traveling without them, when they were all together they were a family of unquestionable unity and commitment, a point of view presented here.

See the handsome man?
He is my uncle too.
He is in show business.
He can sing and he can dance.
My aunt must have liked his song and dance.
But he will never get Daddy's job.
He belongs to another clan.
They have their own government.

The 1962 JFK Coloring Book, *an adult political satire, even featured extended family members such as the president's brother Teddy; the First Lady's sister, "Princess Lee"; and the president's brother-in-law actor Peter Lawford.*

MORT DRUCKER, KANROM, INC.

3

Four Bedrooms, with Crabgrass

The White House as Home

I have a nice home, the office is close by, and the pay is good.
—PRESIDENT JOHN F. KENNEDY

Once you were behind the sliding door—it was a completely private life—you might trip over John-John's toys or Caroline's tricycle. It was so cozy. Here she was at home—a mother, a wife.
—DAVE POWERS, FRIEND AND AIDE TO THE PRESIDENT

*M*rs. Auchincloss," the president had asked his mother-in-law some years earlier after yet another new color scheme appeared in his home, "do you think we're prisoners of beige?"

Jackie Kennedy loved to decorate entire houses. She had her work cut out for her in the White House. From the moment she first walked through what she called the "dreary Mamie Pink bedroom" used by the Eisenhowers to when she thanked the outgoing First Lady for her tour of what would be her new home, Jackie was envisioning how she could make it more attractive and livable.

The day after the inauguration, decorator Helen "Sister" Parish arrived in the private quarters, her arms loaded with paint chip samples, material swatches, and drawings for new cabinets and closets. "We've got a lot of work ahead," the new First Lady warned the chief usher. The very next day, painters, carpenters, electricians, and plumbers swarmed the second floor. "I can't believe what they're doing!" gasped Mabel Walker, Mamie Eisenhower's former housekeeper.

Jacqueline Kennedy's most famous contribution to the public was her historic restoration of the state rooms of the White House—East, Blue, Red, Green, and State Dining Rooms—and those of the ground floor: Library, China, Vermeil, and Diplomatic Reception Rooms. Never seen by the American people and press, however, were the private rooms of the second floor, the family rooms. During the transition she had carefully studied every aspect of the blueprints, and she began assigning new uses to the rooms to suit the purposes of her family. She, said J. B. West, her friend the chief usher—really, manager—of the mansion, "turned the White House inside out."

The chief usher, always "Mr. West" to Jackie, enjoys a smoke in the Entrance Hall. May 15, 1962.

Jackie seemed almost to have a crush on the fatherly chief usher, whom she always properly called "Mr. West." She teased him constantly, breaking him into grimaces of mock horror while really utterly delighting him. He remained the poker-faced straight man while she hatched schemes and tried to make him do silly things. They were partners in crime. Their diagnosis for egotistical staff members was "Whitehouseitis." The First Lady gave the chief usher a pillow as a gift. "You don't have to be crazy to work here," it read; "But it helps!" When Jackie once found West heroically battling a fire that raged in a closed-flue fireplace with his limp arm hung in a black cloth sling, he recalled her "purring" to him as she turned around to leave, "You look so glamorous! Just like Zachary Taylor!" (President Taylor's White

House portrait showed him in his victorious Mexican War uniform.)

The west half of the second-floor residence is laid out like a hotel, rooms flanking the corridor: a perfect rectangle with a bulging "patio" that is the Truman Balcony. A winding staircase and elevator takes one to the third floor, where there are guest suites, oddly shaped storage rooms, a big sunroom and deck where one can barbecue and raise plants. There is a pool (then indoors), a tennis court, a movie theater, two small garden areas, and amazing lawn acreage.

Adele Murphy of Residential Services had frequently helped the Kennedy family in their many moves from city to city, house to house. In the days immediately preceding and following the inauguration, she managed the transfer of furnishings from the Georgetown house—which the Kennedys sold—to either the White House or Glen Ora, the Virginia home they rented. "She always knew exactly where she wanted everything placed," Murphy said of the First Lady.

Jackie got to work right away on the family rooms. At the top of the grand staircase on the second floor, there is a stairwell. The door directly facing the stairs leads to the Treaty Room, with its windows overlooking the south. Immediately to the left is the eastern end of the second floor—where the famous Lincoln Bedroom Suite and Queen's Suite are located, reached by walking up a slight ramp. Beneath this area is the East Room.

Immediately to the right of the stairwell, marked by large wooden sliding doors, is the Center Hall. As one proceeds down it, heading west, there are rooms on either side. On the left side, looking south, is the Oval Room—which is directly above the Blue Room. This is the most formal room in the family quarters, used for some official

Jack and Jackie Kennedy entertain astronauts and their wives in the Yellow Oval Room. May 21, 1963.

welcomes for special guests and presidential meetings. It is oval shaped and extends out, through the
large, curved French windows, to the Truman Balcony. Jackie transformed the Oval Room from
Eisenhower's green-painted Trophy Room, where
he kept military honors, trophies, and other awards
in a large glass case, into a yellow salon. She placed
there some Louis XVI furniture—it was a style
favored by the Madisons—and later said she tried to
suggest the spirit of Dolley Madison in this room
because this predecessor of hers loved bright yel-

low. Two comfortable couches, stuffed with thick
down and covered in pale yellow, were placed at
angles, opening onto the fireplace and the three
French windows beyond. Jack always found these
couches too soft. When the Kennedys entertained
larger numbers of friends or family—which was
quite rare—this is where they came after dining.

A hidden door on the southwest side of the Oval
Room connects it to what was known during the
Kennedy years as the President's Room. This was
Jack's room, in which Jackie put a four-poster bed

President Kennedy's bedroom. The books at far right, in foreground, rest upon Jack Kennedy's TV set, for a while the only one in the family quarters. May 3, 1962.

with white-blue chintz draping, an antique night-stand on which he kept personal items—including a heating pad for his bad back—a rocking chair, an antique coffee table, and a TV set piled high with books, all against chalky white walls. He had the colorful 1917 Childe Hassam painting *Flag Day* hung here at one point. The Kennedys, like the Eisenhowers and Trumans, maintained separate rooms—but also like them, usually slept together. When work got Kennedy up at odd hours, or if he had to work late, or if his back was especially

painful, he used the bed in his room. His bathroom and clothes closet were here. Recalled his friend historian Arthur Schlesinger:

The day began at a quarter to eight. George Thomas, his devoted . . . valet, would knock at the door of the Kennedy bedroom. The president would then ordinarily go over to his own room for breakfast, leaving Jacqueline to sleep for a few more moments. As he sat down before his breakfast tray, surrounded by the morning papers and urgent cables and reports . . . Caroline and John would rush in, greet their father and turn on the television to watch animated car-

toons. When he took his bath, they followed him into the bathroom and played with the little floating animals, yellow ducks and pink pigs that littered the tub. Then more presidential reading with the television set going full blast. At nine o'clock a calisthenics program came on, and Kennedy liked to watch the children tumble on the bedroom floor in [rhythm] with the man on the screen. In a moment, he would go back to see Jacqueline, now awake and having her own breakfast. Then, taking one of the children by the hand, he would walk over to the presidential offices in the West Wing.

Across the Center Hall from the President's Room, on the north side of the house, are two bedroom suites and a large, narrow hallway between them: the hallway's window is directly over the front door of the North Portico. In this hallway, a small room was created for Maude Shaw, the nanny. "She won't need much. Just find a wicker wastebasket for her banana peels and a little table for her false teeth at night," the First Lady explained.

To the right of this hall room was Caroline Kennedy's bedroom. To the left was John Jr.'s room. Both had previously been guest rooms outfitted with hotel-type furniture. Caroline's room had a small sofa crammed with her dolls, her life-size Raggedy Ann kept in a special chair. She had

Caroline Kennedy's bedroom. Her favorite Raggedy Ann doll sits in the far right corner. May 8, 1962.

John Kennedy's bedroom. While he slept in the crib, his nanny, Maude Shaw, often stayed on the bed in the corner to watch over him.

a miniature four-poster bed—with sleeping safety guards. In the corner of the room, Jackie placed an original Grandma Moses painting of a Fourth of July scene. There were pink-white curtains.

John's room had a white-canopied crib—with blue-white curtains. His airplanes, a nun doll, a crib, and an antique rocking chair were scattered about the room. A folk art picture of George Washington hung on the wall. There was also a small daybed that Maude Shaw used when he was an infant. Farther west, connecting to John's room,

was a small area first used as a changing room and to prepare his formula. Its one window overlooks the North Lawn. It was soon made into a makeshift dining room for the children and then, briefly, was prepared as an infant's room for Patrick, the baby who would not live long enough to come to the White House. Behind this small room, just to the south, are tucked a small, hidden, winding staircase and the elevator. The elevator vestibule opens into the Center Hall.

Behind the ninety-seven-inch-high wooden

doors separating the Center Hall from the west end of the house are more rooms. The main area is the West Sitting Hall. It is dominated by a large semi-circular window, which allows the afternoon sun to flood in. This is the living room—where friends and family are entertained, where staff can informally work, where private visitors are received. In the afternoons, at an ornate mahogany French Empire desk with brass hardware, the First Lady often worked on her famous handwritten correspondence, which usually ran for endless pages and was written in a beautiful, looped penmanship. Of all the items in the mansion, this one desk was the jewel she most cherished. "She worried more about scratches-in-transit, or its improper care, than about any other piece of furniture or art," recalled West. It had been the desk of her beloved father, Jack Bouvier, who had died in 1957. William Manchester later described the feeling of this center room, the vital center of the First Family's private life:

The effect could easily be that of a refurbished New York elevator flat. It's not, because the great, barnlike corridor has been toned down by an ingenious use of color, objets d'art, and graceful furniture. Slipcovered French chairs are grouped invitingly on off-white rugs. Lovely chandeliers sparkle overhead. American paintings by George Catlin, Maurice Prendergast, Winslow Homer, and John Singer Sargent hang on tinted walls, and below them are handsomely mounted vases and sculptures . . . The most vivid hues, however, come from book jackets. Altogether there are several thousand volumes, rising in endless tiers: graceful books on art, histories, multivolume encyclopedias, Churchill's memoirs, a few modern novels—and many biographies . . . The portable bar there is stocked with Beefeater gin and Ballantine's scotch . . . White matchbooks bear the gold inscription THE PRESIDENT'S HOUSE, *and the spine of a buckram scrapbook [bears] the simple legend* CAROLINE. . . . *Flowered*

The private elevator of the First Family. It runs up four stories, from the ground floor to the third floor. July 7, 1963.

drapes have been drawn across the broad west window . . . Tiny points of light twinkle on a hall spinet, on a picture of Princess Radziwill, on a framed snapshot of young Jacqueline Bouvier with her father, and another of Caroline romping with hers.

On the southern side of this short, thick, square space is the master bedroom suite; on the northern side are the kitchen and dining room.

Jackie took the master bedroom suite. Proceeding west toward the large window, if one turned left at the first door one came to the First Lady's Bedroom, as it was then called. Two curving walls flank the room. To the immediate left is a walk-in closet—which actually connects with the walk-in closet of the President's Room. At the other end of the room are the two windows, facing south. A door opens at the right into the President's Room, and

Above: *The West Sitting Hall, the presidential family's living room. August 28, 1963.* Opposite: *John colors in the hall; behind him is his mother's favorite object—the desk that had belonged to Jack Bouvier, her father. Behind John is the door to his mother's room. November 27, 1962. Caroline draws as her Halloween pumpkin is carved; her mother's friend Joan Braden sits beside her. The door at far left leads to the First Lady's dressing room. Circa 1963.*

Although this room was called the First Lady's Bedroom, Jackie Kennedy shared it with her husband. The view below is her sitting area. The bust on the mantelpiece later figured in her White House portrait. At left is the bed the Kennedys shared, trimmed in Jackie's signature powder blue. She always liked bed drapery hung from a crown above the headboard. Both pictures, May 9, 1962.

there is small shelving and storage in the little connecting space between the two rooms. Both rooms have fireplaces. When housepainter Joseph Karitas, with drop cloth and brushes, was about to apply beige paint to cover the "Frenchy" blue stripes that had just been painted, Karitas recalled, the president came in at that moment, "barefooted, big cigar in his mouth, magazine in his hand. He said, 'What in the world? She's doing it over already?'" Although Jackie often changed the details of the rooms in her homes—most often her own bedroom—she adhered to a general theme.

Two single beds were put into one frame, creating a king-size bed. She had a headboard covered in cloth: the fabric had shades of light blue stripes with medium-size white daisies sprinkled on it. She had two large white pillows in silk, trimmed in lace, and two smaller pillows, one rectangular, one square, similarly trimmed. Above the bed was a crown post, with light blue silk coming down behind the bedpost. The First Lady usually had breakfast in bed, served on a small bed tray.

There were two bedside tables with white lamps on them, a small periwinkle blue wastebasket, several chairs covered in white and light green silks. On the white wall behind her bed were framed eighteenth-century drawings. On the opposite wall was a framed pastel portrait of her daughter. A terra-cotta bust of a little boy sat on the mantelpiece. The antique Roman sculpture was a sentimental favorite item, a gift from her husband during the Senate years, which she displayed for the rest of her life in her homes. It is in the background of her White House portrait.

In the far southwestern corner of this floor is the First Lady's Sitting Room. One window overlooks the South Lawn; the other overlooks the West Wing. A door on the west side of the First Lady's Bedroom opens into a small hall that leads

Jackie's private sitting room. She dressed behind the screen at far left. Her dressing table is in the corner, and the window overlooks the Oval Office. The walls are hung with family photographs. August 28, 1963.

into this sitting room. As one proceeds back toward the West Sitting Hall, one passes the door to the bathroom on the left side.

The walls of the First Lady's Sitting Room were in the pale blue that became her signature color, once called "powder blue." A coffee table was piled with fashion, history, and European magazines and books, ashtrays, and an antique bronze vase with fresh flowers. Flanking it, and facing the small fireplace, was an overstuffed chair and a chaise lounge, both covered in her blue. Above the fireplace, and flanking a mirror, were framed drawings of eighteenth-century window treatments. On the other walls were family photographs set in pale blue matting with gold frames. A trompe l'oeil painting of important moments of her life covered the two doors of her armoire. She dressed behind an antique Chinese screen. In the very corner of the room, overlooking the Oval Office, was a small desk. Once dressed in her daily uniform of slacks and a sweater or shirt (she usually wore her famous dress suits only in public), she went into the West Sitting Hall, then down the stairs to the ground floor, and bounded out for a vigorous morning walk around the South Lawn.

There was also a prized hi-fi set in the West Sitting Hall right outside the door to Jackie's dressing room. A small record player was on the shelves in the passageway between Jack's and Jackie's rooms. This was where Jack had so frequently played the musical score from the Broadway show *Camelot*. The big hi-fi always had a casual pile of record albums beside or beneath it. The president was a fan of old-fashioned Broadway and movie musicals, as well as Cole Porter and other standards of the late 1930s and early 1940s, when he was in his early twenties. Jackie used to tease him that his favorite song was really "Hail to the Chief."

The First Lady had a better-than-average ear for classical music, but was no expert. She liked certain pieces, usually those she had heard as ballet scores. Having been a fan of sophisticated jazz since her days as a student in postwar Europe, Jackie also got swept up in the bossa nova and samba craze, owning several such records, including the best-selling *Jazz Samba* by Stan Getz and Charlie Byrd. Jackie was twelve years younger than her husband, and her own pop culture sensibilities were formed in the postwar era. In high school she was remembered for her most frequent quote— "Put on another rumba!"

Directly across the West Sitting Room from the First Lady's sitting room door is a mirror image of a same-size room. There is a small elevator there—

As with many Jet Age families, the Kennedys' "hi-fi" record player was a primary form of entertainment: Jack liked show tunes, Caroline and John their children's sing-alongs, and Jackie cool jazz and bossa novas. The console and the record albums were located right outside the First Lady's dressing room, in the West Sitting Hall. June 1963.

used mostly by servants transporting food upstairs from the main kitchen, on the ground floor. There is also a bathroom. In the small square room itself, which has a window facing the West Wing and a window facing the North Lawn, Jackie had a family kitchen built.

"We'll need a kitchen up here," she explained to Mr. West after one too many family meals arrived cold from the main kitchen. "I couldn't care less about the kitchen! Just make it white," she gave as further instructions for the transformation of the dusty-pink bedroom that had been used by Minnie Doud, Mamie Eisenhower's mother. West, Parish, and the new chef designed a modern kitchen with large restaurant ovens—bought from a wholesaler— and stainless steel and white Formica refrigerator and freezer, sinks and countertops. Jackie herself was never known to cook in it.

A door on the east wall of the kitchen opens into the family's dining room—which is called the

President's Dining Room in order to avoid confusion between it and the older Family Dining Room, located on the floor below, next to the State Dining Room. "I want my children to be brought up in more personal surroundings, not in the state rooms. That Family Dining Room is just too cavernous," Jackie explained as her reason for creating the new room out of what had been Mrs. Doud's sitting room. On the walls, she placed rare eighteenth-century wallpaper, "Scenes of Revolutionary America," printed with famous battle scenes.

These eleven rooms formed the primary living space of the John F. Kennedy family in the White House.

Until Jackie finally gave in to her husband's repeated requests for a television set in the West Sitting Hall so he could watch breaking news, there was only one "family" television set, located in the President's Room (his only known light fare was *The Jack Benny Show* and *Maverick*). One TV set per household was standard for average homes, but given the fact that a president—and certainly a Kennedy—could easily have afforded multiple sets, it was interesting that Jackie resisted this. At the 1962 Seattle World's Fair, neither the monorail nor the 600-foot-tall Space Needle drew as many crowds as GE's Television of the Future, which had a four-by-six-foot screen. Television had become the most common cultural denominator in the nation. News shows went from fifteen minutes to a full half hour. Although only 10 percent of the nation had color TV sets, by 1963 the color television would become the most popular status symbol in middle-class homes. Television was particularly influential on children. Among the cartoons a child who was Caroline's age would have been watching was the popular 1961 show *Yogi Bear*. It was no accident that the new breakfast food, Kellogg's OKs, had Yogi on the box hawking the sugarcoated

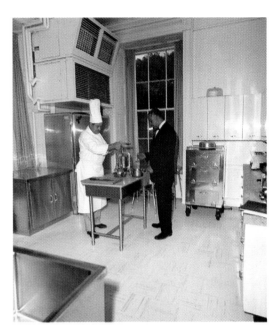

Jackie Kennedy had Margaret Truman's old bedroom converted into a modern kitchen where the family meals were prepared. Chef Rene Verdon and butler John Ficklin are shown here preparing food. Jackie herself was never known to cook in the mansion.

o-and-*k*-shaped oat cereal. Jackie was careful not to let her children become obsessed with television; she considered ominous the charge of Federal Communications Commission chairman Newton Minow that TV in America was becoming a "vast wasteland." However, Jackie's young half sister, Janet, revealed to a friend that the First Lady preferred Richard Chamberlain—who played NBC's Dr. Kildare—over Vince Edwards, who was ABC's Dr. Ben Casey.

Jackie did encourage her children to watch movies. The entire family was entranced with film; Joe Kennedy's favorite room in his Hyannis Port home was the basement screening room, where the entire family gathered to watch first-run movies. In

Jackie Kennedy converted what had been the bedroom of Mamie Eisenhower's mother into a family dining room, officially called the President's Dining Room. She used an antique wallpaper of battle scenes in this room. Here the family usually dined alone or with close friends. This scene is from the Kennedy children's joint birthday party. Eunice Shriver is seen at right, leaning against mantelpiece. Her daughter Maria is in a dark dress at the center table. November 27, 1962.

the White House, First Families had a movie theater with a medium-size screen, projector, and comfortable chairs at their disposal. The president was known to have liked *Bad Day at Black Rock* and

Roman Holiday. Although they might have seen *Splendor in the Grass* with Natalie Wood and Warren Beatty because the young actor was already an avowed Democrat and JFK supporter, there is no suggestion that Jackie was even curious about seeing Audrey Hepburn in *Breakfast at Tiffany's*, in which she wore gowns by one of the First Lady's favorite designers, Hubert Givenchy. Jack walked out of a showing of *The Misfits*, starring Marilyn Monroe. He found it boring. Jackie, however, was an avid follower of Italian surrealist filmmaker Federico Fellini; she later formed a friendship with him, and coaxed Jack to a showing of *La Strada*. She listed *La Dolce Vita* as among her favorite films in 1961. Her other favorites were too exotically esoteric for mainstream American tastes: *Last Year in Marienbad*, *Jules and Jim*, and *Breathless*.

. . .

Jazz records and Fellini films were one thing—those were personal interests—but appearing in riding boots, jodhpurs, and an untucked white shirt, with her long hair tousled by the winter wind, at her first meeting with the household staff—*that* was quite something else. "How can she tell what she is looking at, with all that hair falling in her face?" asked Mabel Walker, the shocked—and soon, the *former*—housekeeper.

Anne "Linky" Lincoln, a high school friend of the First Lady's, was soon hired as the new housekeeper. There were one maître d', four butlers, and three ushers to help run and manage the household. Five maids serviced the private quarters, including Lucinda Morman, who also did personal

The movie theater in the East Wing, put in by the Trumans. In the second chair from left sits Caroline Kennedy, in white; her cousin Maria Shriver faces her, with dark hair and dark dress. Behind her are Avery Hatcher and Agatha Pozen, two of Caroline's classmates. Behind them, in the third row, are Jackie Kennedy with her son on her lap, and her mother, Janet Auchincloss, seated beside her. November 27, 1962.

The White House swimming pool. Jack Kennedy took two daily swims here—before lunch, often with his friend Dave Powers, and before dinner, often with his children. Joe Kennedy commissioned the painting of the seaport scene. At night the ceiling lit up with starlike lights. An adjoining room had free weights and a massage table for the president. August 8, 1963.

sewing for the First Lady. Two native Filipinos who were serving in the U.S. Navy were the housemen for the private quarters, but there were also other housemen who specialized as carpenters, painters, and other tradesmen. One of these housemen, electrician Traphes Bryant, did double duty as the kennel keeper. This staff was salaried by the federal government. When Jackie whispered a question about whether a picture or a sideboard could be moved, they soon learned it was just her polite but definitive order to have it moved immediately.

For head chef in the mansion, the Kennedys hired Rene Verdon, a native Frenchman whose citizenship papers were rushed through. His assistant, Julius Spessot, was a citizen of Italy—and his papers were also processed rapidly. "Tell them that

The household staff was extensive and served all of the family's needs. Pictured here are waiters and kitchen workers; in the bottom photo are chef Rene Verdon (right) and his assistant. January 21, 1963.

the president feels there are too many Irishmen in the White House," cracked Joe Kennedy, "the French and the Italians ought to be given a chance, too." Pearl Nelson, the Kennedys' personal cook from Georgetown, insisted on continuing to cook the family meals, much to Verdon's chagrin. Indeed— there were too many chefs. A pastry chef soon replaced Spessot, and Pearl was retired—after being allowed to live as a guest with full privileges in the White House for two weeks as compensation.

A month into their tenure, Jackie was stunned—and her husband angry—at the high cost of the food served to them and their personal guests: all personal bills were, of course, paid for from the president's own funds. Jackie instructed Mr. West to start shopping for their food at the less expensive wholesalers who supplied the rest of the White House, and not at the expensive little French market in Georgetown, where the couple had had an account since his Senate days.

The Kennedys were famous for their menus of haute cuisine, whether at a formal state affair or a private dinner for friends. For regular family meals, Jackie approved a menu, often speaking in French to Rene—and thanking him for particularly splendid efforts with notes in French. When Jack first met Verdon, in the kitchen, he tried some French out on the chef. "Mrs. Kennedy smiled at his efforts," Verdon recalled. Jack was determined to someday match her facility with the language. For

HOUSEHOLD AND PERSONAL STAFF

GEORGE THOMAS, VALET TO THE PRESIDENT

PROVIDENCIA PARADES, PERSONAL MAID TO THE FIRST LADY

J. B. WEST, CHIEF USHER OF THE WHITE HOUSE

EVELYN LINCOLN, THE PRESIDENT'S SECRETARY

MARY GALLAGHER, THE FIRST LADY'S SECRETARY

MAUDE SHAW, THE NANNY OF CAROLINE AND JOHN KENNEDY JR.

DR. THOMAS WALSH, OBSTETRICIAN TO THE FIRST LADY

DR. JANET TRAVELL, PERSONAL PHYSICIAN TO THE PRESIDENT

LUELLA HENNESSEY, NURSE TO THE FIRST LADY DURING CHILDBIRTH

RENE VERDON, HEAD CHEF OF THE WHITE HOUSE

TRAPHES BRYANT, WHITE HOUSE ELECTRICIAN AND DOG KEEPER

themselves, the Kennedys preferred basic foods for dinner—two vegetables, one often prepared as a soufflé or timbale—and roasts, frequently lamb. The president also liked baked beans. Jackie invariably had a grilled cheese sandwich for lunch, a favorite since her childhood, and a small green salad with vinaigrette dressing. For breakfast she always had orange juice, scrambled eggs, skimmed milk, bacon, and honey—her little son usually gobbling up the latter two treats when he joined her. Both Jack and Jackie enjoyed what she called the "old-fashioned American" desserts they most often indulged in at Rose Kennedy's table—Floating Island and Boston Cream Pie. Jackie had a lifelong chocolate obsession and had some of it in her daily desserts—mousse, soufflé, or just ice cream. As Catholics, both Kennedys abstained from meat on Fridays and always had fresh fish—another favorite of the president's. "Soup was a dish close to the heart of President Kennedy, since it gave him an opportunity to be served the fish for which his New England background had given him a special appreciation," recalled Verdon. "He dearly loved Boston clam chowder, and asked me to prepare it for him on many occasions. I remember particularly a time when he asked for it three days in succession. . . ." Jackie loved cucumbers, but they weren't served to her husband that frequently since they didn't agree with his perpetually upset stomach.

As he was with many details of his personal life, Kennedy was finicky about his food. For breakfast it was juice, toast and jam, soft-boiled eggs, bacon, coffee. At lunch, he often preferred savory or vegetable soufflés. Since soufflés begin deflating the moment they come out of the oven, four of them were baked by the chef and put in the oven at fifteen-minute intervals. The first was ready when the president planned on eating, but since he was frequently delayed, the staggered backups served as the chef's insurance on pleasing the chief executive. Jack was not above coming into the kitchen to make his preferences clear. "Chef, I like my steak broiled, medium rare," he told Verdon one evening; "[I]t looks fried to me. It's a little shiny on top." Assured that it had only been brushed with butter to give it "a better aspect," Jack believed him only after scrutinizing the steak for authentic grill marks.

Verdon always kept the refrigerator stocked with beer for the president. It was his favorite drink, although he occasionally shared a lime daiquiri with Jackie, or less frequently a Ballantine's scotch and water. Kennedy however, usually stuck with his well-known preference for the expensive beer from Holland—Heineken.

The Kennedys paid the salaries of their own personal assistants. George Thomas, an older African-American man, had earlier worked as valet to *New York Times* Washington bureau chief and longtime Kennedy family intimate Arthur Krock—who released Thomas from his employ to serve the president-elect. Thomas lived in a room on the third floor. He helped the president to dress and undress; this was not pretentious, it was simply a matter of having someone on hand to care for the president's clothing and shoes and personal items. In addition, because the president's back was often

George Thomas, a native of Berryville, Virginia, and Providencia Parades, a native of the Dominican Republic, were the valet and personal maid to Jack and Jackie. May 29, 1963.

so painful that he could not bend down to tie his shoes, Thomas was indispensable.

A native of the Dominican Republic, Providencia "Provie" Parades, provided the same sort of service to the First Lady—caring for her notoriously expanding wardrobe of shoes, stockings, dresses, skirts, gowns, sportswear, hats, gloves, bows, scarves, sunglasses, and wigs. Nanny Maude Shaw, a kindly but proper woman from Malta who enjoyed a good laugh and joke, cared for the children. These three, along with Mr. West, were the most intimate members of the household staff.

The First Lady's personal secretary, Mary Gallagher, handled the family's personal finances, paying the bills. The president's secretary, Evelyn Lincoln, took care of his office and personal correspondence, and had access to his private anteroom and desk. Both had worked for Kennedy when he was in the Senate. The Secret Service was simply

The Kennedy children's British nanny, Maude Shaw, had a great sense of humor and was truly beloved by the children. She traveled with the family as one of them. She is seen here with John in his father's secretary's office. From an early age, he loved trying on unusual hats. May 30, 1963.

part of the life—no matter how much Jack and Jackie both initially chafed at the psychological confinement their presence created. For Jackie, there was also a paradoxical fear that their presence could do only so much. She overheard her husband question an agent on his detail about their ability to keep the First Family truly protected. "If somebody wants to do it," the agent replied, "he can do it." She was equally concerned about the effect of agents—and household staff—hovering around her children, inhibiting their normal development by doing favors for the youngsters and doting on them excessively. Months later, however, after Caroline almost drowned in the swimming pool of the First Lady's stepsister Nina Steers and an agent jumped in to rescue her, Jackie became grateful for their presence.

The Secret Service guarded the doors, elevators, and other entrances to the private rooms at all times, but otherwise permitted the family to live not only safely but with some semblance of normality in the family quarters. Whenever they ventured outside the private quarters, however, layers of Secret Service protection came upon them: on the lawn; at the homes of friends and family for private dinners or "drop-bys"; taking a walk late at night or in the morning on the Mall or along the C & O canal (as the First Lady often did); at public events; and in trains, helicopters, airplanes, and cars.

Jack, like millions of Americans, loved the Thunderbird car. He had even asked Ford Motors to provide some two dozen T-birds for his Inaugural Parade: the company apologized, but it was completely sold out. As frequently as possible, Jack wanted to drive his own red-leather-interior white Lincoln Continental convertible. The Secret Service let him do so only for short distances, away from the public and at his private homes in Hyan-

As unobtrusively as possible, Secret Service agents guarded the children even at play. In the process many became close to John and Caroline, tossing them in the air and singing nursery rhymes to them. August 31, 1963.

nis Port, Palm Beach, and Middleburg, Virginia, where country roads could be secured. Otherwise he traveled in the armor-covered presidential limousines, complete with car telephone. He liked to ride with the protective bubbletop cover off—the Secret Service was always skittish about this—and when Jackie rode with him she complained that without the cover her hair was blown by the wind. She had a little bit more freedom, and was permitted on occasion to drive herself and her children in the family's blue Pontiac station wagon into Georgetown to see friends in the late afternoon.

The president and his family always traveled in government helicopters or airplanes. Unlike his extended family members, he and his immediate family could no longer travel in the Kennedys' pri-

Kennedy, at the wheel, enjoys a rare chance to drive his white Lincoln Continental convertible. Jackie is beside him, the Radziwills in the backseat with Jackie's German shepherd, Clipper. Palm Beach, January 1962.

Interior of the presidential limousine, complete with car telephone in control box. June 15, 1961.

The Kennedys in the presidential limousine with the "bubbletop" on. July 11, 1961.

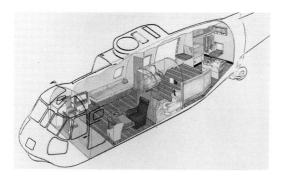

Interior drawing of Marine One, *the presidential helicopter. August 9, 1961.*

Interior cabin of the Honey Fitz, *the presidential yacht. September 9, 1961.*

vate plane, the *Caroline.* In addition to the government-owned yacht *Sequoia,* they used the *Honey Fitz,* named in honor of his grandfather, and the extended family's private yacht, the *Marlin.* Jack also had his own sailboat, the *Victura.*

When the president of the United States looked outside the windows of the Oval Office, he saw one thing: *crabgrass.* He got his wife to deal with it.

"The White House lawns are a disgrace," the new First Lady wrote in one of her famously endless memos to Mr. West. "It is a sea of brown as one looks across the South Lawn. Clover, weeds and *crab grass* are mixed in. . . ."

Jackie's suggestion of sinking water spouts in the lawn, as "it is done in Palm Beach," and the fact that "every place I have lived—with a part-time gardener—the lawn has been beautiful," certainly made her a bit different from the typical suburban housewives. Just like those women, however, she saw to it that every effort was exhausted in the campaign for a uniform sea of emerald grass. At the White House, the top layer of soil was even carefully removed for steaming and sterilization,

then replaced and reseeded. And what grew after all this work? Crabgrass.

Jackie oversaw the general scheme of the gardens, but Jack took an intense and special interest in the redesign of the old rose garden. New plans were drawn up, with geometric patterns brimming with seasonal flowers. Two colorful rows flanked a perfect greensward. This was the area right outside of Jack's office. Loving to be outside in the sunshine at any opportunity, the president used the two colonnades (one that ran along the West Wing, and another, which formed an L-shape with it, running along the French windows of the Cabinet Room and the Oval Office) and the Rose Garden for all of his daytime ceremonies and speeches, large and small. "[T]he beauty of it [the garden] seems to affect even hard-bitten reporters who just come there to watch what is going on," the First Lady wrote her friend, the horticulturist Rachel "Bunny" Mellon, who designed the new Rose Garden, as well as the East Garden, which faced the East Wing. "Jack took Princess Beatrix of the Netherlands to it (I hope she wasn't wearing spike heels) and, of course, he is still planning to

Caroline Kennedy rides her pony, Macaroni, across the South Lawn. Behind her, the Rose Garden is being relandscaped. May 30, 1962.

Little John Kennedy explores the new and blooming Rose Garden, where the president often held ceremonies and events. April 26, 1963.

In the winter, Jackie Kennedy loved using the South Lawn to play with her children. At left, she pulls John on a sled up a mound. Above, she drives a sleigh with her children, pulled by Macaroni—as curious tourists watch from the fence. December 1962 and February 13, 1962.

Caroline Kennedy pushes her brother on the swing set on the South Lawn. Maude Shaw is in the background. April 1, 1963.

Jamie Auchincloss lifts his nephew John toward the ladder to the children's playhouse on the South Lawn.

Jackie lifts John out of the South Lawn fountain after a swim.

drag the Grand Duchess of Luxembourg down there at midnight. . . ."

Jackie Kennedy enjoyed the lawn less as a ceremonial site and more as a playing field. She was particularly fond of winter, when she would break out a sleigh to be pulled by a pony, or simply a sled on which she would pull her children around the lawn. Despite the fact that doing so on the wide expanse of the South Lawn made her vulnerable to tourists and press photographers, she moved quickly enough that it didn't bother her. When it came to her children's playing on the lawn, however, it was a different story.

In her first weeks as First Lady, Mrs. Kennedy had a children's playground installed under some trees in the southwest corner of the South Lawn: a trampoline, a swing set, a playhouse with ladder, a treehouse, a sliding board, a seesaw, and monkey bars. Only as spring warmed the air and the children first came out to play here did their mother realize that tourists had a clear shot for perfect photos of the president's children and their friends playing. A press photographer—with a more powerful lens—could capture images of the children and sell them for magazine and newspaper covers.

Caroline Kennedy jumps on the trampoline on the South Lawn. The First Lady herself enjoyed jumping on it as well.

"If you stand in the children's playground," she wrote to West, along with a map she drew, "you will see that lots of people can take photographs from the place marked X. Could you have some more trees planted—or, perhaps rhododendrons? It must be a solid wall. . . . Who will be the first President brave enough to build a brick wall?"

At times, however, Mr. West knew that the active child's world that Jackie created on the lawn was not just for the children. "Let's put a trampoline right there," she told him on one of her daily morning jaunts around the circular driveway. "And hide it somehow, *please*," she added. After personally directing the transplanting of seven-foot holly trees to hide the trampoline, she grew excited: "Oh, this will be perfect! Now, when I jump on the trampoline, all they'll be able to see is my head, sailing above the tree tops!"

Jack Kennedy squints into the Palm Beach sun. June 7, 1963.

4

CHARMER

Jack Kennedy the Person, 1961

Kennedy refused to show emotion, not because he felt too little, but because he felt too much.
—ARTHUR SCHLESINGER

Emotions move people far more strongly than facts.
—JOHN F. KENNEDY

In the first weeks and months following the January 1961 inaugural, interest in the attractive yet distant man who had become their president gripped the nation. The unabating media coverage of his family, however, indirectly helped to define him. The key to understanding the character of John F. Kennedy ultimately is found in his family dynamics: they shaped his entire perspective. It was the one area of life that engaged him instantly, and it ultimately developed in him the maturity that came at the end of his life. Without viewing Kennedy in the context of both his nuclear and extended families, he appeared remote. "The man is a calculating machine," observed *New York Times* columnist James Reston, "wound up and full of controlled nervous energy." Harvard professor Richard Neustadt characterized him as a man who "mistrusted passion." In 1959, when he began his quest for the presidency, Senator John F. Kennedy granted a series of interviews over the months and years with journalist Ralph Martin. In these informal sessions, he gave rare insights into his character:

I don't think I've ever reacted emotionally to a problem, but that doesn't mean I'm not emotional. It simply means I reason problems out and apply logic to them. We are all the products of our conditioning. . . . I probably have as many emotions as the next person. I have emotional feelings about my family. You can see the way we feel about each other. My brothers and sisters and I see a lot more of each other than many people who are supposed to be emotional. I am not like some people who don't see other members of their families for long periods of time and then well up. I don't do that. This causes people to say "Kennedy is a cold fish." I'm not a cold fish.

Much hyperbole and then so much reactive sensationalism have been used in reference to President Kennedy. He was more complex than either the sycophants or his critics described him. Yet the qualities of the new president could always be better understood through his relationships with his parents, siblings, spouse, and children. This was true even of his famous charm.

Rose Kennedy recalled that when he was still quite small, Jack willfully refused to show up at the designated dinnertime. Already he differed from his many siblings. Rose was an unrelenting disciplinarian. Her rule was that a child could eat only what was being served at the moment he arrived at the table. Jack was "invariably late," but he proudly ate what little remained. Then, his mother recounted, "He would promptly go to the kitchen, where the cook, who loved him very much, would serve him his meals." With dead bluntness, the president's own mother summed him up: "I'm afraid that was the way he was the greater part of his life. He would charm people into giving in to him."

Kennedy's love for and fascination with history were perhaps the greatest gifts his mother gave him. Rose Kennedy excelled in the art of telling stories. She might have been a very successful teacher. Like a mother duck, she led her children through the streets of Boston and its suburbs, visiting historic sites, little heads turning in amazement behind her. As a young child, Jack was always sickly, always battling some new ailment. At four years of age he almost died of rheumatic fever. His siblings played outside while he had to lie in bed and rest. Rose read to him constantly. Perhaps he absorbed everything he could because, as historian Doris Goodwin speculated, it was a way to keep his delighted mother coming back. If reading was initially a distraction, it was soon an escape. His imagination—not to mention his mellifluous command of the language by his teen years—was stirred. From the stories of heroism, escaping danger, and the power of fraternal commitment in *King Arthur and the Knights of the Round*

Table, to the feral impulses of remaining true to oneself revealed in the *Jungle Book* series, to the excitement of new discovery and adventure captured in *Treasure Island*—these sensibilities became part of his developing core and the foundation for his understanding of human nature. "I think he was brighter than the rest of us," said Eunice. "He used to read a lot more."

If the world of ideas and the retreat into books provided the president with a rich inner life, it also helped to create a man who was constantly growing, constantly changing, always opening his mind to new concepts, experiments, and solutions. He sought the views of those who disagreed with him to understand their thinking. He talked to everybody about everything: what do you hear about this, what is that article going to say, give me three good reasons why you believe this.

The new president read several national newspapers each morning and had amazing recall of fact. If the reported claim that the president could read two thousand words a minute was an exaggeration promulgated by the White House and reprinted by reporters, there was no hyperbole in stating that Kennedy was perhaps one of the most prodigious readers to live in the White House. As president, Jack read Shakespeare's *Coriolanus*, George Kennan's *Russia and the West Under Lenin and Stalin*, Barbara Tuchman's *The Guns of August*, and Henry Kissinger's *Necessity for Choice*, about nuclear weaponry. He also read contemporary fiction such as Harper Lee's *To Kill a Mockingbird*, Nevil Shute's *On the Beach*, and Guiseppe di Lampedusa's *The Leopard*. "I've known him for thirty years. There has never been a moment when he didn't have something to read," claimed Lem Billings, "and usually he has been working on at least two books at the same time." This was true of Jackie as well.

Jack's determination always to win but never to reveal fear or physical or mental weakness came from Rose as much as Joe. Forged by Josie's definition of the proper role of wife and mother, Rose did what her husband wanted her to. "I never heard her complain," Joe said of his wife. "Never. Not once." Rose created the family motto, Finish first. For Jack this meant direct competition with his brother Joe, who, in spite of being older, was nevertheless jealous when he discovered how much more naturally intelligent Jack was.

Repressing her own natural talents and interests, as was expected of her, Rose Kennedy developed extraordinary self-discipline and encouraged it in all her children. Indulgence was bad. Physical affection, especially to young sons, was viewed as potentially weakening to their character. "My mother never really held me and hugged me," Jack once told his friend Bill Walton. Still, whatever it was that she did not provide, he appreciated the sacrifices and efforts she made on behalf of her children. "The only things I ever learned from anybody that might have helped [to prepare for the presidency] were some of the early things I learned

Kennedy's lower back was the epicenter of constant physical pain. In this picture of him at Bailey's Beach in Newport, one can see the scar from the failed surgery he underwent in 1954. August 28, 1962.

from my mother," Kennedy confessed. "My mother was the glue."

Jack not only dealt with serious illnesses, he later suffered from life-threatening physical problems. During World War II, he enrolled in the navy and commanded the *PT-109*. While he achieved the status of a war hero after he rescued a crewman's life, he also did permanent damage to the lumbar region of his back. An operation to correct his spinal disk problem at Boston's Chelsea Naval Hospital failed. It left him with a metal plate imbedded in his spine that caused irritation so severe that in 1954 the plate had to be removed. "You know, during my experience out in the Pacific, I really wasn't afraid to die," he recalled. "And I wasn't afraid of dying when I was in the hospital. In fact, I almost welcomed it. Because I didn't want to live the rest of my life the way I was living. The pain was so bad. I could stand the pain, but couldn't bear the thought of living the rest of my life with that kind of pain." Infection set in to the surgical wound. He was given the last rites of the church. Yet he managed to survive. "I've seen him on his deathbed four times," said Joe Kennedy. "Eventually, he always got up."

Jack recovered, but now he had what his friend Dave Powers described as "a hole in his back big enough for me to put my fist in up to my wrist." Nor was the pain gone. It would wax and wane, a constant low-grade irritant. He equated it with weakness and almost never discussed it. "At least half the days that he spent on this earth were days of intense physical pain. I never heard him complain," remembered his brother Bobby. "I never heard him say anything that would indicate that he felt God had dealt with him unjustly. Those who knew him well would know he was suffering only because his face was a little white or the lines were a little deeper, his words a little sharper.

The only picture of President Kennedy carrying one of his children. This might have damaged his back as much as the famous May incident when he planted a tree in Canada. February 10, 1961.

Those who did not know him well detected nothing."

Kennedy had come under the care of Dr. Janet Travell in 1955. She discerned that his left leg was shorter than his right by a quarter of an inch. A lift was placed in his left shoe to compensate for this and place less stress on his back. She also tried to numb the back pain with Novocain. The president was also using other medications. With the discovery during his initial surgery that he had Addison's disease also came treatment to keep it at bay with cortisone. His use of this drug, however, "markedly increased [a] sense of well-being approaching a sense of euphoria accompanied by a real increase in energy, concentrating power, muscular strength and endurance," reported Doris Goodwin. Kennedy's exuberance upon becoming president was cut short in his first weeks by a severe recur-

This is the only known photograph of President Kennedy with Max Jacobsen—who is in the dark polo shirt and light trousers—the so-called Dr. Feelgood, who provided painkiller treatments to the Jet Set of the era. Lee Radziwill is partially obscured by Jacobsen. Stas Radziwill is standing at far right. Kennedy is presenting awards for the "fifty-mile hike" he inspired. Palm Beach. Christmas 1962.

rence of his back pain. Attributed to his bending down to plant a tree at a ceremony in Canada in May 1961, it might have begun earlier, when he impulsively decided to lift and carry his three-year-old daughter through the snow one February day. This new bout of pain led him to try risky experimental injections of amphetamines given by Dr. Max Jacobsen.

Moist heat packs, massage, and electrical treatments were all used to alleviate the pain of tendons, nerves, and muscles in Kennedy's sacroiliac. His beds required firm horsehair mattresses supported by wooden boards. The public never knew that their youthful president wore a tight back brace corset, but there was much publicity about

his use of rocking chairs. While the lack of detail about his true health was not as deceptive as the concealment of the severity of President Franklin Roosevelt's polio, there appears to have been only one photograph of Kennedy as president using the crutches he often used. As his own mother confessed later, "He went along for many years thinking to himself—or at least trying to make others think—that he was a strong, robust, quite healthy person who just happened to be sick a good deal of the time."

Daily he went through an exercise routine, working with light dumbbell weights under the supervision of a naval officer. He played golf regularly. As a golfer, said Palm Beach pro Bert Nicolls, "Jack never fusses. He just walks up and hits the ball." He played fairly well. He was also an avid spectator. Although he found baseball to be a

Kennedy was sometimes in so much physical pain that he had to use crutches. June 16, 1961.

Kennedy enjoyed playing golf and did it well. July 27, 1963.

"slow-going game," every spring the president looked forward to throwing out the first ball of the Washington Senators' season. On the Saturday afternoons before these events, Jack got an old mitt and went into the Rose Garden to play catch with aide Ted Reardon. Despite the fact that he was never a great football player, Kennedy had once enjoyed playing, but now even a game of touch was considered a potential danger to his back. He nevertheless loved football more than any sport and never missed the annual Army-Navy game—sitting with the navy for the first half, with the army during the second half. He relished being in a stadium with such a large and enthusiastic crowd.

Most of all, however, Jack Kennedy loved the ocean. He was an expert swimmer. In Hyannis

Port, he sailed his boat the *Victura;* he relished sailing, even in stormy dark weather, bundled up against the wind. When he once ran his sailboat aground and then the sails collapsed, Bobby teased him, "I often wondered how exactly we lost *PT-109.*" In any weather it was always the ocean that was Jack's favorite place. He famously reflected, "In addition to the fact that the sea changes, and the light changes . . . we all came from the sea. We are tied to the ocean. And when we go back to the sea—whether it is to sail or watch it—we are going back from whence we came."

Jack Kennedy never missed the annual Army-Navy football game each autumn of his presidency. He loved blending into the crowds in the bleachers—as he does here. December 2, 1961.

Swimming was the one activity that relieved Kennedy's physical pain. Here he is treading water in the Atlantic with his niece Maria Shriver and daughter Caroline. July 28, 1963.

The president on his sailboat, the Victura. July 28, 1962.

Interested not only in perpetuating his own image as a healthy young man, Jack called for a national campaign of physical exercise. When Marine Corps commandant General David Shoup showed him a 1908 memo from President Teddy Roosevelt requiring lieutenants and captains to hike fifty miles in three days, it prompted the president to order the same requirement for 1963 Marines. Soon, it was not only Marines stepping up to the challenge but Boy Scouts, businessmen, even children on roller skates. In Washington, Jack predicted that Bobby would "finish if it kills him." In Palm Beach, Stas Radziwill and friend Chuck Spalding also finished the hike.

Jack Kennedy was always preoccupied with death. Norman Mailer observed that Kennedy had "the wisdom of a man who senses death within him and gambles that he can cure it by risking his life." He was the rare person who thought about it every day. Such intense

More than any place, Kennedy loved the ocean. Newport. September 8, 1962.

preoccupation certainly emanated from his own four brushes with death before he turned forty years old—but they were not the only reason. "War had been a hardening experience," said Schlesinger. "Courage, if it is more than reckless bravado, involves the exquisite understanding that death may be its price." The deaths of his two eldest siblings, Joe and Kathleen, in airplane crashes truly traumatized Jack, although he indicated this only to his closest friend, Lem Billings. "The only thing that made sense, he decided, was to live for the moment, treating each day as if it were his last, demanding of life constant intensity, adventure, and pleasure," said Billings. Oddly, Jack told William Haddad, the deputy director of the Peace Corps, that he too wanted "to die in a plane. Quick." Spalding further observed that "[h]e tried

to burn bright, he tried to wring as much out of things as he could. After a while, he didn't have to try. He had something nobody else did. It was just a heightened sense of being; there's no other way to describe it." Kenny O'Donnell concluded that Kennedy "never thought he was going to live to be an old man."

"I feel that death is the end of a lot of things," said President Kennedy, adding in seeming contradiction, "I just hope the Lord gives me the time to get all these things done." If doubt about an afterlife was incompatible with a belief in God, Jack apparently had resolved this some years before, as he had the idea of natural fairness. "There is always inequity in life. Some men are killed in a war and some men are wounded, and some men never leave the country," he said as president with

Richard Cardinal Cushing presides over the Catholic christening of Christopher George Kennedy, son of Bobby and Ethel Kennedy, held by his godmother Pat Lawford. Bobby Kennedy Jr., his parents, and his uncle Jack watch (right photo). Hyannis Port. July 19, 1963.
New Bedford Standard Times

coolness; "Life is unfair." As a young man, he had seriously questioned Catholic doctrine. "We're not a completely ritualistic, formalistic, hierarchical structure in which the Word, the truth, must only come down from the very top—a structure that allows for no individual interpretation—or are we?" he wrote his mother. There are no other further recorded statements about what form Kennedy's Catholicism took. When someone suggested to Eunice that a book about Jack and his Catholicism might be written, she replied bluntly, "It will be an awfully slim volume."

It is fact, however, that Jack always traveled with a Catholic Bible, and also that he prayed before he went to sleep—on his knees at his bedside, according to his friend Dave Powers. He could quote from his Bible, seeming to take comfort from certain passages. He went to church faithfully on Sunday; on his dresser he kept his scribbled list of mass schedules at St. Stephen's, St. Matthew's, and Holy Trinity. There is also evidence that his faith was deeply felt, albeit never divulged. After his death, among his papers was found an original composi-

President Kennedy emerges from St. Matthew's Church with Dave Powers during the Cuban Missile Crisis. He considered this his "home" church once he became president. He is just feet away from the spot where little John Kennedy would offer his famous salute at his father's funeral.

tion in his own handwriting on a small slip of paper. It read, "I know there is a God—and I see a storm coming. If He has a place for me, I believe that I am ready."

On one matter he took a rigid moral stand—the killing of weaker or unsuspecting beings. When handed a shotgun on LBJ's ranch, Jack's machismo took over and he shot a deer as expected. He quickly turned his back the moment the animal took the bullet, but it traumatized him. "He couldn't rid himself of the recollection," William Manchester wrote after being told about it by Jackie. "The memory of the creature's death had been haunting, and afterwards he had relived it with his wife . . . to heal the inner scar."

The president's public knew nothing of incidents related to his true faith. What was glaringly obvious was that he was the first Catholic president, a novel notion for most Americans at the time. During the 1960 primaries, Rose Kennedy—

Kennedy could never pass up a group of nuns who wanted to meet him or shake his hand. Rose Garden. April 19, 1961.

who had been named a papal countess by the Vatican—was forced to keep a low profile for fear that it would alienate Protestants worried that the Vatican would have undue influence with the White House if Kennedy was elected. As president, Jack was sensitive about attention being focused on his Catholicism. It was not just personal, but political. Having put to rest the religious question with his election, he avoided all reasons to reactivate it. Tied to this was also his ethnicity.

"This country is not a private preserve for Protestants," Joe Kennedy had declared to Jack. "There's a whole new generation out there filled with the sons and daughters of immigrants from all over the world, and those people are going to be mighty proud that one of their own is running for president." Grandson of an Irish immigrant, Joe had conquered the business world, become a multimillionaire, and befriended international leaders of communications, industry, politics, and the military—in part so that through his contacts he could place his children at the highest levels of business and society in the mid–twentieth century. As Irish Catholics, they could get only so far. While Joe sometimes seemed to yearn for acceptance among America's eastern establishment ruling class, Anglo-Saxon Protestants, who barred him from their clubs and gatherings, he finally thumbed his nose at their snobbery. Despite being considered an anti-Semite during World War II, Joe Kennedy joined the only Jewish country club in Palm Beach, Florida. "I was born here. My children were born here," he complained. "What the hell do I have to do to be an American?"

As hard as Joe tried, he was unable to keep this sense of rejection from his children—it was, in fact, one reason he built them into what he called "the most exclusive club in the world." Although they never experienced, as Joe had, any serious bigotry

RIGBY in ROME

"It can only mean one thing Giuseppe — a KENNEDY in the Vatican !!"

The Catholic president was sometimes the butt of gentle humor. FUTURE POPE MAY BE NON-ITALIAN, reads the newspaper headline, as one Swiss Guard at the Vatican sighs to another, "It can only mean one thing Giuseppe—a Kennedy in the Vatican!!"

for being Irish, they were acutely aware of it, especially Jack, who wanted to be loved by everyone. Senator Claiborne Pell observed that the president, when he was in exclusive Newport particularly, felt a "bit of a chip on his shoulder about being Irish."

"I'm of the Establishment in this sense of where I've lived, and my schools, but in the sense of the Anglo-Saxon establishment—no," the president explained plainly. To friend Red Fay he further clarified, "Do you know that it is impossible for an Irish Catholic to get into the Somerset Club in Boston? If I moved back to Boston, even after being president, it would make no difference."

Jack's time in London society, while his father was ambassador to England, had awakened a certain British sensibility in him. Ironically, in England he was thoroughly accepted into the elite circles of aristocracy and meritocracy. Of all the history he studied, he loved and knew best that of England. He counted more highborn English friends than any from Dublin. His first two biographers, James MacGregor Burns and William Manchester (of Scottish and English extraction), suggested that Kennedy's love of England was an attempt to rid himself of some embarrassing Irishness. Manchester saw Jack's "reserve, the cut of his clothes, his fondness for understatement, his daughter's nurse and his reading habits" as British, while, because the president "never dances a jig or sings 'Danny Boy,' " he had "little sentiment in him" for his Irish heritage. "Try to imagine him in a cocked derby and all visions of shamrocks vanish." One aide snobbishly declared, "Kennedy's appreciation of Ireland is merely a literary appreciation."

What many of the eastern elite friends and colleagues of the president did not know was that he liked always to travel with a portable record player and his Irish-American standards: "When Irish

Eyes Are Smiling" and "The Wearing of the Green." He relaxed by listening to the familiar songs after a long day of being "on" in public and during meetings. While in the Senate, he had a Boston friend come down once a year just to sing "Danny Boy." Rose Kennedy declared, "Jack delighted in his Irish heritage." Dave Powers recalled how the president, who had not been raised in the Irish neighborhoods of Boston, "could never hear enough of the old Irish stories."

Still, if Jack Kennedy had an internal pride in his ancestry, he did not yet feel comfortable openly embracing it before a world that had been hostile to the Irish for centuries. For him it was not about the stereotypes of corned-beef-and-cabbage dinners or marching in the St. Patrick's Day parade. It was internal, but it was intense. "The Irishness remained a vital element in his constitution," observed Schlesinger. "It came out in so many ways—in the quizzical wit, eruptions of boisterous humor, the relish for politics, the love of language, the romantic sense of history, the admiration for physical daring, the toughness, the joy in living, the view of life as comedy and as tragedy."

If he had ambivalent feelings about being Irish, he had none about being rich. Following other candidates at a rally during his first political campaign, Jack introduced himself by saying "I'm the one who didn't come up the hard way." Joe Kennedy felt he could afford to thumb his nose at anyone—twenty years before Jack's presidency, Joe was already worth $400 million. His children did not have to worry about earning, saving, or investing money. They did spend it, however, sometimes a little too much of it for Joe's and Rose's tastes. The parents were themselves tightfisted; only needed items were bought, and they were well used. The only extravagance Rose indulged in was her annual spring trip to Paris to buy haute couture, but even here she was not excessive. Her purchases were carefully considered, and she wore many gowns repeatedly. When she sent her used clothes to the local consignment shop, Rose always got a receipt for the tax write-off.

The president was famous for never carrying cash, and was forever asking friends to pay for everything from incidentals to restaurant bills to donations when the basket was passed around at church. Jack even asked Joe for cash loans. "Oh, Dad, I don't have a cent of money," he once moaned. Joe pulled out a wad of cash and handed it over to him. "I'll get this back to you," the son replied. With that, Joe muttered in return, "That'll be the day." Bills were sent to "Dad," which meant to Thomas Walsh, the family accountant in New York. Only when Jackie's spending spun out of control did Jack really begin to feel he had to be responsible. When Joe chastised one of his daughters for spending too much of his money, she burst into tears. "Well, Dad," said Jack with a straight face, "the obvious solution is that you'll have to work harder."

Kennedy entered the presidency with an income of about $100,000 annually from his trust, suggesting principal of about $10 million. He donated his entire presidential salary of $100,000 to charity, ranging from hospitals to the Boy and Girl Scouts to Jewish philanthropies and retarded children's associations. In 1962, however, he chose to make what were clearly strategically political contributions with his private funds—the United Negro College Fund and the Cuban Families Committee. Jack enjoyed other benefits as president through his father, like his family's Carlyle Hotel suite in New York, a thirty-fourth-floor duplex with a large living room, two bedrooms, a dining room, and a study. It became the New York White House for Jack and Jackie.

While his wealth was a material luxury few

Americans could ever imagine, Joe also feared the negative effects of it—especially on his sons. Before they could bring a friend home, he ascertained through informal investigation that his children were not being befriended for their money. He also didn't want them to become soft playboys—he wanted them to be as successful in politics as he had been in business. If Jack was secure with limitless wealth, he was also expected to climb to the top. He said of Joe's pushing him into the 1946 race for his first political post, U.S. congressman from Massachusetts, "It was like being drafted. *Wanted* isn't the right word. He *demanded* it."

"An idealist without illusions," is how Jack Kennedy described himself in an honest self-analysis. Realizing the human potential for greatness, he always recognized the flaws that left people short. While his confidence bordered on cockiness, he was especially harsh with self-criticism, and was sometimes overheard yelling to himself, "Goddamn dummy!" His hot anger was

Jack Kennedy was the last president to smoke in public—it was still considered a "cool" thing to do in 1961.

used liberally on his staff, and he peppered it with swearing. Kennedy read and listened to everything said by political commentators and newsmakers about his performance. When he heard an administration decision being criticized on television, he yelled at the box. Once, furious over an article in the *New York Herald Tribune*, he canceled the White House subscription for a time. He admitted that his worst quality was irritability.

He had a hard time relaxing. He would brush his hair with his fingers, play with his tie, doodle, tap his teeth, and pull up his socks. When he was displaying signs of unrest in a meeting, he counted on Evelyn Lincoln to rescue him by saying there was a phone call or a waiting visitor. He was an insomniac, often waking at four in the morning. This came with the job and its monumental responsibilities.

He was also a good actor, a skill he learned not only from a lifetime of repressing some of his emotional and physical pain but also from Jackie's mannered world. Jittery when advisers went on endlessly, nervous when he had to make small talk, he could still hide his feelings by using the power to charm and relax. Like Jackie, he had a sense of the ridiculous, a biting wit, and a sarcasm that was easily mistaken for meanness by the insecure. Dry humor was Jack Kennedy's trademark. His greetings to his postmaster general, at a testimonial luncheon the president could not attend, tweaked the agency's inefficiency: "I'm sending this message by wire, since I want to be certain that this message reaches you in the right place and at the right time." On the only night he ever managed to sneak out to the movies—to see *Spartacus*—Jack spied his agriculture secretary in the row ahead of him and tapped his shoulder, remarking, "This is a hell of a way to write a farm program."

Yet, while he cracked wicked remarks about Richard Nixon, for example, Jack so respected

Nixon's intelligence on foreign affairs that he consulted him during the administration's first international crisis. He burst out angrily at some of his staff who laughed about evidence in the Oval Office floor of Ike's golf obsession: "Most of the people who were now joking about Eisenhower's spike marks were people who would have been only too willing to get down on their knees to shine Eisenhower's golf shoes a few months earlier." He reverted to self-deprecation when he was in a fix. When it looked like the world—or, at the very least, his administration—was doomed, he quipped to historian Schlesinger, "Arthur . . . write the history of my first term—*The Only Years. . . .*"

Although he liked off-color jokes, he despised ethnic jokes. "I don't want to hear it," he would say simply, and walk away. He enjoyed gossiping. When old Georgetown neighbor Bill Walton once visited him, the president was soaking in his bathtub, reading the paper on a board across the tub, as he often did. Suddenly, he got up and ran into the next room and laughingly pulled in Jackie—who had been listening to their gossiping. "You're not supposed to listen to these things!" he teased her; "These are private conversations." She scolded back, "Oh, you two little boys chattering about all this gossip." Winking to Walton, Jack declared, "Eternal vigilance is the price of freedom."

Jack's outward coolness, his detachment, was practiced. Even when he laughed he quickly restrained it; he rarely let out a snort or roar, just a smile or wrinkle of the eye. Among the trio who composed his most intimate circle—Lemoyne "Lem" Billings, Paul "Red" Fay, and Dave Powers—all three had the rare ability to throw the president into laughs so hard that they brought tears to his eyes and made him bend over and hold his stomach. Jack might have discussed more important thoughts and displayed different behaviors with others—he was notorious for compartmentalizing not only aspects of his private life but his friends—but male companionship had always been central to his needs. Manchester characterized the president's circle of friends—including former PT-boat crewman and then Assistant Treasury Secretary Jim Reed, college roommate Torb MacDonald, investor Chuck Spalding, journalists Charles Bartlett and Ben Bradlee, artist Bill Walton, Senator George Smathers, and British Ambassador to America David Ormsby-Gore—as "trustworthy, loyal, helpful, friendly mesomorphs." Despite these men's varying socioeconomic backgrounds and the points at which they met Jack in his life, they were also good-natured people, most of them gentle. "I just seem to be attracted by men like that," explained the president. "Maybe it's chemical."

One person had spent more time with Jack and probably knew his mind better than any other male intimate. "Lem Billings," Jackie told Mr. West, "has been a houseguest every weekend of my married life." Although Billings, an advertising executive, worked in Denmark during the administration, a third-floor White House bedroom was set aside as his own. In the lingo of the era, Lem was a "confirmed bachelor," but his love for Jack since they first met as high school roommates demanded nothing but companionship. Jack had even entered Princeton University so he could be with Lem, although he had to drop out when he developed jaundice. When separated, they corresponded heavily. Eunice became especially close to Lem, but the entire family adopted him as one of their own. Even into their adult life, Jack tried to inveigle Lem into antics. In Palm Beach, Jack offered Lem five hundred dollars in cash if he would interrupt Joe by singing "I'm No Angel," a song popularized by Mae West. Joe, as was his habit, was working in a closed area beside the pool

Jack Kennedy facing his lifelong pal Lemoyne "Lem" Billings, the bachelor who was given his own room at the White House for his visits. Caroline Kennedy is at far left. Hyannis Port. June 5, 1963.

without his bathing suit and was not to be disturbed. Lem chickened out, but when he revealed the scheme to Joe, the old man burst into mock rage: "Only five hundred dollars!?" This incident became an inside joke, and Lem and Jack managed to break into hysterics no matter how often it was recalled.

If Lem was the old school chum, Red Fay was the family man pal. Red and Jack had first met on the *PT-109*. Jackie and Fay's wife, Anita, were contemporaries, as were Caroline and Fay's daughter Sally, and they spent more weekends alone with the First Family than the president's own siblings. The Fays moved from their San Francisco home to Washington after Red was named assistant navy

secretary. Red could always amuse Jack and his family with his standard show-stopping singing of "Hooray for Hollywood." Jack teased Red all the more because Red was initially intimidated by his friend's new position. "I used to kid him all the time," Red said. "But not anymore. You just don't kid the president of the United States."

One man did kid Kennedy—endlessly. Working near the Oval Office, Special Assistant Dave Powers, observed journalist Jim Bishop, had "the wonderment of a priest in his eyes, and the tickle of blarney on his tongue. He is not only the best raconteur in the White House, but he has the sharpest memory for detail. . . . It is begging the issue to say that Dave Powers knows the President's

Jack Kennedy and his friend Red Fay with John at Camp David. March 31, 1963.

mind, knows whom he will see and whom he will not." Powers's famous one-liner was, "My family calls me John's other wife." It was he who always went swimming with Jack. When the family was away, it was Dave who always joined Jack for dinner and then beer on the Truman Balcony. "All these Heinekens of mine that you're drinking cost me a lot of money," Jack teased him. "I'm going to send you a bill for it one of these days."

In many ways, Powers connected Jack to his Boston Irish Catholic roots. Home for Powers was the North End three-story row houses of the Irish working class. Kennedy had heard about Powers's political skill and connections and made a cold call on him for help in his first congressional campaign. They were friends from that point on. Powers even felt comfortable calling the president on his mistakes and was the one person in the office who could be counted on to cheer up Jack. Sometimes he said things that would drop even the president's jaw in shocked silence—but then he always broke up. When Dave escorted the Shah of Iran in to see the president, he told the visiting head of state, "You're my kind of shah." Jack gave Dave a mug that read, "There are three things which are real: God, human folly and laughter. The first two are beyond our comprehension. So we must do what we can with the third." Just when things started getting too misty, however, Dave knew to punctuate the conversation with his amazing ability to rattle off statistics, whether it was voting trends in a state, poll numbers in national surveys, or baseball scores.

It has been suggested that Kennedy was as seductive with men as he was with women, in that he seemed to draw them out. Certainly of the seventy household employees, the clerical force, the politically appointed executive staff, the military aides, and the Secret Service agents, he cared especially for the latter group's well-being because of the risks they took for him. Working late one winter night, Kennedy went out to the agent on the colonnade and insisted he come inside and get warm. The agent said he could not, that he was on duty. The president then returned with his own light coat and insisted that the agent put it on. He finally did so. Jack emerged a third time, a little while later, with two cups of hot chocolate, and they sat down together outside, looking out at the black sky, sipping their hot drinks. "Mr. Kennedy's egalitarianism was, in some ways, even greater than Mr. Truman's," recalled the chief of the Secret Service.

Dave Powers, whose jokes cracked Kennedy up and whose memory of statistics dazzled him. In the pool at Bing Crosby's home in Palm Springs, California. 1962.

The only time the Secret Service did not have their eyes on Jack in the White House was when he was still in his Brooks Brothers nightshirt and terry-cloth robe. Otherwise, the moment he left the private quarters, he was met at the elevator by two agents. On occasion, agents passed a Geiger counter over his watch—just to make sure no minuscule but deadly capsule of uranium had been placed there.

Because he spent most of his day in his office, Jack ordered it redecorated. He wanted chalk-white walls. He carefully chose the items to be displayed: the antique blue flag with white stars that had flown on a ship commanded by one of his favorite naval heroes of the American Revolution, Commodore John Perry; antique models of the American navy's most legendary vessels, the *Constitution*, the *Wasp*, and the *Saratoga*. His antique desk, made with timbers of the *Resolute*, had been given to President Hayes by Queen Victoria. On his desk, Jack meticulously placed his most personal item: the coconut on which he had written an S.O.S. to rescue his stranded *PT-109* crew.

Such attention to detail had not come naturally to Jack. He had been influenced by eight years of marriage to a woman who was fanatical about beauty and quality. By the spring of 1961, Jack had absorbed Jackie's visual lessons. "Perhaps because of his constant exposure during the television age, [he] was more interested than any of the other Presidents in every nuance of what the press and the public would think about him and his family in the White House. He fretted about the colors of the walls, the height of the fences," recalled J. B. West. "He was always entirely serious about the White House."

Jack learned antiques from his wife. He stunned Steve Smith when he ran his hand under a desk and explained, "You can tell by the boards—the underside—what age it is, whether it's of the period or a reproduction." Jack stood back and smiled at the rarity. "It's a beautiful table," he said. Then he turned away rather airily and explained that he "favored heavy Chippendale." To his brother Ted, Jack quipped like an exasperated decorator at a chair, "It's not even a *good* reproduction!"

By presidential directive he ordered "all the Lowenstoft bowls in the house filled with flowers—very low." For "my garden," as he called the Rose Garden, he made his wishes clear: "What I want is blooming flowers on the three sides, and especially along the portico where I receive groups. And I would like to look at those flowers as I walk from the Mansion to my office. And I would like them changed from season to season." He designed the steps, platform, and microphone panel he used for ceremonies in the garden. He often held meetings on the flagstone patio, and whenever he saw Rachel Mellon working in the garden, he rushed to speak with her about his flowers. He hated brown patches anywhere. At his orders, the ugly spot would be sprayed with green lawn paint. "Get Macaroni out of my garden!" he yelled when he saw his daughter's

pony munching on some shrubbery, and Evelyn Lincoln ran out and shooed it away.

Jackie also imparted a consciousness of detail about his personal appearance. George Thomas pressed Jack's eighteen or so dark, lightweight suits, custom-made from the New York tailor Sam Harris. Kennedy popularized the two-button suit jacket. He changed his slightly starched monogrammed shirts sometimes four times a day—but never wore any with button-down collars, declaring them "out of style." The president's eight pairs of shoes were always carefully polished.

Equally as sensitive as his wife to the composition of photographs (tucked into his dresser mirror were snapshots of Caroline wearing her mother's high heels, a color Polaroid of Jackie, and an old photograph from their early married years with Bobby and Ethel), he was always aware of how he looked in public. His gray eyes were nearsighted, but he never wore his glasses in public—and often misplaced them. He wore only Wayfarer sunglasses as a trademark, but because so many people pinched them as souvenirs, he had a bag of them kept by his military aide.

Jackie watched his weight—limiting whipped cream from his desserts on occasion, much to his mock chagrin. Kennedy was six feet tall and weighed 175 pounds most of the time—he was always conscious of his weight. He gained about 10 pounds during the course of his presidency. Several days before making a major speech on television, he would go on a crash diet. He always traveled with a scale, so he could check his weight daily. He drank coffee at breakfast, milk or tea with lunch. He traveled with his own supply of bottled Poland Spring water.

He was most vain about his famous head of chestnut-colored hair. At the end of one work day, Special Assistant McGeorge Bundy found Jack having a recommended "health" gel worked into his scalp. Jack told Bundy that he didn't "plan" his "hair very well." Bundy recalled, "He was just terrible about his hair. He had that damn comb in his pocket and went through that hair at least fifty times a day. I don't know what he would have done if he lost his hair." The president sometimes lightened his fingernails with a white manicurist's pencil.

Jack Kennedy plays with Caroline and John on the terrace, just outside the entrance to the pool area. March 28, 1963.

One thing he didn't mind being seen doing was smoking. He smoked about two cigars a day, with a preference for the long and thin H. Uppman cigar; the same expensive smokes that had been the favorite of King Edward VII of England. Sometimes, however, the president was caught puffing on the popular Owl brand cigarillos.

Despite his immaculate presentation in the office, and his careful screening of any situation or person who threatened his dignity, there were two visitors who had carte blanche entry into the Oval Office and also could tackle him to the ground, mess his hair, and even tickle him—his two children. Many late mornings, the president looked up from his desk in the Oval Office to find his wife popping in with their son in tow. He loved these interruptions, especially if a foreign visitor was there and he could introduce them to the famous Jackie and "John-John," a nickname created by the press that the family never used. "Tell me a secret," was Jack's usual greeting to his son. He'd cup his hand as the boy whispered in his ear and would then exclaim, "You don't say!" John always broke into a laugh. When John wandered into the Cabinet Room during a meeting, Jack would sit the boy on his lap if there were not intense discussions. Caroline was known to ride her tricycle through the West Wing.

The most overlooked yet perhaps greatest force in the life of President Kennedy was his love for his children. There was tied up in them a consistent emotional expression that he displayed in no other area of his life. On the day of his marriage, Jack had asked Cardinal Cushing, who had performed the ceremony, to look after Jackie and any children they had if he died young. "Most men don't care about children as much as women do, but he did," Jackie observed. She also compared herself and Jack to icebergs: most of who they really were as human beings was submerged from view; they sensed this and it drew them to one another. They also shared a view of childrearing—exuberant

Caroline visits her dad at the office. May 15, 1962.

adventures, discipline, and open displays of affection.

From almost his first day in office, the president usually took Caroline by the hand to walk with him to the office. When she got there, Caroline got to "work" in Evelyn Lincoln's office, requesting her sheaf of scratch paper and either drawing with pencils or typing some words on the secretary's typewriter. She immediately noticed a dish of candy. Mrs. Lincoln told her it was for people who worked there but added, "It really is so when you

come over, you can have some candy." Caroline—and soon John—took full advantage of the candy dish. Sometimes, the president joked, he really thought they came to the office not so much to see him but to get candy or some of the little novelty gifts his secretary learned to keep in her desk for them when they visited. As time went on, Caroline got bolder and brought her crew of classmates over to invade Mrs. Lincoln's pencils, papers, and, of course, candy dish.

On the walls of Lincoln's office, Jack had cre-

ated a gallery of framed photographs. On one wall were official events and foreign visits. Another had political cartoons and honorary degrees and awards given to him. It was the third wall, however, that attracted the most attention. Here were the family pictures, and they were constantly being updated. And it was not only visitors who were drawn to the intimate images; Jackie herself would wander over to inspect them, often ordering copies for herself. John was, typically, drawn to those that had "Aaplanes!" which he shouted out as he pointed to them in the photographs.

The children were omnipresent in the Oval Office. Some mornings as Jack was heading out of

Caroline and her classmates invade Mrs. Lincoln's desk, and the president pitches in. May 15, 1963.

Caroline playing hide-and-seek under her father's desk, viewed from the back side. The footstool was one of many made for Kennedy to raise his legs to relieve tension on his back. May 16, 1962.

Caroline pays a call on her father's secretary, Evelyn Lincoln, and Dave Powers, showing off her Christmas card and toy snowman, fetched from her school bag. December 4, 1962.

the family rooms to the West Wing, John yelped, "Don't leave me!" If he caught his father's eye, Jack finally said, "Okay, let's go to work," and brought him to play in Mrs. Lincoln's office throughout the morning hours. Inevitably, the boy somehow managed to sneak into Jack's office, open the small wood panel of the president's desk, climb in, and hide. When Jack began a meeting, a scratching came from the desk. "Do I hear a rabbit?" Jack asked, prompting the boy to pop out. Shooed away because his father had to work, John dubbed his father a "foo-foo head." Jack put on a stunned face. "John Kennedy, how dare you call the president of the United States a foo-foo head?" With a tap on his father's bottom, John then called Jack "Bad Daddy." That night, as he was being tucked in, he whispered into his father's face, "Foo-foo head."

The Italian prime minister, Amintore Fanfani, shows Caroline the doll in native dress that he brought as a gift for her. January 17, 1963.

As did other proud fathers, Jack kept signs of his home life around him at work. In the small working room beside the Oval Office, he kept Caroline's gift to him of a pink piggy bank, family vacation pictures taken by Jackie, and the children's latest artwork. He showed off the homemade card Caroline made for his birthday to the staff, passing it around as if he were a junior executive bursting with pride at his firstborn.

Such reminders of the children in the Oval Office, however, served a greater purpose than just momentary distraction and laughter for Jack. In Mrs. Lincoln's office, he kept a rocking horse that his sister Eunice Shriver had brought to the Cabinet Room for use by some retarded children who had met with him there. The toy was used not only by the children but by the president as inspiration. "We keep that rocking horse in here," he explained to a cabinet officer, "to remind us of the younger generation and

John plays with Mrs. Lincoln's typewriter at her office desk, right outside the Oval Office. May 30, 1963.

Below: *Fanfani and Jackie steady John as he struggles after opening his gift of a toy dog.* Right: *Then, Jackie struggles with her dog, Clipper, in getting the toy dog back. January 17, 1963.*

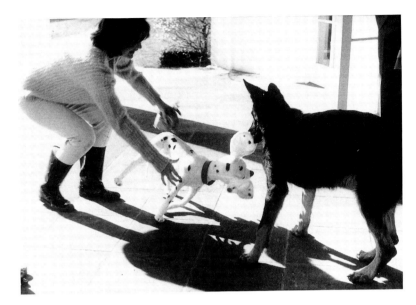

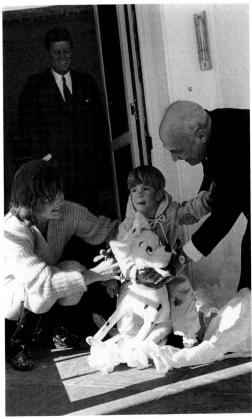

what our responsibilities are in making this country a safe place in which to live."

Before lunch Jack would go for the first of his two half-hour swimming sessions in the pool, a workout with weights, calisthenics, and a back massage. It was his evening swim, however, that he relished. This was when his children often joined him. First came a race over to the pool—which, of course, he always let them win—and then splashing in the 90-degree water. The children demanded that the president swim "like a fish," underwater, and that Dave Powers—who almost always joined them—swim "like a whale," doing the backstroke and spouting water. If a call came through, the president hushed the children. When he hung up, there were shrill calls for him to jump into the pool. Caroline showed off her ability to put her head underwater and John tried to imitate her.

On evenings when Jackie was away, the children came to the Oval Office dressed in their pajamas and bathrobes, ready for bed. As he opened the door and first glimpsed them, Jack would quip, "Hello there, Sam, how are you?" John would shout back loudly, "I am not Sam, I'm John. Daddy, I'm John." Then it was the same with his daughter. "Hello there, Mary." Caroline very seriously replied, "No. My name is Caroline."

"You can talk when he comes home at night," Jackie said of their home life in the White House. "That's been wonderful for the children." The children having eaten dinner earlier in the evening with their nanny, Jack and Jackie usually dined together and then worked next to each other in the West Sitting Hall, he spreading papers out on the sofa and floor, both of them writing in longhand on legal-size yellow notepads. While he worked, Caroline often sat on her father's lap, quietly drawing pictures. When the important executive documents of the president were returned for filing the next morning, often shuffled among them were drawings by Caroline with the word *Daddy* written in crayon.

Caroline's father bids her farewell from an afternoon visit to his office just before she heads out on her pony, Macaroni. June 22, 1962.

5

I N   A   C R I S I S

The Extended Kennedy Family, 1961

Nobody tells Jack what to do unless he wants to be told.
—JOE KENNEDY

Everyone asks if Jack has a complex about his father, and if Bobby has a complex about Jack.
—JACQUELINE KENNEDY

Less than three months after his inauguration, Jack Kennedy realized the vital role his extended family would play in his success, even more acutely than he had during the campaign. On April 17, 1961, during the Congressional Reception, at about ten in the evening, while Jack and Jackie began dancing to the tune of "Mr. Wonderful," Bobby lowered the boom on his lighthearted brother. The attorney general had just received word that an invasion of Communist Cuba, approved by the president, had collapsed into the first and worst debacle of the administration. "This thing has turned sour in a way you wouldn't believe," Bobby explained to his brother.

Just after the inauguration, President Kennedy approved a CIA plan drawn up during the Eisenhower administration—one assured to be a success by the Joint Chiefs of Staff, CIA chief Allen Dulles, and others. The mission was an invasion of Cuba by 1,200 Cuban nationals who had escaped to America from the new Communist regime of Fidel Castro. The day before the action, Jack sent his fellow cigar smoker and press secretary Pierre Salinger to buy as many Cuban cigars as he could; shortly they would no longer be available in the United States. But a cigar shortage was the least of Kennedy's Cuba problems. Human lives were at stake. The troops came ashore in an area of Cuba known as the Bay of Pigs, but were quickly captured by Castro's forces. It turned out to be the greatest disaster of the Kennedy administration.

"My God, the bunch of advisers we inherited," Jack initially complained to Jackie. "Can you imagine being President and leaving behind someone like all those people there [CIA]?" In the end, however, Jack "blamed only himself," according to Arthur Schlesinger. With his macho ego, humiliated before the world, he regarded it as his own personal failure. After the Bay of Pigs, he became even more intense. Even Lem

Billings, who had always been a person who could make Jack laugh, was unable to do so. The event, he said, made it more difficult for even the president's most intimate friends "to get close to" President Kennedy. Jackie later confessed to Arthur Schlesinger that the president "had cried when the news of the Bay of Pigs came in."

Soon enough, as he always could in a crisis, Jack Kennedy counted on the support of his extended family. "Tribal loyalty" is how historian William Manchester characterized it: "Let one of them be threatened and the others hold up knuckles. . . ." Eunice repeatedly referred to the Bay of Pigs as "one little mistake." Joe tried to buck Jack up by saying it was better to make mistakes as soon as possible, so one learned lessons early on. Joe further responded by attacking his son's critics, saying they offered no solutions. Rose Kennedy was visiting her son in the White House at the time. She recorded in her diary: "Jackie walked upstairs with me and said he was upset all day. Had practically been in tears, felt he had been misinformed by the CIA . . . Jackie seemed so sympathetic and said she had stayed with him until he had lain down as she had never seen him so depressed except once at time of his operation." The following weekend, at the family's Virginia retreat, the president angrily hit golf balls into a cornfield. Jackie was extremely solicitous of his comfort and relaxation. "It was the only thing on his mind," said Chuck Spalding, "and we just had to let him talk himself out."

At this juncture, Jackie's approach to her husband was tentative. He did not invite any sympathy. Characterizing her role in reaching out to the president during the Bay of Pigs as "very subtle," Spalding conceded, however, "She wouldn't come out and put a sympathetic arm around him, or anything like that." Had she tried to do so, it was likely that Jack would have rejected this as a sign of sympathy, not support. Her understood task was to keep away people who would want to rehash his mistakes. Her role would deepen, however, as their marriage grew and, later, when a global catastrophe threatened.

As the invasion was taking place, the president had momentarily distracted himself by strolling out into the Rose Garden, where he spotted Caroline and some of her friends running on the lawn. As he always did when he wanted to call children or pets, he clapped his hands loudly and they came to him. Caroline ran into his arms, and he gently lifted her and spun her about. Now, in the aftermath, even his daughter was not spared ridicule. As one of the bitter jokes at the time went, "Caroline is a nice kid, but this is the last time she plans an invasion of Cuba." This particular joke set off the president's formidable anger: he felt that any sarcastic mention of his children, other than in good humor, was "dirty politics."

What also developed in Kennedy, however, was doubt about the infallibility of military experts and advisers. Part of his rage at himself was that he had followed their advice rather than seeking a perspective from those whose judgments he most trusted and who would have had his own best interests at heart. Despite all the military advisers who had urged the badly planned invasion, Kennedy's prestige and reputation were most directly damaged, and he had to assume full responsibility. Victory, he said, had many fathers, but defeat was an orphan. The one person to whom he now knew he could always turn for advice was his brother Bobby. He had realized, "I should have had Bobby in on this from the start." His immediate response in the wake of the disaster was to place Bobby on a board of inquiry that investigated where the failures had been made. "We'd been through a lot of things together," the attorney gen-

President Kennedy and the attorney general in the Oval Office. FBI director J. Edgar Hoover, a nemesis of the brothers, stands second from left. September 19, 1961.

eral later wrote, "and he was more upset this time than he was any other." In seeing clearly that Jack had been poorly served, Bobby "vowed never again to let it happen." On every important issue facing the president, the attorney general would be his most intimate adviser. This was above and beyond his running of the Justice Department: his influence was felt in all domestic policy and proposed legislation as well as foreign and defense issues. Perhaps most important, noted Schlesinger, "After the Bay of Pigs, Robert became his brother's eyes and ears around the national security establishment."

Loyalty to and protection of his brother became Bobby Kennedy's driving mission. This, in a sense, allowed Jack to continue to play the charming good cop while Bobby viewed everything as a matter of, as one friend put it, "the white hats and the black hats, the good guys versus the bad guys." Even Bobby's wife viewed political figures as "goodies" or "baddies," based on whether or not they were blindly in line with everything the president believed. It was a dynamic that played out their personalities. When Jack gave Bobby the book *The Enemy Within*, he inscribed it: "For Bobby—the Brother Within—who made the easy difficult." Spalding observed, "It wasn't that Bobby was more passionate than Jack. It was simply that . . .

Bobby Kennedy greets his nephew John and niece Caroline in the Oval Office. 1963.

Bobby's emotions were closer to the surface and Jack's were buried. Jack had greater control."

Jack's closest confidant in everything was Bobby. He was the only person who could not only demand absolute support for Jack's decisions but also could speak with total candor to the president. They so frequently talked to each other on the telephone that Eunice suggested they somewhat "shared" the presidency, complementing each other and cryptically communicating to each other in the presence of others by, as the president put it, "osmosis." They could read each other by looks or body language. Such fraternity, however, did not mean that the attorney general escaped his brother's suspicions. "Far from being influenced easily by Bobby, the President was quick to point

out an error or weakness in one of Bobby's proposals," observed aide Kenny O'Donnell. For his part, Bobby sent a memo to the president suggesting that he more frequently heed the advice on a variety of noncrisis issues from "The best minds in government." At the bottom of the handwritten memo, the younger brother wrote the explanatory footnote "Me."

Around Bobby's office were signs of a new and different sort of attorney general: finger paintings by his children, a gigantic lacquered sailfish, a stuffed tiger, and a large, mean black dog who sat in the corner. He worked in shirtsleeves and rumpled pants, his legs often on the desk, a football always on the desk. Like his brother, he was intensely focused on his children. After his showdown with Governor George Wallace over the forced integration of the University of Alabama, Bobby wrote to his son David, "Shortly after you left my office, the two Negroes attempted to register . . . Jack called up the National Guard and tonight at 6:00 they are registered and preparing to attend classes tomorrow." He wrote his older son Michael, "I hope when you are Attorney General these kind of things will not go on." At the so-called Hickory Hill Seminars, evening discussions with various experts, Bobby's wife, Ethel, and sister Eunice often peppered the speaker with a litany of probing questions about his beliefs. Jack seemed bemused by what he considered the naive eagerness behind the idea—yet the next morning he always wanted to know what the speakers said.

Ethel Kennedy drove her children to school each morning from their suburban Virginia home. Deeply anchored to a literal belief in her faith, she and her husband said evening prayers with their children and hung religious pictures on their walls. Ethel Kennedy thought the work of the Peace Corps was excellent—but she wished they wouldn't distribute

The attorney general and his wife at breakfast with some of their children.
<small>COURTESY MAX KENNEDY</small>

birth control devices. Ethel Kennedy casually picked up special guests of the administration from the airport in her big white convertible: the CIA director found himself crammed in with kids; Marian Anderson was trapped as Ethel demonstrated her singing voice. She did her bit as the boss's wife, too—arranging for a snack area and patio for Justice Department employees, complete with tables and umbrellas. At her parties, guests were warned that they might be thrown into the pool; the warnings were based on the fact that at one party a wooden platform over the pool collapsed and she, as well as Arthur Schlesinger, fell in.

The president relished the tales of his extended family that seemed to entertain the nation—whether the stories were true or apocryphal. In fact, his own telling of stories at his family's expense soon became a trademark element of his humor. At a Teamsters' dinner, Jack Kennedy let loose a series of Kennedy jokes that showed his self-deprecating wit at its best: "Vaughan Meader was busy tonight, so I came myself. I listened to Mr. Meader's record album, but I thought it sounded more like Teddy than it did me—so he's annoyed. . . . If anyone here feels pressured by his boss into coming tonight, I know just how he feels. Jackie

Ethel Kennedy (to the right of the piano) presides over a children's party in the East Room.

made me buy a ticket to the National Cultural Center dinner . . . I was proud of the Attorney General's first appearance before the Supreme Court. He did a good job, according to everyone I talked to—Ethel, Jackie, Teddy . . ."

Although Rose Kennedy was dismayed about the publicity over the pool antics, there were times when she, too, could propagate jokes about her family. "There's never been a woman who's been mother of two or three Presidents," she told one audience. "So I've told my other sons, 'Get busy!' " Rose occasionally substituted as First Lady for Jackie at events for visiting dignitaries. On one such occasion, when she was told by the wife of the Ecuadorian president that her son didn't want to be president, like his father and grandfather, Mrs. Kennedy took umbrage at the notion that there was something wrong with politics as a family business: "I think it's a thing to be praised." To

Bobby she wrote in June of 1961, "I think you should work hard and become President after Jack. It will be good for the country. And for you. And especially good for you know who—ever your affectionate and peripatetic mother." She wrote the letter at a particularly happy moment. She was in her favorite room in her favorite hotel in her favorite city—the Paris Ritz's rose suite—and relishing what would be her favorite moment of his administration, the president's first European visit.

At seventy-one years of age, the physically fit Rose Kennedy had no ambivalence about whether she wanted to be acknowledged as a public figure or remain a private citizen: at one state dinner, after Chief Justice Earl Warren offered a toast to her, the First Mother arose and waved to the guests. She presented a protocol problem at White House functions since there was no specific ranking for a president's mother. Finally, since she had

Jack listens to his mother, Rose, at a fund-raiser dinner for the Joseph Kennedy Jr. Foundation, while Jackie and LBJ kibitz. December 12, 1962.

been an ambassador's wife, the State Department placed her just below the spouses of the vice president and chief justice.

The First Mother also refused to be left out of the youthful image of the Kennedys. She swam and golfed daily. When she told some reporters that she took note of the summer season's bikinis at Cannes, she insisted they record this fact, "Because everyone thinks I'm so saintlike." At her homes, in the afternoons, she was often found with notes to herself pinned to her dress to keep herself abreast of

all of her planned activities—and "frownies," paper patches intended to reduce wrinkles, on her face. She didn't wear them at the White House—but she did insist on a daily afternoon rest. Rose Kennedy was not going to let anyone prevent her from enjoying her unique status—even the president himself. However, when she demanded of the president's military aide that she be permitted to exit *Marine One*, the presidential helicopter, first—signifying respect for an older woman—Jack refused. He got off first. When she came down the stairs and saw a

Rose Kennedy presides as White House hostess with her son, greeting entertainers at the post–state dinner performance in honor of Haile Selassie of Ethiopia. October 4, 1963.

crowd, she proudly introduced herself: "I'm Rose Kennedy, mother of the president." She commandeered the Lincoln Suite while staying at the White House. Once the president was giving a tour of the rooms to actress Carol Channing; he peeked into the Lincoln Bedroom and then closed the door. "Sorry! The tour is off! Mother's *in* the Lincoln Bed!" Rose was taking her nap.

In public, Rose always addressed her son as "Mr. President." Occasionally, she walked out on the lawn and peeked into the Oval Office as he worked, but she generally kept her distance from him, rigidly obeying her own rule never to disturb him. "I never wanted to intrude on his time . . . I wouldn't think of going to talk to Jack. I think if he had something particular to say he'd come to me or ask me . . . to expect to see him at lunch or dinner, no, I never expected that. I knew if it were possible

he would send for me, but otherwise he would be engaged and he had a good deal on his mind." Privately, she continued to offer motherly suggestions and religious reading—and the titles of new movies disapproved of by the Catholic Church—to all of her adult children. The president was no exception. She suggested he wear striped ties on television because they looked stylish on black-and-white sets. She reminded him to keep his nervous hands out of his coat pockets, a habit she noticed in news coverage. After one of his speeches, she might sometimes call a speechwriter about better word choices.

Jack appreciated his mother's talents, believing that, when it came to crowd pleasing, she was "a natural politician." As First Mother she continued to deliver public speeches about what it took to raise a president. She had never been afraid to needle him in public. When he appeared late for a speech at which she was introducing him, he came in with a hat and asked, "How do I look?" She quipped, "You would have looked better two hours ago." Building up her collection of personally inscribed pictures from heads of state, she wrote Khrushchev for his. When he learned of this, Jack told her to stop—such contact must go through the State Department. Rose gave as good as she got. "Dear Jack," she responded, "I'm so glad you warned me about contacting the heads of state as I was just about to write Castro. Love, Mother."

Jack seemed to retain a prickly caution with his mother. Doris Goodwin characterized Jack's and Rose's relationship as one of "lifelong detachment." When Rose was once leaving for a three-week trip with her sister, six-year-old Jack told her boldly, "Gee, you're a great mother to go away and leave your children alone." In his young adult years, Jack learned to keep secrets around his mother, sharing aspects of his private life—particularly those decidedly irreligious ones—with his brothers, sisters, and father, but never Rose. Instead, he humored her with jokes and teasing. He never sprang bad news on her—but knowing how much she had sacrificed in her life for her family, he never denied the nation's First Mother her part in his presidency. He included her in all variety of events—a luncheon for the Greek premier, a reception for one thousand people, and the famous Pablo Casals concert in the East Room. And, on her annual springtime Paris trip for designer clothing, she wanted to be part of her son's and daughter-in-law's regal celebration by that city. "Jack was against her going, but there wasn't anything he could do about it because Mrs. Kennedy was determined to be in on everything," recalled Lem Billings.

Paris might have been Jackie's city, but it was also Rose's. Not only was she included in the official greeting ceremony hosted by President Charles de Gaulle and in the official motorcade, but she attended the state dinner at Versailles as well—as did Eunice and Jackie's favorite cousin, Michel Bouvier, who was working overseas, and his wife, Kathy. Between the official events, the elder Mrs. Kennedy, as she always did, roamed the ancient streets incognito in her sunglasses and green celluloid forehead visor, going from designer house to showroom, inspecting and gathering some of the season's new couture. Jackie was expected to wear—or at least to claim that she wore—American fashions, but Rose reveled in her Balenciagas, Diors, St. Laurents, and Nina Riccis. She also endlessly practiced her French, with records while at home and with a tutor while in France. Although she spoke the language well, she never lost her Yankee accent. Rose always spoke French in France, even under the hair dryer at the beauty salon. Unself-consciously, she wore a black band over her eyes to block out distraction and said her prayers in French, as she held her rosary beads.

She always wore a scarf, she explained: "When I pass a church I go in to say a prayer, and all the churches in France are so cold."

Rose seemed as fearless as her son. She enjoyed picking up hitchhikers just to see their reaction when they realized who she was. She loved to walk late at night, rather than take taxis, and once convinced Truman Capote to walk with her some thirty blocks. "[S]he talked the entire way," he recalled, "going on about things like how Central Park didn't frighten her at night and how she wasn't afraid of anything and every other subject you can think of."

The president's mother remained with the presidential entourage and went on to Vienna, where she met the Khrushchevs and compared Nina to "a neighbor you'd call in to baby-sit." Before they left for Vienna, de Gaulle warned Jackie that Nina Khrushchev was *plus maline que lui*—more sneaky than the premier. Jackie was already wise to the Soviet couple. Khrushchev made some remark about wanting to shake her hand instead of that of the president. Jackie was not flattered. Khrushchev talked of the superior educational standards in the Ukraine. "Oh, Mr. Chairman, don't bore me with statistics," she shot back. He was amused by the challenge. Finally they found common ground while talking about dogs. She asked him about Strelka, the famous Russian dog that had been sent into orbit. He offered to send her one of Strelka's pups. She accepted. Throughout the evening, Jackie carefully scrutinized the personalities of the Politburo members she met. She had already provided her unsolicited assessment to Jack that only Andrey Gromyko could be trusted.

After Vienna, another family encounter became charged with political purpose. Because he had been asked to serve as godfather to Christina

Jackie Kennedy and her sister, Lee Radziwill, in Greece, seated for a performance in an ancient open-air theater. May 1961.

Radziwill, who had been born the previous autumn, President Kennedy had an ostensible reason for going to London. While Jack was in fact at the christening ceremony, his brief trip to the English capital also permitted him to meet with Prime Minister Harold Macmillan without an official agenda or expectations. From there Jack went home. But Jackie and her sister Lee jetted off to Greece together, the first of several international trips they would take.

Although it was billed as a "private" trip, wire service photographers, Greek reporters, and a slew of European paparazzi stormed Jackie and Lee, known from that point on as "Princess Lee." Although her kind husband, Stanislaus—

nicknamed Stas—could claim a Polish royal title, he was deposed. Still, the title added luster, and Lee did not dissuade people from using it. Peasants and the press clustered narrow streets just to glimpse the First Lady and the princess. There were reports that Jackie had danced to folk music and done the cha-cha to "Never on Sunday" in a Hydra nightclub. There were photographs of Jackie and Lee strolling through a Poros lemon grove. When the sisters toured Cyclades Island on a yacht, the Greek government warned swimmers and paparazzi alike, "We are instructed to spear any large sea life moving toward the Kennedy party." The cobblestones of the entire village of Mykonos were whitewashed, and the entire island

Extended Family of John F. Kennedy, 1961–1963

Rosemary Kennedy, born September 13, 1918, unmarried

Eunice Mary "Eunie" Kennedy, born July 10, 1921

    Married on May 23, 1953, to (Robert) Sargent "Sarge" Shriver, Jr., born November 9, 1915

    Children:

        Robert "Bobby" Sargent Shriver III, born April 28, 1954

        Maria Shriver, born November 6, 1955

        Timothy Perry Shriver, born August 29, 1959

Patricia "Pat" Kennedy, born May 6, 1924

    Married on April 24, 1954, to Peter Lawford, born September 7, 1923

    Children:

        Christopher Kennedy Lawford, born March 29, 1955

        Sydney Maleia Lawford, born August 25, 1956

        Victoria Frances Lawford, born November 4, 1958

        Robin Elizabeth Lawford, born July 2, 1961

Robert Francis "Bobby" Kennedy, born November 20, 1925

    Married on June 17, 1950, to Ethel Skakel, born April 11, 1928

    Children:

        Kathleen Hartington Kennedy, born July 4, 1951

        Joseph P. Kennedy II, born September 24, 1952

        Robert Francis Kennedy Jr., born January 17, 1954

        David Anthony Kennedy, born June 15, 1955

        Mary Courtney Kennedy, born September 9, 1956

        Michael LeMoyne Kennedy, born February 27, 1958

        Mary Kerry Kennedy, born September 8, 1959

        Christopher George Kennedy, born July 4, 1963

Jean Ann Kennedy, born February 20, 1928

    Married on May 19, 1956, to Stephen Edward Smith, born September 24, 1927

    Children:

        Stephen Edward Smith Jr., born June 28, 1957

        William Kennedy Smith, born September 4, 1960

Edward Moore "Teddy" Kennedy, born February 22, 1932

    Married on November 29, 1958, to Virginia Joan Bennett, born September 9, 1936

    Children:

        Kara Anne Kennedy, born February 27, 1960

        Edward Moore "Teddy Jr." Kennedy, born September 26, 1961

of Delos was closed to tourists because the Bouvier sisters were coming.

Being with someone from *her* family was one way Jackie could briefly put off the inevitability of being with people from *his* family. It wasn't that the First Lady and her in-laws fought or disliked each other. They just had radically different sensibilities. Jackie, in fact, saw her sister-in-law Jean Smith socially. She highly respected Eunice's intelligence. There was a mutual admiration society among Jackie and Bobby, Teddy, and Joe. Like Jackie, Joan marched to the beat of her own drum,

The extended Kennedy family at Hyannis Port. Bottom row, left to right: Stevie Smith Jr., David Kennedy, Joe Kennedy II, Chris Lawford, Jackie Kennedy holding her baby John, Bobby Shriver, Sargent Shriver, Bobby Kennedy Jr.; second row, left to right: Jean Kennedy Smith, Sydney Lawford, Pat Lawford holding Vicky Lawford in her lap, Maria Shriver, Steve Smith holding son Willie Smith in his lap, Courtney Kennedy, Jack Kennedy holding daughter Caroline in his lap, Kerry Kennedy, Kathleen Kennedy, Joan Kennedy holding daughter Kara in her lap, family friend Lem Billings, Eunice Kennedy Shriver holding son Timothy in her lap, Michael Kennedy. Summer 1961.

in her case, classical music. At the family's summer compound in Hyannis Port, when the others went off sailing, swimming, or playing some competitive sport, Jackie would paint with watercolors while Joan would play her piano. "They think we're weird! Weird!" Jack's wife giggled to Teddy's wife. Yet, unlike Jackie, Joan was unable to see her uniqueness from the clan as an asset. "Why worry if you're not as good at tennis as Eunice or Ethel when men are attracted by the feminine way you play tennis?" Jackie implored Joan to realize.

In early summer, there was some rivalry between Rose Kennedy and her daughter-in-law, who returned from Europe renowned around the world. Rose tried to draw a line about mothering her grandchildren. When she was at the White House, she refrained from her favorite nighttime habit of "informal storytelling or hearing prayers" with Caroline and John—but at Hyannis Port, well, Rose admitted she indulged in this. "You want Caroline to be like you," Jackie said to her mother-in-law, "and I want her to be like me." Oftentimes the older woman gave strict instructions that seemed condescending or repetitive to the younger woman. In time, however, a deeper sense of understanding of what each went through would develop, and with that would come a genuine bond. After the Casals dinner, for example, Jackie wrote a thank-you letter to "Dearest Belle Mere" for *her* "immeasurable luster" that night.

Conflict between a new and forming nuclear family and a larger extended family ruled by tradition and habit is inevitable. Jackie's response was physically to separate herself and her children from the clan in Hyannis Port. For Jack, this conflict only fueled the competition for the attention of "Mr. President" (as everyone in the family called him—while they called Bobby, Bobby), and he somehow successfully managed to please both his

wife and his extended family—to be part of them, yet in his own league. In the process he had made himself the delightful leader of his siblings, their spouses, and their children, even eventually of his parents and then the nation and world. But this could be deceptive. "The self-assured manner concealed a more explosive insecurity," observed Doris Goodwin. "It was not the confidence of one who had inherited the world, but of a man who believed he could win it if he tried."

Jack particularly enjoyed the public attention that his loving crowd of about a dozen towheaded little nieces and nephews received. He genuinely enjoyed taking the children into the Hyannis candy store and newsstand, where they invaded the racks of Necco wafers, button candy, and Bantam taffy sticks—and had Rose pay the bill. Then, tradition had it, the president would pile the Lilliputians onto the back of his motorized golf cart and drive them back to the family compound—before the eyes of the national press. It was much the same on Sunday mornings, when he took a group of them to church. When little Maria Shriver sold lemonade and postcards of her uncle to raise money for the mentally retarded or when Chris Lawford tumbled from the golf cart, it made news. In Hyannis Port, however, tourists continually jammed the streets near the president's home and poked through the hedges—sometimes to be met by nephews and nieces charging a nickel to answer the question "What does Jackie eat for breakfast?"

With Lem Billings and Red Fay spending weekends during the summer of 1961 with Jack on the Cape, the adults relished the cruises out into the ocean. Although any member of the Kennedy family could use Joe's *Marlin*, one had to be invited onto the president's yacht, the *Honey Fitz*, or his sailboat, the *Victura*. The *Honey Fitz* was ninety-two feet long, and

President Kennedy leaves church in Hyannis Port with his niece Maria Shriver, nephew Bobby Shriver behind him, and niece Sydney Lawford. After they had all changed from church clothes, he often took them all for candy at the local news and stationery store. Summer 1961.

New Bedford Standard Times (top)

President Kennedy on the yacht Honey Fitz. *From left to right, family friend Chuck Spalding, Steve Smith, Jack Kennedy, Stas Radzi-*
will, family friend Dave Ormsby-Gore, Jean Kennedy Smith, Jackie Kennedy in large hat. 1961.

although there were telephones for the president to use and at least two Secret Service speedboats always alongside it, these outings offered Jack true relaxation. He had a chance to put on his swimming trunks, take off his shirt, and soak in the sun while gossiping or discussing philosophical matters with his sisters, brothers, in-laws, and closest friends. He could read, smoke cigars, nap, eat lunch or ice-cream cones, or play with the children at his leisure. Sailing was a bit more of an ordeal, the Secret Service naturally nervous about the president's vulnerability, as there was a greater chance he would tip into the ocean or run aground. There were other political risks on the ocean, however. When Jackie put on her bathing suit and took off on her water skis with John Glenn, the telephoto lenses of photographers were

Jackie and Jack Kennedy standing in their sailboat the Victura as it runs aground. July 28, 1962.

Jackie Kennedy water-skiing in Hyannis Port Bay. Summer 1961.

BOSTON HERALD

Ted Kennedy plays the family's favorite game, touch football, with his brother Bobby and sister-in-law Ethel.

capturing the scene for the next morning's newspapers. Then came days of critical editorials and mail. "I never quite figured out why some people thought it was unbecoming that she was water-skiing in a bathing suit," Glenn later reflected. "She got a huge kick out of it. She was also very apologetic, thinking that *she* had gotten *me* in trouble."

In the late afternoons, the president had to refrain from the family's famous touch football games because of his back, so Bobby now taught the younger generation of grandchildren to play the game. "Except for war," he said, "there is nothing in American life—nothing—that trains a boy better for life than football." In the evenings, the president most enjoyed going to his parents' house, where, in the basement, there was a small movie

Jackie Kennedy carrying a tray and following her son John in the living room of Joe Kennedy's home. Rose Kennedy's piano is behind them. 1961.

theater. Here the whole family watched first-run films sent to them by friends in Hollywood. The Joe Kennedy home was headquarters for the extended family. They all gathered in it for dinner—although Jackie wanted her family to attend only once a week—followed by games for the grown-ups in the large living room or sing-alongs around the piano, Rose or Joan on the keys, and Ted breaking into his famously toneless baritone.

However, for most of that first summer when the president visited, Joe and Rose Kennedy stayed out of the limelight. As was their custom, they rented a summer home in Antibes, France—Joe making headlines when he was spotted with his shapely

Jackie Kennedy in discussion in the front parlor of the "big house," the home of Joe and Rose Kennedy, overlooking the water. 1961.

young French caddy. From Europe, Rose would go directly to Palm Beach for the winter. She wanted to avoid the media circus in Hyannis Port that summer, and consequently she did not visit her own mother for months. Unknown to the press, however, ninety-five-year-old Josie Fitzgerald lived in the shadow of the famous "compound," on a back road, Lighthouse Lane—appropriately enough, between her family and her church, St. Francis Xavier.

Overlooking Hyannis Bay, the Kennedy compound consisted of a loose grouping together of shingled and clapboard houses, partially protected from public view by tall hedges and rambling flowers, placed along or near Irving Avenue. The main house

was the one Joe and Rose had bought in 1926. With fourteen rooms, it directly faced the water. Its porch wrapped around the seafront side, and there were large wicker chairs and settees on it. A flagpole marked the circular lawn area, which was surrounded by the asphalt drive. In front of this was the wide expanse of lawn where the presidential helicopter always landed after having picked up the First Family at Otis Air Force Base, where *Air Force One* had brought them in from Andrews Air Force Base in Washington. When in residence, Joe Kennedy was always on the porch to watch his son's arrival.

The president's house looked large from the outside but was considerably smaller than his father's. There were only three bedrooms, and

Jack Kennedy walking to his Hyannis Port home. Dave Powers (left) holds the president's hat. May 10, 1963.

Jackie had made it a cozy New England home—yellow cushions, chintz chairs, colored glass bottles the couple had collected together on top of the small window ledges. The dining room was somewhat plain, all in traditional pinewood, with Jack's cushioned chair at the head of the dining-room table. A small linoleum-floored kitchen had not been changed since the late 1940s.

With increased frequency, the president used his Hyannis Port home to hold meetings—not only in the summer but, when he wanted to escape Washington, off-season as well. Jackie was less than thrilled about this but did not complain. She

The dining room of the president's Hyannis Port home. 1961.
BOSTON HERALD

In the living room of the president's Hyannis Port home, conferring with Sargent Shriver. 1962.

President Kennedy with reporters in the living room of his Hyannis Port home. Large framed family pictures were on the walls. 1961.

was even less enthusiastic about family just popping in. Jack, not wanting to be as isolated, more frequently visited the homes of his siblings, usually bringing Caroline along with him.

Summer was the only time, for example, that he had a chance to see much of his sister Pat and her husband, Peter Lawford. As it was, she was only there a week. Fiercely loyal to her brother, Pat sometimes seemed a little ambivalent about her own children, often globetrotting with her sisters or husband. Barely a month after the July 2 birth of her daughter Robin, she took off for Europe with Peter—joining her parents for part of the time—and did not return even when the infant was hospitalized. In September, after her return, Pat acted as a substitute First Lady at several occasions, but the Lawfords were more removed from the Kennedy White House simply because they lived in Santa Monica, California. Close friends of Marilyn Monroe, Judy Garland, Frank Sinatra, Dean Martin, Sammy Davis Jr., Shirley MacLaine, and Joey Bishop, the Lawfords were the Hollywood connection for the president and other members of the family. The president was even named an honorary member of the famous Rat Pack. His nickname was "Chicky Baby."

Pat Lawford was rarely in Washington. On September 26, 1961, however, she played the role of First Lady by welcoming the poster child for the Leukemia Society.

Although Joe Kennedy was not fond of Peter Lawford, and there were already strains in Pat's marriage to him, Jack Kennedy enjoyed the company of his actor brother-in-law. They had become genuine friends, and the president was even protective of Lawford's career. When Arthur Schlesinger asked Jack if he'd have any problem with his writing movie reviews for a new magazine, Jack sent back a note saying it was fine—"As long as you treat Peter Lawford with respect." Still, Lawford's heavy partying soon enough drew in Jack: it was through Lawford the president met the most unsavory characters.

"I wish I'd saved one boy for the business," Joe Kennedy reflected that autumn. "Here I am, seventy-three, and I could drop dead any minute, and I have to keep working because they're in these other things." He would not have to worry. His daughter Jean's husband, Steve Smith, who had managed Jack's campaign finances with a mean accounting ability, would become the family's point person on money. Throughout 1961, however, Steve Smith was working closely with the

Peter Lawford, the movie star brother-in-law, talks to Jack during a sailing voyage in Maine. Kennedy teased Lawford about this picture, in which it looks as if the president is taking Lawford's policy advice seriously. August 11, 1962.

president as a consultant to the Development Loan Fund at the State Department. Steve Smith was an intense, chain-smoking, defensive team player who fought for the Kennedys as if he had been born one of them. "My political philosophy? John F. Kennedy," Smith quipped. Although Jean went with Steve and Vice President Johnson on a Southeast Asian trip, her life was the traditional one of being a wife and a mother to her two young sons. In later writing to LBJ about the Asian trip, she referred to herself as "Little Sister." It was an apt description for how she viewed herself—with some sense of a less certain status among her elder siblings Eunice, Jack, and Bobby. Naturally curious about the private areas of the White House, she never pressed Jack and Jackie for invitations. Instead, one afternoon when she, along with Eunice and Ethel, stopped by the White House to swim in the pool, she wandered through the family quarters. Thinking the First Family was away, she was mortified when she awoke the napping president.

Jean was the second youngest of the president's siblings, and it was the youngest child—her brother Ted—who was always her closest friend and the favorite of the family. The twenty-nine-year-old Ted was the lighthearted delight for all of the Kennedys. "Teddy was our surprise baby," Rose revealed. "He's probably brought more joy into our lives than we ever thought possible. He has so much joy in him." Teddy was indeed the loved child. Eunice had even taken him along on her 1953 honeymoon.

Earlier that year, on February 5, Ted had accepted a dollar-a-year post as assistant district attorney in Suffolk County, near Boston, and moved with Joan and their baby, Kara, to a rented Beacon Hill apartment. In his effort to make a case that he could deservedly earn a U.S. Senate seat,

The president confers with Steve Smith, the businessman brother-in-law, outside the Oval Office. Smith was initially a consultant to the Development Loan Fund, then served as deputy director of the State Department's crisis center, went to New York to assume a leading role in directing the family's financial affairs, and then, in 1963, returned to Washington, to the Democratic National Committee, where he headed early planning efforts for the 1964 reelection campaign. July 18, 1963.

he had the total support of his family—led by Joe. The president, however, continued to be leery: not only would the "dynasty" charges against him be taken more seriously, but if his younger brother lost, or even ran a bad campaign, it would directly impact the public perception of the administration.

Jean Kennedy Smith served as surrogate First Lady at the state dinner for the president of Ireland. She also greeted alumnae of her alma mater, Sacred Heart College, at the White House. October 15, 1963.

The president's youngest brother, Ted, talking to presidential aide Larry O'Brien. Ted Kennedy was traveling the world throughout 1961, laying tracks for a 1962 Senate run.

Any sense of friction that might have existed because Jack did not want yet another brother riding on his coattails was deflated by Ted's teasing but pointed reminder to the president that when he made his first congressional run in 1948, he always had himself introduced as "John *Fitzgerald* Kennedy" to make the obvious connection to the legendary Honey Fitz. Soon enough, Jack was needling him back: "Teddy wants to make it on his own and is thinking of changing his last name. To Roosevelt."

Despite the fact that his own political experience had been limited to the less-than-successful management of western states for Jack's presidential campaign, Ted was an impressive political apprentice. In May 1961 he toured Europe, meeting with Italy's president and Yugoslavia's vice

president, and discussing with them the administration's foreign policy—despite the fact that the trip was billed as "strictly unofficial." In July, he did the same throughout Latin America. He would spend his thirtieth birthday that coming February overseas again. This time it would be for an exhaustive three-week-long series of meetings with Western and Eastern European and Middle Eastern leaders: the Belgian foreign minister, the Greek premier, the German chancellor, the Israeli premier. He would talk about Common Market trade agreements and meet with labor leaders, students, and American businessmen. He would step across the border into Communist East Berlin, and *Pravda* would declare it all a Cold War tactic to outpsych the Soviets.

Such a junket was obviously arranged because Ted was the president's brother. Yet, Jack, rather than seeing himself as the inspiration for Ted's as-yet-unannounced launch into politics the next year, pointed to his father, explaining:

[M]y father . . . made his children feel that they were the most important thing in the world to him. . . . He held up standards for us, and he was very tough when we failed to meet those standards. . . . If it hadn't been for that, Teddy might just be a playboy today. But my father cracked down on him at a crucial time in his life, and this brought out in Teddy the discipline and seriousness that will make him an important political figure.

As 1961 began to wind down, and the senior Kennedys left Hyannis Port for their winter home in Palm Beach, speculation about Ted's possible run for the Senate seat mounted. The old man still resisted all entreaties, knowing when the time was right and when it wasn't. "We aren't ready to announce that yet," he flatly responded to yet another reporter's question about the potential race. Launching Ted, however, was the last piece of a plan Joe had confessed to in the September 7, 1957, *Saturday Evening*

Joe Kennedy with his son Ted before the father took off with Rose for their annual summer vacation in Antibes, France. Joe was a driving force in convincing his sons Jack and Bobby that it was Ted's "turn" to have their support for his Senate run. 1961.
SATURDAY EVENING POST

Post: his sons would be president, attorney general, and U.S. senator simultaneously. That vision still gave Joe a sense of purpose.

Throughout 1961, Joe Kennedy relaxed enough to talk openly about his role in launching Jack's career: a year earlier he would never discuss it. "I got Jack into politics. I was the one," he finally offered to a reporter. "I told him he had to." Such admissions, however, seemed like old news. In the late autumn, strolling the shore at Palm Beach, he made a rare confession to his friend Frank Waldrop, who assumed Joe was flying high with his son in the White House. "I get awfully blue sometimes," the old man said simply, then turned.

The senior Kennedy seems to have had some bouts of ambivalence. He said that if strangers were around, he would address Jack formally, but he emphasized, "I'm certainly not going to call my son 'Mr. President' when we're alone together." While he still encouraged his family's irreverence (he particularly loved Jackie's painting of the clan on the beach with an overhead plane carrying a banner that read, "You can't take it with you. Dad's got it all"), the gruff former ambassador seemed increasingly sensitive.

"Hell, I don't know how it feels to be the father of a president," he snapped at a reporter. "I get letters saying how proud I must be. Of course I am. But I don't feel any different. I don't know how it feels. Jack doesn't belong anymore to just one family. He belongs to the country. That's probably the saddest thing about all this. The family can be there for him. But there is not much they can do sometimes for the president." For Joe, this must have been a painful realization. During the transition, when he was asked by Jack to recommend the best possible Treasury secretary, the old man said he felt he was no longer in the position to do so. He began to feel displaced. "My life won't change much," the First Father mused to a reporter. "I have the notion I'd like to go abroad and stay a little while longer than I should—but probably not."

Father and son wrote letters to each other and often spoke several times a day: it was a two-way street, Jack asking advice, Joe offering it unsolicited. "I want to help," he told his son-in-law Stephen Smith, "but I don't want to be a nuisance." Joe successfully urged the reappointments of J. Edgar Hoover as head of the FBI and Allen Dulles as head of the CIA. Neither man proved to be helpful to Jack. There were two incidents that Joe insisted on, however, that caused public embarrassment for the president: the naming of loyal family crony Frank X. Morrissey to a federal district court judgeship, and the effort to dismiss a

tax problem of another friend of Joe's, James Landis. Ultimately, the president went against his father's wishes on both counts—Morrissey was not named for the post, and Landis had to face the IRS.

During his one 1961 visit to the White House, in the spring, Joe Kennedy entered the West Wing ranting and raving in his signature style, this time about the president's proposal to increase the Defense Department budget. "Damn it, I taught Jack better than that! Oh, we're going to go broke with this nonsense," the patriarch yelled—then stopped, smiled, and lowered his voice. "The election is over. I can disagree with him anytime I want to now." Disagree he did. Joe opposed Jack's foreign aid proposals and his efforts to hold Berlin, calling it a "bloody mistake." When Kennedy's showdown with big business resulted in a stock market drop, Joe Kennedy cracked, "To think I voted for that son-of-a-bitch."

The father never had any real influence on his son's policies, however, both recognizing their polar differences—Joe had become a reactionary conservative on nearly all issues. Sometimes Jack diminished his father's advice by sarcastically quipping, "We've heard from the Ambassador." He now matched his own father with an equally hurtful wit. "Caroline's very bright," Joe told Jack. "Smarter than you were at that age!" The president shot right back, "Yes, she is. But then consider who *she* has for a father!" When Jack decided against the Morrissey appointment, he told his brother to break the news to their father. "What shall I tell Dad?" Bobby asked Jack. "Tell him he's not president," Jack replied.

Still, both men had not only a loyalty but also an obvious love for each other; Jack once told a friend, "Do you always agree with your father? No. But you love him." Lem Billings observed that Joe "didn't want his love for his children to overwhelm them, and talking about impersonal matters was one way to avoid that." The affection between them was still evident. Joe thoughtfully bought the golf cart Jack needed to get around the Hyannis Port compound to relieve his back. "Jack still writes a letter to his mother," Joe recalled. "And when he comes over to use [my New York] apartment, he still takes my socks if I happen to have some new ones around."

Still, although it was apparently unspoken, it was clear to anyone around them that a fundamental family dynamic had changed forever. The focus, the attention, the homage and adulation, had shifted away from Joe Kennedy to Jack

Kennedy. Perhaps that turning point most sons face with their fathers was enhanced by the president's realization, "I don't have to do anything that my father wants me to do."

If his sons were his pride and joy, however, Joe Kennedy showed increasing appreciation of his daughter Eunice's intelligence and ambitions to succeed with her projects on behalf of the mentally retarded and the disabled. She still always loyally came to him for advice on or approval of her ideas. "Competition—that's what makes them go on. They are all competitive, including the girls," he said proudly in late 1961. "In fact, Eunice has more drive than Jack or even Bobby."

The president rides with his sister Eunice Shriver, who was acting as First Lady for the arrival ceremony of the president of Yugoslavia. April 30, 1963.

That would certainly have been the assessment of many government officials who found themselves increasingly harassed by the First Sister. Eunice loved being a part of her brother's presidency. One night she called while he and Jackie were entertaining guests, and finally the president turned over the phone to Leonard Bernstein, one of the guests. "Oh, come on, what are you doing?" she asked, eager to be included in everything. Jackie's friend Joan Braden thought that Jackie might have slightly resented her sister-in-law because "Eunice was such a confidante of Jack's, and she [Jackie] wanted to be the only one." One night Eunice invited a mutual friend over for dinner; he accepted only to call back and turn her down because the president had suddenly called to ask him to dine at the White House that evening. She berated the friend mercilessly. "Eunice," Jack finally said to her in a call to calm her, "you can have anyone you want for dinner. I can't." At that, she softened and was overcome with tears, reminded of just how isolated his social life in the mansion had to be. Among his sisters, Jack relied heaviest on the ideas and unbounded love shown him by Eunice. She was frequently in the

White House—for ceremonies, for parties, for childrens' events to which she usually took her own children—and never hesitated to phone the Oval Office.

Her husband, Sarge, was just as frequently in conference with his brother-in-law. In the first weeks of the administration, Shriver pressed hard on his idea of creating a government program of volunteers working in undeveloped countries—the Peace Corps. Around the White House, Shriver was somewhat derisively called "the Boy Scout," not only for his manners and uprightness but also for his eagerness to help his brother-in-law. Many advisers had warned Jack that the Peace Corps was a risky, no-win proposal. He created it, but had it budgeted as part of the Agency for International Development. Initially, Joe Kennedy helped fund the first office and staff, but Shriver wanted it to be federally funded and an independent agency. Kennedy put him on the carpet: Shriver had to lobby Congress to get support. It was up and running by April. Jack soon had to confess that he had given Sarge "one of the most sensitive and difficult assignments which any administrative group in Washington has been given almost in this century." Under Shriver, the Peace Corps would not only survive but thrive. It

President Kennedy gives his "Boy Scout" brother-in-law, Sargent Shriver, a pen he used to sign the Peace Corps funding. The Oval Office. September 22, 1961.

would remain a permanent part of the federal government. "Sarge does everything well," the president said.

Eunice had her own ambitions. She had not forgotten the story she had read about care for the mentally retarded. The story had been buried in the back pages of the *New York Times* amid all the pomp of the forthcoming inauguration parties. She was not making idle chatter about doing something serious for the mentally retarded; by her unrelenting insistence to her brother, she saw her first goal achieved with his creation of the President's Panel on Mental Retardation in the spring of 1961. Knowing full well how quickly even the most well-intentioned of government investigatory and advisory commissions ended up suffocated or drowned in the bureaucracy, she did nothing less than walk her panel through its conception, birth, and growth. Eunice Shriver decided to sign on only as a "consultant," giving herself more flexibility as maestro of her vision.

As Laurence Leamer, chronicler of the Kennedy

Eunice Shriver, the leading administration activist for the mentally handicapped, brought several children to meet her brother the day he officially created the first federal panel on mental retardation. Shriver is standing second from left. November 14, 1961.

Joe Kennedy on the golf course at Antibes, France, with his son Bobby. 1961.

women, wrote, "Eunice wanted her commission to be the beginning of a revolution in the understanding and treatment of those with mental retardation." It was a tall order, but her passion drove her: Eunice attracted the nation's medical and scientific leaders to the panel, making Dr. Leonard Mayo, director of the Association for the Aid of Crippled Children, its chairman. She not only wangled the Cabinet Room for their first meeting but got the president to welcome the group in the Rose Garden. She upbraided weary and overworked presidential aides, pushing them to get not only national publicity for the mental retardation panel but federal funding as well. As generous as was her impulse, the president had other more politically viable priorities for his budget. Yet even Jack Kennedy was no match for Eunice Shriver. After one of her loud arguments with the assistant secretary of health, education and welfare, Wilbur Cohen, who was charged with drafting the administration's legislation proposals, the president met with him in the Oval Office. "Has my sister been giving you trouble again?" he asked Cohen. "How do you know?" the incredulous assistant secretary asked. The president replied, "I know my sister."

Frankly, President Kennedy was himself harassed by her. When she learned that a group interested in mental retardation was coming to the capital, she wanted to host a White House reception for them. Jack tried to gently tell her no by saying, "Well, Jackie isn't here." She would not take the bait. "Well, could I still have them at the White House?" He relented.

Privately, the president must have been rather astounded by his sister's steamrolling to ultimate success. It certainly would have been able to alter, ever so gently, his idea of women as activists. In small, personal, almost unstated ways, Kennedy did show a growing sensitivity to the rights of women. Hearst reporter Marianne Means was fighting hard to file stories as serious and political and newsworthy as her male counterparts in the White House press corps in her attempt to earn a column for herself. Observing this, the president told one aide, "Give her some stories. Give her all the help you can." He had genuine respect for and considered seriously the advice he was given by Esther Peterson,

Just one hour after this picture was taken of Joe Kennedy with the president, the elder was felled by a stroke that left him paralyzed and speechless forever. December 19, 1961.

the co-chair of his Presidential Commission on the Status of Women. Peterson was a person who refused to be thought of as a second-class citizen. Kennedy also trusted a woman, Dr. Janet Travell, as one of the two physicians in charge of looking after his precarious health.

What seemed to set Eunice Shriver apart from not only her sisters and sisters-in-law but also most women of that era was her absolute self-confidence. She refused to accept any limitations that either her family or society at large attempted to place on her because she was a woman. Her credo seemed to be a line she would be heard to repeat constantly to her father in the coming months: "You can do anything you want to." It was just the sort of advice the father would need to hear from the daughter.

In the summers on the Cape, Joe would go down to Allen's Farm in Osterville, Massachusetts, and ride his horse every morning. In the winters in Palm Beach, he could still beat his sons Jack and Bobby at golf. He was on the golf course on December 19, 1961, accompanied by Ann Gargan, the daughter of Rose's late sister Agnes. His own children were busy with their lives, so Joe came to rely on having one special person dote on and protect him, a living shield against anything and anyone he didn't care to engage. A convent dropout, Ann had been misdiagnosed with multiple sclerosis. With her medical care covered by her aunt Rose and uncle Joe, Ann's nerve problem finally resolved itself. She was drawn to Joe. She seemed to understand people who were suffering and frustrated. Joe seemed to understand her.

Earlier that day, Joe had taken Caroline and John to the airport to see Jack off from Palm Beach. The president had stopped to see his parents there on his way back to Washington from Colombia. At the air-

port, the president's secretary observed that Joe's "face seemed flushed and he was a little unsure of his steps." He went to play golf with Ann. He felt weak. He returned home and went to his room. Jackie was swimming in the pool with her children. Rose was playing golf. Bobby telephoned his father. His father did not answer. Ann found Joe unconscious in his bed, and he was rushed to St. Mary's Hospital. "Dad's gotten sick," Bobby told Jack in an abrupt telephone call. The president immediately flew back. Ted Sorenson, the president's speechwriter, was with Jack on the *Air Force One* flight back to Florida. "It was with difficulty and incredible self-discipline that he engrossed himself in our work on that sorrowful flight." The crisis "broke his spirits but not his stride."

By the time the president joined other family members around Joe's hospital bed, last rites of the Catholic Church were being said. Joe Kennedy had suffered a major stroke. He lost all movement on his right side and his ability to speak and move independently. It had not even been a year since he had stood for his son, the newly inaugurated president, in the parade stand, but in some way, at that moment, he had lost the primary motivation for being Joe Kennedy. It was great to see Bobby in the cabinet and perhaps Ted in the Senate, but after seeing Jack in the presidency, the great object of Joe's lifelong work, the seemingly endless push ahead was over.

As he lay in St. Mary's, it looked as if Joe Kennedy's life was over. "Age," admitted Rose, "has its privileges. One is to reminisce and another is to reminisce selectively. I prefer to remember the good time . . ." Later, in recalling her husband's demise, however, Rose Kennedy's self-imposed restraint seemed to break. "Next to Almighty God, I had loved him," she wrote of Joe, "with all my heart, all my soul, all my mind." She bought a

Bound for life to a wheelchair and the help of his wife's niece Ann Gargan, who assumed the role of his caretaker, Joe Kennedy is being transported from the family plane Caroline, a shell of the man he had once been. Spring 1962.

black dress in anticipation of his funeral. As it would turn out, however, she found herself carrying the dress back and forth with her, from Palm Beach to Hyannis Port, season after season.

Joe began to rally, and he soon recognized his family. All he could say, however, was "No" repeatedly, and by considering the tempo with which he said it—or through other noises he made, the look in his eyes, and the contortions he made with his face—his family learned to somewhat interpret what he wanted. Soon, they were speaking as if he were directly involved in the conversation, most frequently completing a subject by turning to him and asking, "Isn't that right, Dad?" They ignored the effects of the stroke to ask him questions, tell him about their days, sing songs to him, and try to make him laugh. Though he was wheelchair bound, the family included him on their sea excursions, holidays, and evening dinners. He often sat on the porch of his home in Hyannis Port watching the day's activities, with his children and grandchildren coming up to kiss him or say hello. Ann Gargan loyally became his protective caretaker, but her presence did not stop the others, especially Eunice, from encouraging him to try aggressive physical therapy.

Jackie was especially sensitive. She would kiss his crippled hand and the side of his face to assure him it did not matter, and placed her head in his lap as if he had all of the same old power to offer protection. When he drooled, she just wiped his mouth. She put her children at ease around him, allowing them to ride on his wheelchair with him.

When he came to the White House, she wrote endlessly detailed memos to Mr. West about providing for his comfort in the Lincoln Suite: a hospital bed, a Victrola, a soft drink setup made to look like a cocktail bar, and a medical lift in the bathroom. She arranged to take her meals and those of her children with him. She paid for the meals of his nurses and met him at the airport, asking that he be allowed to ride in the front seat of the convertible, as he liked.

In the hours after the stroke, Jack questioned the meaning of life. "Saddened to see the old man suffering both physical and mental agony in his permanently crippled and virtually speechless condition," Sorenson recorded, "the president wondered out loud about the decision facing doctors who work desperately to keep alive any man hovering between a peaceful death and a fraction of life." Still, the president put on his optimistic mask. He treated his father gently. On one visit, the president placed a puppy in the lap of his father, and Joe seemed to respond. Sometimes daily, he told his father on the phone about the decisions and crises facing him, even though Joe could only respond with grunts. Out of his father's range, however, Jack seemed haunted by what had happened. "He's the one who made all this possible, and look at him now."

Now having to assume the role of head of his clan, the president seemed to be enlightened with a new lesson. "My father's one motive," he was often heard to say following Joe's stroke, "was love of family."

Jack and Jackie steal a private glance in a public moment, at a state dinner for the Peruvian president and his wife. September 19, 1961.

6

QUEEN OF THE CIRCUS

Jackie Kennedy in Private, 1962

I always push unpleasant things out of my head on the theory that
if you don't think about them they won't happen.
—JACKIE KENNEDY

I'd known a lot of attractive women in my lifetime . . . but of them
all there was only one I could have married—and I married her.
—JACK KENNEDY

When Americans watched Jackie Kennedy end her famous television tour of the White House on February 14, 1962, they saw her joined by the president in a tableau that was true to life—a gingerly handled, carefully spoken respect of boundaries with some stolen loving smiles. It is easy to think that they were destined to be together. Contrary to the now-entrenched legend of a dinner party introduction, they had first met on a train speeding up the eastern seaboard in 1949. College junior Jackie Bouvier, scribbling a letter to a Newport friend, unwittingly recorded their first meeting. Her description of him would be a blueprint for their marriage—he was, she wrote, a charming, confident, and handsome but insistent flirt to whom she responded with indifferent amusement, yet absolute attraction.

Millions of words have tried to unravel the marriage of Jack and Jackie Kennedy. Romanticized versions of the sort Jackie preferred made it out to be near-perfect bliss with, at worst, a sort of heroic heartache occasionally suffered by her. Cynical analyses of the marriage by people such as Gore Vidal paint it as a solely Machiavellian pairing—he needing a politically viable wife, she interested in money. Neither is accurate. What is true is that, at the start of 1962, after eight years of marriage, he wouldn't give up his womanizing (even Jackie told him he "met his love too late"), and material objects effectively soothed her resulting insecurities. It is also true that this dynamic was beginning to change after a year in the White House and that there was a more consistent and growing pattern of their expression of mutual love and devotion.

However odd and offensive it was to others, both husband and wife had been raised to believe that outside relationships were routine. "I don't think there are any men who are faithful to their wives," Jackie Kennedy famously said. "Jack kept assuring us that she didn't suspect when it was obvious that she knew exactly what was happening," admitted his friend Jim Reed. "He was so disciplined in so many ways. Discipline was, after all, the secret of his success. When it came to women he was a different person." Jackie made sure her husband knew when she was coming home—so she was certain never to confront him with another woman. It was a chicken-and-egg question: did her being away encourage the relationships, or was she so often away as a means of avoiding them? When one woman asked why he was "taking a chance on getting caught in a scandal," he responded, "I don't know, really. I just can't help it." Doris Goodwin thought that his drive to conquest suggested "a deep difficulty with intimacy." Garry Wills suggested that it was his "way of cackling at the gods of bodily debility which plagued him."

All of those reasons might be valid, but even had they been understood by him, they likely would have had little impact on Jack Kennedy. Like most men of his class in the early 1960s, he would rather spend his time physically enjoying himself than emotionally expressing himself. Asked by historian James MacGregor Burns if he was ever "desperately, hopelessly in love," Jack just shrugged and said, "I'm not the heavy lover type."

The remark to Burns seems harsh initially. However, it again seems to be a case of Jack Kennedy creating a wall of machismo between himself and other men. He himself admitted privately—but only to his parents and only in writing—that he was deeply in love with Jackie from the day they were married, as she was with him. As pub-

lished in 2001 by his niece Amanda Smith in Joe Kennedy's correspondence, Jack Kennedy sent a telegram to his parents just three days after his wedding, on their honeymoon:

"At last I know the meaning of rapture. Jackie is enshrined forever in my heart. Thanks mom and dad for making me worthy of her[.] Your Loving Son Jack."

Joe Kennedy himself had been wary of his son's ability to drop the privileges he took and the benefits he enjoyed as the young, rich, and handsome thirty-six-year-old bachelor. Joe wrote to Jack's friend Torb MacDonald a month after the Kennedys' marriage had been announced—and two months before it took place. Torb and Jack were about to embark on the latter's last vacation as a bachelor:

Jack needs a rest. Unquestionably he has the best time with you.

I am a bit concerned that he may get restless about the prospect of getting married. Most people do and he is more likely to do so than others. As I told you, I am hoping that he will take a rest and not jump from place to place, and be especially mindful of whom he sees. Certainly one can't take anything for granted since he has become a United States Senator. That is a price he should be willing to pay and gladly. I understand your love and devotion to Jack and I know you wish him nothing but the best and I hope you both will have a good vacation.

Jackie, like other society women of the early 1960s, accepted the fact that Jack "really hated public demonstrations of affection." Though pained by any of his straying with people she knew personally, she determined not to react with anything more severe than long respites without him. "I don't care how many girls, as long as I know he knows it's wrong, and I think he does now," she told Adlai Stevenson. "I think she probably suffered to beat the band but nobody ever saw the hurt," said Chuck Spalding. To prove it, she would "pick out the two prettiest, brightest women," claimed Bill Walton, "and put them on either side of him" at dinners. It was also true, noted Goodwin, that Jack didn't "understand the devastating effect on Jackie." He simply had a compartment for the relationships, apart from his wife. He told Lee Radziwill, "I love her deeply and have done everything for her. I've no feeling of letting her down because I've put her foremost in everything."

One cannot ignore the fact—without justifying anything—that relinquishing his past was not made any easier by being president. As Faye Emerson wrote in her 1962 article "We All Love Jack," published in *Eros* (a sort of intellectual *Playboy* without centerfolds), "The females of this country have a crush on JFK. They dig him." A 1962 poll of women college students found that Jack Kennedy had more "sex appeal" than matinee idol Rock Hudson. When he saw the photograph of himself being physically hunted by women on the beach at Santa Monica, he pointed out, "*They're* chasing and *I'm* running!" The women attracted to the president were even categorized by Emerson: "jumpers" were those young women who bounded into the air, shrieked, and threw kisses at Jack; "touchers" were the matrons who fought their way to the front of the rope line only to gently hug him in a motherly fashion. There were also young marrieds who "daydreamed themselves in Jackie's shoes" and glamour girls who "stumbled over their sables to stand near him."

Even the "swinger" culture of the Jet Age supported him. *Playboy* abounded with

THE FIRST LADY'S EXTENDED FAMILY

JOHN VERNOU "JACK" BOUVIER, FATHER, BORN MAY 19, 1891, DECEASED 1957

  MARRIED JULY 7, 1928, TO JANET NORTON LEE, DIVORCED IN 1940

  THE FIRST LADY'S SISTER:

    CAROLINE LEE "LEE" BOUVIER, BORN MARCH 3, 1933

      MARRIED MARCH 19, 1959, TO STANISLAUS "STAS" RADZIWILL, BORN IN 1914

      CHILDREN:

        ANTHONY "TONY" RADZIWILL, BORN IN AUGUST 1959

        CHRISTINA "TINA" RADZIWILL, BORN IN AUGUST 1960

JANET NORTON LEE, MOTHER, BORN DECEMBER 3, 1907

  MARRIED IN 1942 A SECOND TIME, TO HUGH DUDLEY AUCHINCLOSS, BORN AUGUST 28, 1897

  CHILDREN:

    JANET JENNINGS AUCHINCLOSS, HALF SISTER, BORN JUNE 13, 1945

    JAMES LEE "JAMIE" AUCHINCLOSS, HALF BROTHER, BORN MARCH 4, 1947

HUGH AUCHINCLOSS, STEPFATHER, MARRIED AND DIVORCED TWICE BEFORE MARRYING JANET BOUVIER

  MARRIED FIRST TO MARIA CHRAPOVITSKY, BORN 1900

  CHILD:

    HUGH D. "YUSHA" AUCHINCLOSS, STEPBROTHER, BORN SEPTEMBER 16, 1927

      MARRIED IN 1958 TO ALICE LYON

      CHILDREN:

        CECIL AND MAYA AUCHINCLOSS (TWINS), BORN IN FEBRUARY 1959

  MARRIED SECOND TO NINA GORE

  CHILDREN:

    THOMAS "TOMMY" AUCHINCLOSS, STEPBROTHER, BORN SEPTEMBER 17, 1939

    NINA AUCHINCLOSS, STEPSISTER, BORN JANUARY 12, 1937

      MARRIED IN 1957 TO NEWTON STEERS

      CHILDREN:

        IVAN STEERS, BORN IN JULY 1958

        HUGH STEERS, BORN IN JUNE 1962

straying husband advice. Jokes about traveling salesmen and dumb mistresses were popular comedy. The series of spy novels featuring James Bond, Agent 007, by Ian Fleming, was the basis for a number of films, the first released in 1962, the second in 1963. Red-blooded American men ravenously consumed the books: Jack Kennedy actually expressed his admiration for the spy character. "Why couldn't this have happened to James Bond?" he even sighed after the Bay of Pigs. Bond, of course, always got all the beautiful women he wanted. The media comparisons between Bond and Jack were the strongest coded message about

Jackie Kennedy hated having every aspect of being examined, photographed, and analyzed by the public. On top of this, she was naturally shy. She is seen here being escorted into one of her least favorite First Lady activities, the annual Congressional Wives luncheon, as women reporters carefully watch her from the door behind her. Spring 1961.

DEFENSE DEPARTMENT

the president's habits. The worst words even tabloids like *Confidential* printed were "whispers" of extramarital "tender little friendships." The mainstream press wouldn't touch it.

However, if all was not perfect, it was getting better. Among his most guarded aides, Ted Sorenson even admitted that the longer the couple was in the White House, the more it "strengthened instead of strained their marriage . . . he found with her a happiness and love he had never known before. . . . Their marriage was not always smooth in its early years, but it brought them both an increasing amount of happiness . . ."

While fame reduced Jackie's privacy, it also increased her sense of self, and with that she shed a layer of insecurity. "You don't know how it is," she had told friend Joan Braden just before the election. "Everyone flirts with Lee and you, but nobody flirts with me." Sometimes she cried about her feelings of inadequacy to her husband: "Oh, Jack, I'm so sorry for you that I'm such a dud." While, according to Arthur Schlesinger, Jack would say he "loved her as she was," it was easy to see how a man of his personality would withdraw from such a need for a romantic validation.

Then came her crowning moments in Europe and, in December 1961, Latin America. "I think that's when she really began enjoying it all," said Jean Smith. "Up to that point, she was just his wife." Jack even teasingly called her "Sex Symbol" after she became the object of many a world leader's affections. With her White House restoration and other projects, Jackie began to rediscover the sense of personal purpose she had just barely attained as a budding writer the year before her marriage. Granted, she still needed to hear that he loved her. After she suggested to him that an attractive blond friend was his "ideal," he responded, "You're my ideal, Jackie."

Jack Kennedy's pride and appreciation of his wife grew steadily through his administration, prompted by her popularity and other people's responses to her. Here she speaks to some of the released Cuban expatriates who had been taken prisoner by Castro after the failed Bay of Pigs effort. She addressed them in Spanish. Miami Orange Stadium. December 1961.

With her growing confidence came her willingness to challenge his ego and keep his arrogance in check. "Jack always said how smart Jackie was," Steve Smith recalled. "And she could cut him down and did—there was no question about it. When she felt strongly about something, she let him know it and let everyone else know it." Bill Walton offered that, in conversation, she would "beat him down." Charles Bartlett noticed that she deflated him when he got "over-serious or pompous."

As she relaxed, Jackie became more fun—which delighted Jack to no end. One night at one of their private parties, enjoying her champagne, Jackie even kicked off her heels and danced in stocking feet on the marble Entrance Hall with a friend. But this quality could quickly vanish and be replaced by what her mother called "Jackie's introverted-

ness, stiffness." Jack characterized his wife as "sensitive by contrast to my sisters, who are direct and energetic." Jackie was idiosyncratic—she changed her mind with her mood. Even when she smoked the cigarettes Jack abhorred nobody knew which brand it might be that day—she liked Salem or Marlboro or Newport or Winston.

By the time they entered the White House the couple had learned to identify—if not yet accept completely—each other's deficiencies and attributes. In doing so, they began to recognize just how similar they were. While he had been an outcast as an Irish Catholic, she had also felt alienated in her youth because her parents were divorced Catholics; she later confessed to friend Peter Duchin that she never really felt accepted in the WASP social culture of her youth. They both had a need for independence, they both found escape in the world of books, they were both able to view people and situations with a jaundiced eye, they could both detach emotionally when they wanted a protective wall; they were smart people, and they recognized the similarities in one another. "My husband was a romantic," Jackie later said of Jack, "although he didn't like people to know that." That very well described her, too.

At first, Jackie resented being the president's wife and resisted assuming aspects of public life. With great privileges came tiring and irritating intrusions into daily life. She could not even go out for her solitary morning walk within the White House gates without tourists' producing movie cameras to record her coughing. She hated daytime appearances that required her to waste accumulated hours sitting for makeup artists and beauticians—let alone what the coloring, teasing, spraying, and drying did to her hair. "I may be bald in a year," she cracked.

Slowly she had begun to figure out ways around it. After Jack returned excitedly one Sunday with the news that he had walked the Mall without being recognized, he coaxed her to go out with him for a walk that very night. "Noting their exhilaration afterwards," observed reporter Ralph Martin, "one might have thought they had been down the Grand Canyon rapids on a rubber raft." Jackie soon tried it alone, considering it a great victory that she and a friend were able to linger peacefully in a restaurant one night until eleven in the evening without being besieged by the public. Wigs not only helped disguise her appearance—they also began saving her from daily hairdressing.

Jackie also found that in making concessions to the First Lady role, she could also get concessions from her husband. The president himself had to broker a deal with her to be hostess at one mundane event. "Mrs. Kennedy is going to do it. It cost me," he told his press secretary, who speculated that she made a trade for a new dress. "Worse than that," said Jack. "Two symphonies." By acting the part, she soon enough discovered that her expensive tastes were indulged, whether it was the gift of a belt encrusted with diamonds and emeralds or gelding horses from heads of state. "He can never really get mad at her about anything," said one friend, but Jack was put to the test with her tastes. The cost of her horses remained a bone of contention. Remarking on a "hell of a bill" for the horses' upkeep, Jackie told one friend that it had come just after a "big lecture" about family budgets. Jackie didn't want the "boom lowered" for overspending, joking that she might be left with just a pony to ride. "Don't you hate facing the economic facts of life? I do!" she sighed to her friend. "That Jackie," the president told a friend, shaking his head. "She thinks she can keep on spending forever. I don't understand what the hell she's doing with all those things. How much does she need?" When Princess Grace asked him how he knew she was wearing a Givenchy gown, he quipped, "I ought to. I've paid for enough of them." Yet it was Jack Kennedy who loved nothing more than, as Schlesinger noted, "picking out presents for her"—especially the most exquisite indulgences. The fact is, in coming to recognize how much she had sacrificed of the life she had really wanted, the president never once told her to send something back or denied paying for what she bought.

After a year of his presidency had passed, Jack and Jackie both came to see for themselves just how heavy the public expectations were on them both. They also had more time to talk about their mutual pressures. Despite their travel schedules, they were alone together more often. Ironically, it was the presidency, which Jackie had feared would isolate them, that drew them closer. "The one thing that happens to a president is that his ties with the outside world are cut. And the people you really have are each other," she said, adding with a confident note, "I should think that if people weren't happily married, the White House would really finish it."

At one point in her life she had wanted to be a ballet dancer, then an editor, then a journalist, and then a novelist—but joked that she would end up "Queen of the Circus." She did not want to be First Lady, a figure of public responsibilities. But she did not want to go on as "Mrs. Kennedy" alone—there were so many of them. Instead, throughout 1962, as she told her stepbrother, she was to be known as "the president's wife."

"What I wanted to do more than anything," she explained with great seriousness, "was keep my family together in the White House." She found that the only way to do this was, as Jack's press secretary said, "force a separation between his private life and work . . . when Kennedy was finished, once he went back upstairs, he went to his wife and that was the end of it. No staff, no more interruptions every half hour."

Jackie's routine was similar to that of tens of thousands of upper-middle-class young wives of that era—except that instead of watching for a car to pull into the driveway, she looked for the lights of the Oval Office to go out. As Jack came home from work, washed up, and changed his clothes, she would raise no unpleasant subjects, have his daiquiri ready, and make sure the hi-fi set was playing. "The president kissed his wife, asking about the children, and wanted to know how Jacqueline had spent her day. He noticed, and complimented, her hairdo," recalled Peter Lawford of one night upstairs in the White House as Jack came home from work. On the rare nights when the children were already in bed before their father was home from the office—usually about seven-thirty—the couple sometimes had friends and family in for small dinners because, she explained, "Jack was even more isolated than I." She always tried to end the evening with a surprise such as a performance by friend Jim Symington, famous for his political parodies of popular songs. While she failed to coax Jack to do his Noël Coward impersonation, her dinners did successfully distract him. As one night was ending, and composer Igor Stravinsky was bestowing European double-kisses to guests, Jack took it all in, then piped up, "What about me!" It is not known if Stravinsky kissed Kennedy.

During the day, whether dictating correspondence to secretary Mary Gallagher in the West Sitting Hall or looking over clothes in the First Lady's Sitting Room with maid Provie—who was perpetually worried that Jackie didn't eat enough—the First Lady could watch Jack at his Rose Garden ceremonies from her sitting room window or go downstairs to be with him to watch important events on the news. While taking her morning stroll on the lawn, she popped in to see him, sometimes sneaking up behind the windows of the Oval Office and tapping on them—which startled him and, when he turned around and saw her, broke them both up into laughter. Around the house, before lunch, or before dinner, she went into his lavatory or closet and tucked limericks she wrote or cartoons she drew into unexpected places. She loved making him laugh.

While she was behaving the way he thought wives and mothers should conduct their lives ("He told me I'm getting to be just like his mother," Jackie gasped to her secretary), she was—euphemistically speaking—seducing him. He had already come to rely on her photographic memory

and encyclopedic knowledge of history and literature for his speeches. If he still cut off her questions about policy and politics, he patiently listened to her shrewd assessments of policy makers and politicians. Perhaps more conventionally, he took genuine pride in her restoration project, especially astonished by her administrative and management skills—the sort of strengths he assumed that only men had. Encouraged, she would rush over to his office to tell about or show her new discoveries. When he learned that the typewriter Woodrow Wilson had written the Fourteen Points on was available, he instantly arranged for its donation and display in the West Wing; it was his. "My wife has collected everything," he said shyly; "this is the only thing I have produced." He increasingly made affectionate and teasing references to her in his speeches, usually about how beautiful she looked. Photographs show that, if she was there, and if they managed a glance at each other, he and she broke into smiles.

When both were in town and there were no small dinners, Jackie put on her reading glasses at night and worked quietly beside Jack—as he worked—sitting with him on the cushy sofa beneath the half-circle window in the West Sitting Hall. Sometimes she retreated to her room to do her watercolor painting. It had now become her favorite creative outlet; she worked on her primitive oil canvases only in the summer. She usually retired first; he followed. "Jacqueline had become to John Kennedy what she had always hoped to become," friend and reporter Laura Berquist said in retrospect, "his haven, his refuge, his separate world."

It was in the middle of the day, however, that husband and wife had their time completely alone together, in their bedroom. The ritual was never public knowledge, nor even common gossip. As far as their office staffs knew, they were simply having a long lunch together. Only Mr. West, Maude Shaw, George Thomas, and Providencia Parades knew what happened after lunch. If there were other people occupying the First Lady's attention at that moment, the president told his valet, George Thomas, to get her. "The president says that if you don't hurry," Thomas would tell her, "he'll fall asleep." As she later told Schlesinger, once the children were safely kept in the nanny's charge, she "drew the curtains" in the bedroom for her "hour of the day" with Jack Kennedy.

"Mrs. Kennedy dropped everything . . . important, to join her husband," West later revealed.

During those hours, the Kennedy doors were closed. No telephone calls were allowed, no folders sent up, no interruptions from the staff. Nobody went upstairs, for any reason . . . the discreet White House [domestic] staff, which always must know when to stay away from the second floor, was attuned to the intimacy that actually existed between the young couple . . . when George Thomas, whose job it was to wake Mr. Kennedy, would find the president absent from his bedroom, the valet would tiptoe into the room next door, and gently shake the president—so as not to awaken the president's wife.

Jackie was always to be uncomfortable with public knowledge of their intimacy. The bedroom was off-limits to everyone except the children, his valet, and her maid. She was known to blurt in front of others her private nickname for him—"Bunny"—only once. When, later, the chance to explain their intimacy arose in Schlesinger's book, she responded to his first draft, "Eliminate descriptions of what went on in bedroom . . . it sounds . . . as if I just pour out all details of my married life. . . . Let us leave out all bedroom scenes . . . no mention of me or a bedroom . . . they seem to me to be real peeping behind curtains. It is no reader's business whatever happened in a bedroom with me and JFK."

Before the year was over, Judith Campbell and Mary Meyer—Jack's two most reckless ongoing relationships—would be history. He would still be traveling around the country enjoying the "jumpers" or having Dave Powers visit with a "friend" when Jackie was away, but probably without realizing it, Jack Kennedy was metamorphosing into a notorious family man.

The fairest analysis of Jackie came from the person she trusted and relied upon most, and consequently to whom she revealed herself, Chief Usher J. B. West. He left a richly paradoxical portrait of the woman as she was at the age of thirty-one years, when she became First Lady:

There was wonder in those eyes, determination, humor, and—sometimes—vulnerability . . . Her interests were wide, however, as was her knowledge, and she had a subtle, ingenious way of getting things accomplished . . . the most complex personality of them all. In public, she was elegant, aloof, dignified and regal. In private she was casual, impish, and irreverent. She had a will of iron, with more determination than anyone I had ever met. Yet she was so soft-spoken . . . that she could impose that will upon people without their ever knowing it. Her wit—teasing, exaggerating, poking fun at everything including herself—was a surprise and a daily delight. She was imaginative, inventive, intelligent—and sometimes silly. Yet there were subjects that did not amuse her one bit. Relaxed and uninhibited, she was always popping up anywhere, wearing slacks, sitting on the floor, kicking off her shoes, her hair flying in every direc-

Beneath the dazzle of her physical appearance and style, Jackie Kennedy was an intelligent and intense woman of substance. As such, her moods could be unpredictable. March 13, 1961.

tion . . . a total mastery of endless, endless detail . . . highly organized, yet rarely held herself to a schedule. For others, she insisted upon order; for herself she preferred spontaneity. She took advice readily, but only when she asked for it, and she strongly resisted being pushed.

Of all her family members, however, the one person Jackie seemed to most dislike receiving advice from—and who gave it without solicitation—was, naturally enough, her mother. While Janet Auchincloss did not want Jackie to become a "colorless creature" by conforming entirely to convention, she did believe her daughter *should* change

her look, because "there must always be room for improvement . . . you have to keep your own identity . . . within bounds. There are certain things that obviously you can't do when you are very much in the public eye." On the subject of women all copying the "Jackie Look," the First Lady's mother remarked, "I don't think they all loved it. I used to get a good many critical letters about her." Janet was rarely able to get her phone calls through directly to her daughter. When the calls did go upstairs and Jackie's secretary was with the First Lady, Jackie had her secretary pick up the phone and say that the First Lady was not there.

Janet Auchincloss had a famous temper, and during the hysterical months of her divorce from Jack Bouvier, Jackie was sometimes the unfortunate recipient of her rage. "My dear sweet mother," Jackie sometimes sarcastically called Janet. "That was Jackie's way of getting back at me for divorcing her father," Mrs. Auchincloss offered. When Janet wanted White House guidebooks she had to buy them like everyone else. She finally had to ask a curator to show her through the family rooms for

Jackie Kennedy and her mother stand together watching the swearing-in of Franklin Roosevelt Jr. as undersecretary of commerce. The Cabinet Room. March 23, 1963.

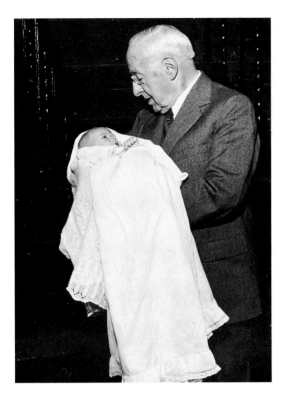

her first peek. The First Lady's grandfather—Janet's father, Jim Lee—was never invited to the White House. On the other hand, Janet always made herself available to serve Jackie's needs. Ultimately, Jackie was grateful for her mother's lessons and taught her own children to curtsy, bow, formally address people, and behave politely in public. She never showed disrespect to Janet and was even rather protective of her. Jackie, for example, never confronted Janet about reinventing herself from an Irish Catholic granddaughter of a New York City public school superintendent to an Anglo-Saxon Episcopalian collateral descendant of Robert E. Lee. She recognized how important that identity had become to her mother.

As is often the case with mothers, however, Janet was often more open and free with children other than those for whom she had to be responsible. To children of an activity director on the SS *France,* she advised "Learn Chinese!" as a way of enjoying life more in the wider world, and long into

Although James Lee was the only grandfather in history to see his granddaughter become First Lady, the staunch Republican real estate mogul never visited her in the White House. Only after she left Washington did Jackie take her children to see him. He is seen here at the christening of one of his great-grandsons.
COURTESY MIMI CECIL

Jackie's mother, Janet Auchincloss, second from left, was always there to help her daughter by substituting for her as hostess at the last minute. September 18, 1962.

Despite her often forbidding demeanor, Janet Auchincloss had a great sense of humor and loved to laugh when among old friends. She is seen here at the Newport Preservation Society Ball in Marble House, with her friend Cynthia Cary.
COURTESY JAMIE AUCHINCLOSS

adulthood they remembered her kindness. She not only always let the local newspaper delivery boy for her Georgetown home use her own upstairs bathroom as he made his rounds, but even invited him to stay for tea with her, Jackie, and the grandchildren. Her son recalled that when Janet was really relaxed, she could be devilish, and her distinctive laugh became infectious to anyone around her. Whatever issues Jackie still had with her mother, she never let them interfere with bringing her children close to their grandmother, and many afternoons she would drive them over to Janet's home, first in Virginia, then, in 1962, in Georgetown, while the incognito First Lady prowled nearby antiques and book stores for an hour or so.

Jackie was especially close to her half sister, known in the family as "Little Janet," and had almost a romantic friendship with her supportive and gentle stepbrother Yusha. Her half brother Jamie began a lifelong interest in politics because of Jack and shared with Jackie a love of reading history books and biographies. Jackie saw less of

her stepbrother Tommy and occasionally saw stepsister Nina and her children, who played with Jackie's, but "Nini's" husband, Newton Steers, was an outspoken Republican and was hardly welcomed by the Kennedys. At one private party, Gore Vidal—who was also a stepchild of Hugh D. Auchincloss, by his second wife (Janet was his third)—got into an argument with Bobby Kennedy and found himself banished from the circle. As to her Bouvier relatives, Jackie saw even less of them, the exception being her beloved cousin Michel. She invited her twin aunts Michelle and Maude to a 1961 luncheon and a day at Glen Ora, where her cousin Shella joined them. Two years later, Shella, Maude, and her daughter Maudie came for lunch in the family quarters and had a picture taken in the Lincoln Bedroom.

The anticipation of the arrival from Europe of "Princess Lee," however, excited not only the maids and butlers in the White House but the First Lady. "Jackie was happiest when her sister was around because Lee was the one person with whom she could relax and pour out her feelings. They were like schoolgirls together," said Jackie's secretary. When Lee came for her lengthy stays in the White House, she was put up in the Queen's Suite, her hair washed with imported beer carried up on a silver tray for her. Both women liked clothing and jewelry, and the warm and generous Stas Radziwill would tease, "These girls are frightfully greedy," but Jackie frequently sent packages of her clothes to his displaced relatives in Communist Poland.

Jackie and Lee had endured the trauma of their parents' painful divorce together, and although it would have been natural for Lee to envy Jackie when suddenly the world was celebrating her personal style, they depended on each other's company. In every way, Jackie tried to share her privileges and status with Lee. Living in Europe and moving in Jet

Author and social commentator Gore Vidal was not a blood relation of Jackie Kennedy, but they shared a stepfather in Hugh Auchincloss, through two of his three different wives. After an argument with Bobby Kennedy and savage commentary on the Kennedys, he was banned from their circle. Jackie is at far right, Vidal right behind her. Alice Roosevelt Longworth is at center, over emblem, Eunice Shriver behind her. Family friend Bill Walton is at far left. The Washington Horse Show. October 27, 1961.

Set society, Lee introduced Jackie to her celebrated acquaintances who had grand entertainments on yachts and in castles. Such high life was escapist adventure for Jackie, and on every transatlantic trip she made as First Lady, Lee was with her.

On what was an official trip this time, the Bouvier sisters again traveled in March and early April 1962. Jackie first made an official call on Pope John XXIII in the Vatican, escorted by cardinals, bishops, and other Roman Catholic officials, to lend support to her sister's efforts to have her first marriage annulled. Then it was on to the duo's famous visit to India and Pakistan. Along the way they charmed Nehru of India—who gave Jackie tiger cubs, and whom Lee called "the most gentle, intriguing, sensual man I have ever met"—and Ayub Khan of Pakistan, who gave Jackie one of her

most beloved horses, the gelding Sardar. Mostly, the sisters had a crash course on Indian, Pakistani, Hindu, and Moslem cultures. Lee Radziwill later recalled of the trip, "There were times when we were so completely exhausted by our schedule that at the end of the day, laughter overcame us as we exchanged stories of whom and what each of us had had to cope with. Then it was back to smiles and nectarine juice at the banquet table until I thought I would collapse." On her way home, Jackie seemed upset at herself for having been "so far away alone, without Jack or the children," but she felt closer than ever to Lee. "I was so proud of her," she said. "Nothing could ever come between us."

Jackie's closest confidante during the White House years was her sister, Lee Radziwill. Seen here are the sisters on the walk leading to the Oval Office, with Tina Radziwill, daughter of Lee, and Jackie's dog, Clipper. January 1962.

During a spring 1962 trip to India and Pakistan, Lee Radziwill took second place to her famous sister, and it certainly could not have been easy. A woman who walked sixteen miles to see Jackie called her "Durga, the goddess of power." Her picture was hung in the cooking areas of some Indian homes with a burning votive candle in front of it, and was placed beside pictures of Hindu gods. One

admirer wrote her a letter in his own blood. Rosewater was sprinkled at her feet, lotus garlands strewn around her neck. In India, the Bouvier sisters cruised down the Ganges in a flat boat with a canopy of thousands of marigold flowers, watched a snake charmer at work, and rode an elephant. In Pakistan, they rode a camel. "A camel makes an elephant feel like a jet plane," declared the First Lady. March 1962.

Jackie also wanted her children to be as close to their maternal cousins as they were to the Kennedys. Consequently, Stas and Lee Radziwill were frequent visitors for long stays around holidays and summer with their children, Tony and Tina, who were comparable in age to Caroline and John, respectively. Lee Radziwill was with her sister at Hyannis Port and Glen Ora—the Kennedys' weekend home in Virginia—as often as she was at the White House.

At Jackie's insistence, Jack had rented Glen Ora, about an hour's drive southwest of Washington. It was located in Middleburg, Virginia, where the Orange County Hunt Association held its autumn and spring foxhunting, and where the Gold Cup horse race was held. Jackie's friend Eve Fout and her husband, Paul, and their children were permanent residents and sponsored Jackie's membership into the hunt. Also nearby were Paul and Rachel Mellon, who were of a slightly older generation, although the First Lady knew the famous millionaire's wife well enough to call her "Bunny." When she was "riding to the hounds" on her horse Bit O'Irish—a whimsical reference to her own half-Gaelic ancestry—tromping through swamp, brush, branches, and over stone walls and wood farm gates, the First Lady said she felt "clean and anonymous." In the house, Jack was particularly

Glen Ora, the private house in Virginia hunt country that Jackie called "home," while she called the White House "Washington." January 1962.

proud of a large blue ribbon Jackie had won and had fluttering on a large lamp shade, but he never used the riding outfit she bought for him and she called off a search for his "perfect horse." Content with a difficult three-hole golf course put in for him, he found Glen Ora too slow for him every weekend, and seldom visited.

"Glen Ora is my salvation," said Jackie, "I'd die if I didn't have some place to get away from the terrible pressures around here." Consequently, she was there for many of her famous Thursday-morning-to-Tuesday-night "weekends" with her children. She particularly wanted to do things with them that she didn't have time for in the White House. Although Maude Shaw was there, Jackie took over changing John's diapers, giving the children baths, reading to and feeding them, and snap-ping them into their pajamas at bedtime. She could go out to dinner with the Fouts at the local Red Fox Inn. She knew when fresh cookies were sold at the local bakery—and formed a lifelong friendship with the baker. Caroline and her mother lunched at a drugstore counter—arguing over whether Caroline would drink milk or soda with her hamburger. Jackie waited on line at the B&A Grocery. She even fetched the morning paper at the newsstand—picking up multiple copies for company.

The old 1810 yellow stucco country house that the First Family rented from Gladys Tartiere had stone gateposts with terraced gardens. Although it appeared somewhat rustic, Jackie gave it the Fifth Avenue touch: she redecorated its six bedrooms in French antiques with the help of Sister Parish; she had the terraced gardens uprooted and redesigned.

Jackie on her favorite horse, Sardar. The stables at Glen Ora are behind the fence. September 25, 1962.

There was a guest house, a farm hand's house converted into the Secret Service headquarters, a cave, and huge horse stables. The sign at the end of the road leading to the house said POSITIVELY NO TRESPASSING, and here she could truly be alone with her husband and children. Being a wife and mother was, Jackie told the Fouts, "exactly what I should be in this period of our life."

Jackie could humorously caption a photograph of her and Jack watching television with, "This is the last time Caroline goes on 'Meet the Press!'" but when it came to stopping even the most talented photographers from taking pictures of her children, she meant business. After the initial official pictures were taken—that was it. *Look* photographer Stanley Tretick said she had a way of affirming this rule that "strikes terror to your heart. . . . This is one thing that old Joe Kennedy liked about her, that she was a tough babe." Not only did she directly approach lurking photographers who anticipated shots of her nearby playing children, she wrote to them and to writers who sought to have their copy illustrated with such pictures. "Caroline was being recognized wherever she went," Jackie wrote in denying permission to one writer. "That is a strange enough thing to get used to at any age—but pretty sad when one is only three. Every article just increases interest in her—her little friends and cousins see it and mention it to her and it is all bad for her."

What always underpinned Jackie's famous style was a substance that was rooted in her intelligence and absorption of knowledge. In preparation for motherhood, for example, she had read dozens of articles and books on raising children and child psychology, including the era's famous works by

Jackie drastically changed the interior of rustic Glen Ora into that of a French country manse. Franklin Roosevelt Jr. and Lee Radziwill sit in the Glen Ora living room. 1962.

Dr. Benjamin Spock. She was determined that neither of her children would be "singled out and fawned over." She was particularly angry about satirist Vaughan Meader's use of Caroline as a character on his comedy album *First Family*, finding it to be in "appalling taste that he should make money out of a five-year-old child." Asked in 1962 about her further goals as First Lady, Jackie answered personally: "More time with my children, for they are both at an age where it is important that their parents be with them as much as possible." In various remarks during her tenure, she reinforced constantly her focus on her children:

It's hard enough to bring up children anyway, and everyone knows that limelight is the worst thing for them. They either get conceited, or else they get hurt . . . I wanted to take my daughter to the circus last week, and I decided I just shouldn't because I'd ruin it for her. I worked so hard to make her little ballet school a private thing . . . And there were all the photographers waiting . . . Someday she is going to have to go to school, and if she is in the papers all the time that will affect her little classmates and they will treat her differently . . . It isn't fair to children in the limelight to leave them to the care of others and then to expect that they will turn out all right. They need their mother's affection and guidance and long periods of time alone with her. That is what gives them security in an often confusing new world.

Caroline Kennedy. November 11, 1963.

Had they not been presidential children, however, Caroline and John would still not have lived like "normal" children, as Jackie always said she tried to raise them: they had a nanny, cars, planes, ponies and other pets, beautiful clothes—total material comfort and security, even indulgence. While their mother jetted to Paris or Rome, "Miss Shaw," as they always called her, took care of them; she was a loving woman with a careful sense of teaching the children the mannered behavior their mother wanted them to have. She had a good sense of humor, and the policemen and service staff loved teasing her for being English. One day, when Caroline left her talking doll in the Oval Office with its recording device still on, the tape that repeated whatever was said to the doll picked up the president's voice—

and cursing. Called down to fetch the doll, Miss Shaw listened to the recording, heard the president cursing, and in frantically trying to record her own voice jammed the mechanism. Finally, the tape was pried out from the back of the doll. She told Caroline the doll had lost its voice. She could be befuddled but was always resourceful. Shaw had to be more than a nanny; the president's children were recognizable in public. Although she only laughed when they once escaped her and made a plunge into the South Lawn fountain—naked—the nanny had to shoo away people asking for three-year-old Caroline's autograph or coming up to pat John's head.

Three Secret Service agents—Lynn Meredith, Bob Foster, and Tom Wells—were on what their colleagues dubbed "the Diaper Detail." They played ball and miniature golf with the children, taught them nursery rhymes, and showed John how to ride a bike. The head of Jackie's Secret Service detail, Clint Hill, became an honorary member of the Diaper Detail. When Jackie went out with her children, she liked to sit in the front seat with them—squeezed beside an agent. She much preferred to drive herself, and when the agents let her, the children climbed all over them. The entire household staff looked after the children as they grew and began to explore the far reaches of the mansion.

Despite all the help she had, Jackie was an unusually intense mother who gave love without reserve, hugging and kissing her children freely. Shaw washed and dressed John as a baby, but Jackie always fed him his morning bottle. Each day she was in residence she spent special time with each individually and together—a walk on the lawn, reading a book, exploring nature, shopping, riding horses together, and just talking to them as small adults—never in baby talk. On her official schedule, her time with her children was inviolate and permanent—nothing interrupted it, and she more than willingly relinquished public duties to her mother, sisters-in-law, and mother-in-law rather than cancel her time with her kids. "Let's go out and kiss the sky," she whispered to her daughter as if she were some sort of big sister princess of magic. The traditional mother would never have a radiator removed from a hidden wall just to create a secret hiding place—but Jackie did. She managed to take the children for short walks through Lafayette Square, or out to Glen Echo Park, where there was an old carousel for them to ride. Mr. West concluded from watching her play with abandon with them, "This was the real Jacqueline Kennedy."

On rainy days, she sometimes treated them to cartoons in the movie theater. In the evenings, she always joined them for their early dinner, John in his high chair and Caroline in an adult chair with pillows on the seat. Sometimes, when she and Jack ate their later dinner together, the children were permitted to spend a little time with them before they were sent off to bed. Regardless of his schedule, if he was in Washington, their father always went to their rooms to say good night to his children and say prayers with them. When their behavior forced her to, Jackie could dish out reprimands and punishment. Usually, a stern and disapproving tone of voice kept them under control. "Someone, her father or me or the nurse will draw the line," she once said. "They are properly disciplined, I can assure you. I hate spoiled children." John tried to pull rank, once getting into a waiting car and asking for a ride. When the driver said no, the little boy snapped, "You'd better do it or my daddy will make you!" Only once, when Caroline disappeared while playing, did a panicked Miss Shaw slap her—then she immediately apologized.

Jack Kennedy was not as much of a disciplinarian as his wife had to be. When Caroline began pouting that she wanted to watch *The Lassie Show*, he immediately ordered up a portable television—against Jackie's limited TV viewing hours rule. He loved tickling the children until they fell to the floor, even if he was running late. Unlike Jackie, he was less encouraging of their independence. Rather lonely for Caroline's company when she was out at a friend's party, he cracked, "She's got to start staying home at night." Not until she was a week shy of her sixth birthday—on November 22, 1963—would he grant her permission to spend the night at a friend's house.

He even let them into cabinet meetings—when they insisted. While the president was in closed conference, Caroline popped down to fetch him for a scheduled event. Mrs. Lincoln agreed to scribble a note and slip it to Kennedy. She went into the Cabinet Room without realizing that Caroline was behind her. "Mommy wants you!" the First Daughter shrilly announced in front of the entire cabinet. The president did as he was told and the meeting broke. John wasn't so lucky. As Jack was about to begin a cabinet meeting, at which he initially per-mitted his son to sit in one of the large chairs around the table, Jack opened by asking the men, "What have we got today?" John shot back first—before being carried away by his nanny, who was quickly called in—"I got a glass of water!"

Both parents were constantly teaching the children. Before Jack went off on a trip, he always showed the state or country he was visiting on a map, and drilled Caroline on state capitals—as his own mother had done with him. When Jackie was leaving, she filled out postcards for them to be given while she was away, explaining where she would be. Both parents read to them, and Caroline was a fast and early reader, proud of her growing little library. Jackie specifically raised the children with those of other races. Besides Avery Hatcher, the African-American student in Caroline's class, John's best friend was Gustavo, the son of his mother's maid. "One remarkable thing about the children," noticed Shaw, "is the complete unawareness of any difference between themselves and colored people." When Caroline once asked George Thomas why he was darker than she was with her tan, he simply said he was in the sun longer. She never asked about it again.

It really wasn't until 1962, when John was able to walk, that he seemed to develop his distinct personality. When he was a baby, Jackie often wheeled him in his carriage around the south grounds. As he began to climb, she put in an intercom so she could hear him when he was napping. As he began to walk, she would encourage him to go find the goldfish in the South Lawn fountain, and he would waddle down, then run back to her, saying, "Dogs chased fish away." John went wild at the sight of helicopters; his father once joked that when the public saw a picture of the boy running toward him they would think he was attached to his father—when in fact he was scrambling to climb into the

John Kennedy had full access to the Oval Office and Cabinet Room—he was removed only when his father had to have quiet. These pictures, by Stanley Tretick of Look magazine, were donated as part of the Cowles Publication archives to the Library of Congress and deeded for public use. October 1963.

John Kennedy was more of a terror than Caroline, taking things apart to explore their mechanics, roughhousing with the dogs, or falling off a ladder—and losing a tooth. August 31, 1963.

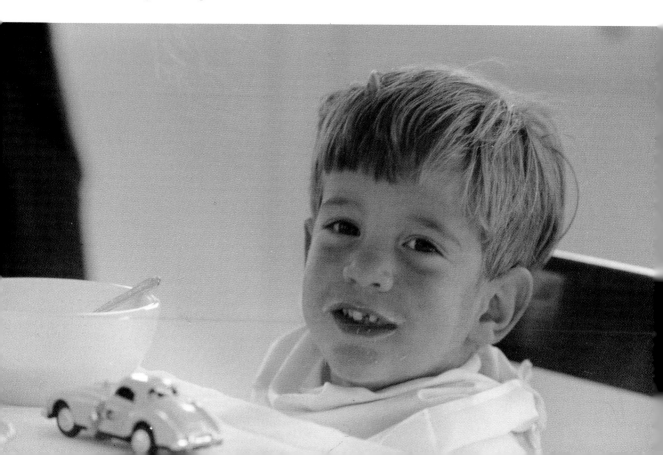

John Kennedy was obsessed with helicopters and airplanes as a little child, so much so that he was nicknamed "Helicopter Head" by his family. He cried whenever one left the White House grounds and he was not on it. At Camp David, however, he looked and listened overhead for the anticipated arrival of one with his father, shouting, "Chopper! Chopper!" as it came into view. When it landed he ran up to enter. He often went to play in the copter by himself. One weekend, while it was parked at Camp David, he dragged his father down to it and they sat beside each other with helmets on, making an imaginary flight. October 11, 1962 (crying); March 31, 1963 (climbing in, and at pilot seat).

John Kennedy had a habit of begging for the hat of anyone he saw with one—and putting it on for the camera. Here, he imitates a Secret Service agent by borrowing the man's sunglasses. September 14, 1963.

John Kennedy always got himself into the middle of things— like the Marine Band—much to his sister's delight. He is seen here trying the drums with her, trying the piano, and finally just dancing around with his lollipop. May 29, 1963.

helicopter that had just delivered the president. He also liked the sound of twenty-one-gun salutes and took in arrival ceremonies of state visitors on the South Lawn from the Truman Balcony—although his yells of "Ken-dee, Ken-dee" were not appreciated, and his dropping of a toy gun sent the Secret Service into a frenzy. When he heard the Marine Band, he looked for a parade.

John was often in trouble, stealing sugar cubes from the tea service, letting snakes from a snake farm near Camp David run over his arms. Whenever he saw an officer—or *anyone*—with a hat, he had to try on the hat. He imitated adults and began laughing when they laughed. He was a cute little fellow and doted on by everyone.

When it came time to cut John's hair—which Jackie didn't want to have done—the president had to take command. Coming into the kitchen one summer night, dressed in Bermuda shorts, slippers, and a white shirt, Jack solemnly asked the chef for a pair of scissors and began trimming away—Jackie wincing with suggestions, Caroline crying.

The domestic staff found Caroline to be a "good, good child." Jackie's "inherent shyness," observed

Jack Kennedy was unable to lift his son—who always wanted to be tossed in the air—because of his bad back, and encouraged his male friends, Secret Service agents, even the elderly German chancellor, Konrad Adenaeur, to do so. However, he could lie flat and hold him up. Most often he teased the boy with his foot, and then John would try to grab it so his father could not escape. When it was time to go, the president would tickle him and John would let go. In the third-floor hallway of the White House. May 29, 1963.

Caroline would interpret her brother's baby talk for her father. She gave up Neddie, her donkey-on-wheels toy, only reluctantly when John wanted it as his own. She insisted that his hair be brushed with the little silver brush set that had been her gift to him on his birth. He grew immediately attached to "Cannon," as he first pronounced her name, and she enjoyed helping Maude Shaw feed him, bathe him, and

put him to sleep. She always came running to his crib when he called for her, and had what Shaw called "the knack of bossing John without putting his back up." When he began asking for candy from Secret Service agents, from whom he knew he would always get some, Caroline was "horrified" at his boldness, according to Shaw. Sometimes she smashed his sand castles when he went jumping into the ocean, and he came out howling with shock. When he dropped food, she mimicked Maude Shaw's exasperated feminine sigh, and when he played rough, she assumed her mother's pose, silently extending her arm and making a "stop" signal with her palm. She could

reprimand John, even scold him, when he got too close to her territory—tugging on Macaroni's bridle, running off with one of her dolls. But her love for her brother was more evident. She patiently permitted him to play with her and her toys. She put a protective arm around him when they were in crowds. And most of all, she loved laughing at his antics or when he showed off. September 30, 1963 (pony); May 29, 1963 (doll); May 29, 1963 (seated); November 27, 1962 (playing).

Of the two children, Caroline was the more hesitant, the shyer, when she was introduced to strangers—including kings and presidents. April 24, 1961.

Caroline Kennedy was especially close to her parents and could talk endlessly to them about her ideas and observations. August 25, 1963.

Shaw, was "passed on to Caroline, and, like her mother, she needs to be given confidence." When she could not ride a two-wheel bike, but a younger cousin could, Caroline would not practice in front of him—until she, too, could ride. With her parents and nanny, however, she was uninhibited and full of constant chatter, questions, and observations. Carefully examining the plates of caviar the chef was preparing, she asked what it was—and then asked for a sample. He said most people didn't like caviar the first time they tried it. She pulled back in thought. "Never mind, then, I'll taste it the second time." Journalist Jim Bishop thought Caroline to be "sensible and sometimes quietly serious, as though she comprehends more than a child should." Joe Kennedy long remembered her half-hour discussion of the personality and character of the family's Welsh terrier, Charlie. If she had her mother's imagination, she also copied her mother's airs. Seeing a generic historical figure on a scotch bottle, she exclaimed, "Oh, look, there's Louis Quatorze!"

Despite Jackie's best effort to prevent it, Caro-

line was highly conscious of the attention she attracted. On one occasion when photographers came toward her, the four-year-old put up her hands and yelled, "No pictures!" On yet another occasion, when emerging with her mother from a plane, she piped up, "Where *are* the photographers?" Even her mother was amused when Caroline announced to the White House press corps that the president was "upstairs with his shoes and socks off doing nothing."

Caroline was especially attached to her father, worshipping everything about him. He taught her poetry, and fulfilled his promise to include in one of his speeches a poem she had memorized. As they sailed, she loved to hear his ongoing, spontaneously created tales of the mysterious "White Whale" and the one-legged sea captain who always failed to get the whale—which always ended with Jack taking socks from his unsuspecting friends and throwing them into the yacht's wake to "feed" the whale. There were other stories he based on the children—the girl equestrienne who won the Grand National and the boy who piloted a boat that sank a destroyer—and the surrounding woods of Glen Ora, from which the mysteriously shy girl Maybelle and the sad giant Bobo the Lobo never emerged. Although she had the sort of toys that little girls were traditionally given—ironing board, tea set, dolls' dresses—her favorites were those her father brought her: a toy giraffe and a life-size Raggedy Ann.

Her parents tried to integrate into "normal" family life those aspects of official life in the White House that the little girl could not ignore—and she responded as a child would. When Caroline popped down from the family rooms to peek over the railing at a formal party her parents were giving and the Marine Band struck up an original song, "My Pony Macaroni," she asked for "Old MacDonald," then showed guests that she had on

Caroline Kennedy and her kindergarten class pose for their class picture. May 7, 1963.

The school functioned as a cooperative among the mothers, each one taking turns as a teacher's helper—including Jackie.

Elizabeth Boyd and then Alice Grimes instructed the group. Seven girls and four boys—the children of friends of the Kennedys—formed the class. The parents paid for all supplies, school furniture, lockers, and teachers' salaries equally. Class began just before nine. A different parent car-pooled the children to the White House, while Caroline headed upstairs. Each child brought his or her own lunch. There were reading exercises from a storybook, printing lessons, naps, snacks of orange juice and cookies, prayers, art time, calis-

her "very best dress." Introduced to John Glenn, and knowing only that a chimp had earlier gone into space, she only remarked, "Where's the monkey?" Protestors carrying signs and chanting outside her house—which she watched from her window—were harder to understand. "What's Daddy done wrong?" she asked her mother. It was often explained to the children that they were only borrowing the house, and when the likes of Margaret Truman or Franklin Roosevelt Jr. came to visit, Caroline and John were told that they, too, had lived in the house as children.

Jackie's most unusual innovation was starting a kindergarten in the White House Solarium. An outgrowth of a Georgetown play group of children started by some mothers who were friends, it had originally moved each week to a different home. Jackie wanted her daughter to continue to be exposed to other children, and so she created the kindergarten on the third floor, with a space on the eastern end of the floor serving as the art room.

Caroline Kennedy lying on the ramp that leads to the Solarium, where Jackie Kennedy established the kindergarten class. Jackie is seen in the doorway. May 24, 1963.

Caroline and some of her classmates reading books. The Solarium was fully outfitted with kindergarten furniture—desks, chairs, book-cases, coat hangers, easels, sandbox, map, and more. 1963.

thenics, and, four times a week, French lessons taught by Jacqueline Hirsch. When Jackie was overseas for a long stretch and Caroline seemed particularly lonely for her mother, Hirsch focused on teaching the child a lengthy "welcome home" greeting in French. When the girl repeated it for both her parents, Hirsch recalled, "I have never seen two people so happy about children's achievement."

White House usher Nelson Pierce was ever efficient when Jackie told him, "It would be nice if the children could see a mother rabbit and her babies." A member of his church was president of the Rabbit Breeders' Association, and through him

Jackie Kennedy had a White House usher get a pregnant rabbit, Anabelle, for the class. Caroline is at center; her best friend, Agatha Pozen, is at right. May 7, 1963.

Pierce obtained the pregnant rabbit Annabelle. She gave birth to four babies, and the class was delighted to watch them grow—until the day their mother ate them. "Imagine trying to explain that to children," Jackie later told a friend.

Being in the White House did have its privileges. The children were always allowed to watch state arrivals on the South Lawn, poking their little heads through the balustrades of the open-air area just outside the Solarium windows. They got to greet special guests like Native Americans in headdresses or the astronauts. Playtime was also on the South Lawn; the children invaded Caroline's and John's playground. Many times, the sound of two loud claps from the West Wing was heard. This was the president signaling for Caroline and her pals, and they came running. He

Both of her parents took an active interest in Caroline's education. Watching a class performance in the third-floor hallway, in front row, are Jackie, Jack, and Janet Auchincloss. John Kennedy lies on the floor, watching. Caroline is third from left, in white baker's hat. May 29, 1963.

always enjoyed taking a late-morning break for a few minutes and talking to the children. Jackie made sure that even though Caroline was attending school in her home she took a bag lunch up to the classroom like the other students. She was not allowed to come down to join her mother or brother for lunch in the family rooms. Caroline preferred this anyway. She was not fond of vegetables, although Jackie saw to it that there was always at least a carrot or celery stick in her bag. Class broke up at about one-thirty, when Caroline and some of her friends could be counted on to drop by the kitchen to see if there were any fresh cookies to be had. If it was not too close to dinner, they were allowed to indulge.

As all the mothers of the children did, Jackie Kennedy served her kindergarten duty as "teacher's helper" on a regular basis—teaching the children to pray before their juice and cookie snack, drawing with crayons for them, and trying to talk to her daughter. May 24, 1963.

There was another hidden extra in having one's school in one's home—but not just for the First Daughter. "Somebody's been up here making the biggest mess! And it's not the first time, either," Alice Grimes told the chief usher one morning. "Something is going on in this nursery school at night!" Caroline, it was discovered, was playing in the sandbox—with the First Lady, who coaxed her up there.

If she had come into the White House insecure about everything from her marriage to being photographed, by 1962 Jackie had relaxed—and it was evident to everyone. "She always treated me more as a friend than an employee," said one staffer. "She always introduced me to anyone who happened to be around, no matter how important they were—kings and queens, it made no difference." The person making this statement, Traphes Bryant, was the White House dog keeper.

The winter home of Joe and Rose Kennedy, where the extended family gathered for Christmas dinner and Easter.
BOSTON HERALD

7

THE DYNASTY

Gatherings and Celebrations, 1962

It doesn't really matter as far as you and I are concerned, what really matters is the children.
—JACK KENNEDY

I am Teddy Kennedy's brother!
—JACK KENNEDY

Jackie returned from India in time for her family's annual trek to Palm Beach for the 1962 Easter holiday, an important one for Catholics. For short trips, the First Family used the mansion of their friends Charles and Jayne Wrightsman if they were away. Otherwise, for lengthier stays and their annual Christmas and Easter sojourns, Jack and his family stayed at the home of Captain Michael Paul, who made it available to them. Staff often accompanied them, and the president continued to conduct meetings and public ceremonies at the Paul house.

A large Easter dinner was usually held at Joe and Rose's Palm Beach estate, a rambling house with windows opening to a vast emerald lawn, and beyond that a seawall protecting the property from the crashing Atlantic. Decades of use by the growing family had left the interior furnishings threadbare, and although it was comfortable, it was not as elegant as the fashionable mansions that flanked it. On Easter 1962, Jack and Jackie had their own friends over to the Paul house in the late morning, before dinner.

Every year, Jackie gathered her children and any of their friends who were visiting, such as Sally Fay, and took them into the kitchen. After spreading newspapers on the table, she broke out the famous Paas brand of Easter egg dyes and they all colored the eggs. It was a time Jackie guarded fiercely. When asked to host an art-related event at the White House by the president's arts adviser, Jackie said, "We can do it almost any time but not in the early weeks of April, because that's near Easter and that's going to be Jack's vacation and I want to keep that absolutely clear."

The family returned from Palm Beach to the White House in time for them to inspect the latest addition to their menagerie, the gift to Jackie from Pakistan's president Ayub Khan of one of his prize geldings,

The Kennedys leaving Mass on Easter Sunday in Palm Beach, Florida. Below: The president in his "traveling" rocking chair, which was always sent with him on trips. Caroline is on his lap, Jackie behind them, stealing a smoke. That year, the president and his family gave his father—for use by the whole family—a jukebox. Jackie Kennedy teaching her son to color Easter eggs and create stands for them in the kitchen of the Paul family home, which the Kennedys always rented in Palm Beach. April 20, 1962 (leaving church), April 13, 1963 (all others).

Jack Kennedy at Glen Ora with his Welsh terrier, Charlie, a favorite of Caroline's. Charlie was not hesitant in snapping at little Tony Radziwill. February 18, 1962.

which she named Sardar. Jackie was not above accepting exotic gifts from potentates; soon enough she received another horse, from the president of Ireland. "Tell her, it's hurting me politically," the obviously nervous president told his chief of protocol to tell the First Lady. "I understand what you're saying," she responded to the go-between. "But there's a problem: I want the horses." She won that round.

Not since Theodore Roosevelt was president did a First Family have so many pets: deer, parakeets, ducks, dogs, cats, hamsters, fish, horses, and ponies. Jack and Jackie had both grown up with many family dogs—and, in Jackie's case, ponies and horses. They felt owning pets was a way to teach the children to lose fear around animals and to be

gentle caretakers. Jackie often took the children to a nearby county park in Wheaton, Maryland, to feed sheep and other penned animals at a small farm, then eat lunch at picnic tables.

"You be nice to those dogs," the president once yelled at his son as he roughhoused a bit too much with them, "they're your friends."

The Kennedys arrived in the White House with their Welsh terrier, Charlie, a particular favorite of Jack, who considered the dog his own. Joe Kennedy gave Jackie a German shepherd which she named Clipper. When asked by a pestering press corps what Clipper liked to eat, the First Lady stared at the dog, then stared at them·and said simply, "Reporters." They got the point: he was a menacing protector of his mistress. In June

Although checked for any Soviet bugging devices before being allowed into the family menagerie, Pushinka was a democratic dog for all to enjoy—even the work crew in the basement. August 28, 1963.

1961, two nervous Soviet officials accompanied by the Soviet ambassador carried a small, frightened white puppy into the Diplomatic Reception Room. "How did this dog get here?" Jack asked upstairs. Jackie confessed, "I'm afraid I asked Khrushchev for it in Vienna. I was just running out of things to say." And so, Pushinka came to live in the White House with the Kennedys. Besides these three dogs, two others—Shannon and Wolf—would later join the crew.

Among the various other pets, Tom the kitten was kept first at Janet Auchincloss's house and then made his home in the Solarium of the White House. There was even a press "interview" with

Caroline's pet bird, Maybelle, carefully being taken out of her cage. The bird was later given a South Lawn funeral and burial. August 1962.

The White House ducks in the South Lawn fountain didn't stay long after Charlie, the Welsh terrier, grabbed one by the neck and nearly killed it. Besides, the ducks were in the habit of eating the tulips. June 22, 1961.

Tom before he was finally banished to the home of Mary Gallagher, Jackie's personal secretary, because of the president's severe allergy. In Caroline's room, two parakeets were watched over by the president's daughter. Hers was named Maybelle and John's was called Bluebell. When their mother was in the room, she supervised their careful handling of the birds, permitting the pets to be held by the children—but she warned them not to let go since the birds would fly away. Ducks, kept in the South Lawn fountain, also were briefly part of the Kennedy animal family. Their days were numbered when Jackie noticed that were they eating the tulips that surrounded the fountain. Jackie

also struck upon the romantic notion of having some deer roam the lawn. A gift of several was brought to the White House, and they stayed until the First Lady was warned that they were unpredictable around children and not suitable as pets. They were sent off to the New York Central Park Children's Zoo. Certainly the most renowned of the Kennedy pets was Caroline's pony, Macaroni, a present from Vice President Lyndon Johnson. Caroline rode Macaroni on the South Lawn on a few occasions, but he was otherwise kept with her mother's horses at their weekend home.

No Kennedy pet story, however, garnered more national attention than the woeful tale of Caroline's hamsters. Caroline was frantic one morning when she noticed that one of her hamsters had escaped its cage. A hamster hunt of serious proportions got under way involving Secret Service

The two deer presented as pets to the Kennedy children didn't last long on the South Lawn. They were given to the Children's Zoo in Central Park, New York. November 6, 1963.

agents, maids, and even the president. Sadly, he discovered, the hamster had met its maker in the presidential bathtub. A burial on the South Lawn followed. Pierre Salinger even addressed the issue of whether it was hamster suicide with a somber national press corps.

That spring, however, concern turned to the human members of the Kennedy family. Ted Kennedy had made it official on March 14—he was a candidate for the United States Senate seat from Massachusetts. On April 27, Jack conducted a secret White House meeting on strategy for Ted's campaign and to provide general advice. Some of the Boston political figures who attended were even flown down to Washington under assumed names. The president was clear that he did not want his staff involved actively, but claims that he was opposed to Ted's running because of the potential backlash against the administration might have been exaggerated.

Jack had always been especially fond of his little brother, and according to Mrs. Lincoln, Ted "adored" Jack. At some of the most emotionally difficult moments in Jack's private life, it had been Teddy who was always there for him as a companion. Following Jack's 1954 back surgery and near-death experience, Ted was the one—along with Jackie—who saw his brother through the depressing recuperation; after Jack lost the 1956 vice presidential nomination, it had been Ted who accompanied him on a sailing voyage. Mrs. Lincoln observed that, at least during Ted's 1962 campaign, there was none of the "aggressive rivalry" that Jack experienced with Bobby.

Jack was more involved, and engaged emotionally, in Teddy's campaign than he let on. When Ted was eager to attack his opponent for the Democratic nomination, the president leaned on his crutches in his father's house and looked over some briefing papers given him by the candidate. "Listen," he told him, "stay on the issues and leave the personal attacks out. He'll be gone and forgotten when you are a United States Senator." Ted Sorenson helped prepare questions and answers that would be asked in town hall meetings around Massachusetts. Jack discouraged aides from telling his brother that they didn't think he did well in a debate at the state convention. Jack himself gently broke the news to the friendly *Boston Globe* Washington bureau chief about how Ted had asked a friend to take a Spanish exam for him at Harvard, and how the younger brother had been expelled for it. The careful language describing the incident as offered by the president was printed word for word in the *Globe*. The March 30 story called it the "Examination Incident."

The appealing prospect of Ted's living in Washington was far more than that of another Democratic Senate vote; Jack had always enjoyed the company of this brother. Whereas Bobby would bring up work and issues and crises, Teddy would simply make Jack laugh or explore ideas in convivial conversation. Many times, when Jackie was away, Jack would phone Ted and ask him to pop over for dinner—and the evening usually ended with a long talk on the Truman Balcony.

"It's certainly true that I'm more isolated socially," the president told a reporter. "In the beginning I tried to carry on the life I had led, going out, seeing people; but I soon realized that was impossible. Apart from state dinners, I suppose I see only three or four people socially. But I have no feeling of withdrawing. After all, everyone's life is circumscribed. And in many ways I see and hear more than anyone else."

To counteract potential isolation, the Kennedys hosted a handful of private parties—one for the Radziwills, one for Eugene Black, another welcom-

Jackie Kennedy (back to camera) seated at one of her private dinner dances. Across the table from her at left is Lyndon Johnson, at right her friend Jayne Wrightsman. After dinner there was dancing in the East Room. Meanwhile, President Kennedy holds a group of guests captive in conversation in the Cross Hallway. January 21, 1963. Jackie liked to dance to the samba, the cha-cha, the Twist, and even—according to William Manchester—the Alley Cat. At a private party with her sister Lee, Jackie Kennedy danced the Twist with her friend and designer Oleg Cassini—and captured on film by her friend Paris Match *editor Benno Graziani.* BENNO GRAZIANI (RIGHT)

ing the Ken Galbraiths back from India, and another in honor of Jean and Steve Smith before they moved to New York from Washington. At the March 1961 party for the Radziwills, seventy-two guests came for cocktails at eight-thirty in black tie and gowns, then dined at nine round tables in the State Dining Room. Lee was in red, Jackie in white. The president entertained the guests by having two larger-than-life blown-up photographs brought in—one of Stas Radziwill, the other of Oleg Cassini. Their resemblance was remarkable, and that fact launched a witty monologue from Jack. Then there was dancing until three in the morning to the orchestra of Lester Lanin. He played

Whenever the Bouvier sisters arrived in Europe, it brought out adoring fans, local political leaders, and, of course, the paparazzi. Lee is seen, as usual, behind Jackie with sunglasses on.

again at the White House party for the Smiths in February 1962 until the wee hours.

Jackie's favorite dancing partner was the vice president: "He was a good dancer . . . dancing then was still traditional . . . the Twist was just starting. But nobody really knew how to do it." Indeed, the Lanin orchestra did play the Twist at one party, but reports that the president danced it were exaggerated. He had simply been shown a few steps and followed it a bit, as a joke. Jackie, however, was, in the words of her mother's friend Molly Thayer, "a wicked twister." Rose Kennedy recorded during the

gathering of the extended Kennedy family in Hyannis Port for the Thanksgiving holiday in 1961 that there was "Lots of discussion about 'the Twist'—the new dance which has great vogue at the moment [−] throw your hips around—NO one knew much about it but Jackie[,] at [the] end[,] in a Schiaparelli pink slack suit[,] gave a three-minute performance to the jungling-rumbling music of Joan [playing the piano]."

Besides these private parties on the state floor, Jackie tried to regularly host small dinners in the private dining room for close or special friends—including Marlene Dietrich and Isaac Stern. When Jack stayed up well past ten on one of these evenings, in a convivial, joking mood, Jackie assured the guests, "Don't worry . . . if he wants to stay up, let him stay up. He hasn't done this in ages." When Jackie was away, Jack always had friends over for impromptu dinners.

And Jackie was away again that summer. After a few weeks in Hyannis Port, the First Lady was again overseas with her sister and her family for a two-week vacation, this time bringing Caroline along for her first trip to Europe. Starting in Rome, the Bouvier sisters went to a dinner-dance with Italian High Society hosted by Count Fernando "Dino" Pecci-Blunt, a Harvard acquaintance of the president, at his Capitoline Hill palace. Then, they—along with Caroline, Stas, Tony, and Tina—headed to Ravello. They stayed in an eleventh-century villa, El Episcopio, perched on high cliffs above the Amalfi Coast, south of Naples. It was intended as a private vacation and a chance to see the Greek ruins at Paestum—despite a Colorado minister's condemnation of her for "permitting" paparazzi to photograph her wearing a bathing suit. There were daily trips to the public beach—where a section finally had to be cordoned off—for swimming with the children, speedboating, and suntanning. Fiat Motor Cars owner and president Gianni Agnelli and his wife, Marella, were frequent visitors, and there was a side trip for some heavy-

duty shopping in Capri. Jackie invited the Agnellis to come to Newport a few weeks later.

It was hardly a "private" respite. Given honorary citizenship, the American First Lady won the nation's affection when it was learned that she immediately contributed funds for those displaced in a nearby earthquake. After a late supper, the adults often went for strolls in the narrow streets, trailed by cheering Italians and swarming paparazzi whose hundreds of camera bulbs flashed like lightning bugs in the summer night air. It was all quite surreal, the midnight hours in cafés, with live tableaus of stout Italian widows in black coming to stare at her, little children excited at being able to stay up so late to see the American lady, and the

Jackie being driven along a European port. Summer 1962.

spontaneous serenades on mandolins that broke out on street corners as she passed by under strings of lights throwing off their artificial glare. Jackie later joked that she had actually filmed a scene in a movie by her favorite director, Federico Fellini.

Caroline was as great a celebrity as her mother. She and Jackie stayed out evenings to watch townspeople perform the traditional tarantella in their honor, and the First Daughter was presented with a native costume of her own. Photographers went into a frenzy when Jackie was seen feeding Caroline a plate of spaghetti after a swim. Caroline sent her father a postcard from Italy that he cherished, and even placed in his dresser mirror: "I like Italy better than Hyannis but I like Hyannis a little bit more because there's fairs. I miss you Daddy very much."

Jack, meanwhile, was with John, not in Hyannis Port but in Newport, visiting his in-laws. Little has been written about Jack's relationship with his wife's family. It was at the 1953 Kennedy wedding that the matriarchal Mrs. Auchincloss realized the full extent of her son-in-law's toughness and determination to get his own way. "Mummy is terrified of Jack because she can't push him around at all," Jackie said shortly after her marriage. While it was true that Janet developed an immediate respect for her son-in-law, she,

The president sails in Narragansett Bay, near Newport, Rhode Island, with, right to left, Yusha Auchincloss, Jack, Janet's daughter, known as Little Janet, unknown, future senator John Kerry, and Janet Auchincloss, who sips her chowder. August 26, 1962.

too, in a sense, fell in love with him as had Jackie, Lee, Little Janet, even Yusha and Jamie. Janet doted on Jack—making sure he wasn't too hot or cold, asking if he needed anything to eat, if he was tired—whatever it was, she wanted to make sure he was served first and fast. Although a lifelong Republican, she became even more vociferous in her defense of the president than Jackie was.

Janet's husband—Jackie's stepfather—was a Standard Oil heir, and as a couple, Mr. and Mrs. Hugh Dudley Auchincloss were a formidable entree into the most privileged world of eastern seaboard society. Hammersmith Farm, their twenty-eight-room mansion and estate, where the Kennedys had their wedding reception in 1953, had a staff of sixteen servants. Thirty-two gardeners manicured the thirty acres of gardens and lawns. In the fall of 1961, the Kennedys had welcomed the Indian prime minister to Newport for several days. As they helicoptered over the mansions and yachts, Jack cracked at him, "I wanted you to see how the average American family lives." Nehru was not amused.

At Hammersmith, Caroline and John played with their stepcousins Cecil and Maya Auchincloss and Ivan and Newton Steers. Sometimes the sailors—who particularly liked Caroline—tied mul-

Secret Service agents, Caroline Kennedy, and household staff members of Hugh and Janet Auchincloss await the president's arrival at the Auchinclosses' Newport summer estate, Hammersmith Farm. September 26, 1961.

Urged by his father to jump into the pool, and with his uncle Yusha Auchincloss beside him, John Kennedy plunges in. Standing behind Yusha are Janet Auchincloss and Little Janet. Standing at far right is Maude Shaw. August 26, 1962.

ticolored balloons to the railing of the *Honey Fitz* in her honor as they sailed Narragansett Bay. She spent hours in the boat as her father read and her mother water-skiied. The Kennedys used the golf course at the country club across the road from Hammersmith. At the private Bailey's Beach Club, they used the Auchincloss family cabana.

Newport had its unpleasant moments. As the president and First Lady and friend Jim Reed spent the day at Bailey's Beach Club, it was painfully evident that they were being studiously ignored by the starchy Republican membership. When they left, Jackie nodded toward the thick throngs of tourists craning for a glimpse of the president. "Those are the important people," she said. In fact, Jackie seemed more ambivalent about Newport than did her Irish Catholic husband. In earlier years she had heard so many anti-Semitic remarks in society there that she was permanently disenchanted by the town. Although she loved Hammersmith and her stepfather, who was wonderful to her, Newport still represented a part of her life associated with her parents' divorce.

Jack Kennedy loved Newport because of the sea. He found that he could go sailing there every day of the summer and early autumn—there was something about the ocean there that especially entranced him. Instead of being just Jack, among a clan of other Kennedys, he was always treated as a prince in Newport. Janet always saw to it that the presidential flag was properly flown when he was "in residence." Little Janet, whom Jack especially liked, was a lovely, bright, and fun girl with a

humorous and extremely kind nature. Jamie treated Jack like a god. Yusha recognized Jack as a man as sensitive as himself, and the president was always touched by his generous impulses. The two also formed a kinship. The president's stepfather-in-law was called "Uncle Hugh-dee" by both Jack and Jackie. Hugh Auchincloss was an intelligent and witty man, but rather quiet compared to Janet, who tended to speak bluntly. Despite being a Republican, Auchincloss, out of loyalty to Jackie, supported President Kennedy personally, if not politically. He was not outrageously generous during the campaign, however. He managed to come up with only a $250 donation to his son-in-law's White House bid.

When Jackie returned from Italy with Caroline, Jack was at the airport to meet them. His comments about Jackie's beauty on her return seemed to touch off a softening sentiment between the couple. Photographs show them especially close and comfortable

Jackie and Caroline, on their arrival home from their summer trip to Italy, are escorted by the president. August 1962.

Jackie and Jack sailing in Newport with her mother and stepfather, partially obscured behind Janet Auchincloss. September 1962.

with each other as they sailed during the golden September afternoons. Before they left, Jack inscribed a photograph of Jackie and him: "For Mummy and Uncle Hugh D—with thanks for helping to create the best half of this photograph."

He and Jackie were in Newport during the September 18 Massachusetts primary election but went to Boston to vote. Later that day, back at Hammersmith Farm, he rushed the Auchinclosses through dinner as he anxiously waited for the returns. The president was extremely nervous about Ted's possibly losing even though the campaign, headed by Steve Smith, was a steamrolling

President Kennedy with his stepnephew and stepniece by marriage, the twins Cecil and Maya Auchincloss.

The grandchildren and stepgrandchildren of Hugh D. and Janet Bouvier Auchincloss, two years after the Kennedy administration ended, photographed at Hammersmith Farm: Top, left to right: Maya Auchincloss, Cecil Auchincloss, Caroline Kennedy, John Kennedy; bottom, left to right: Tina Radziwill, Tony Radziwill, Burr Steers, Hugh Steers, Ivan Steers.
COURTESY YUSHA AUCHINCLOSS

wonder in organization. Jack's and Ted's conversations, however, had remained limited to the time they saw each other at Hyannis Port. Ted and Joan had bought a nearby home on Squaw Island, where the president was also using a home (security and space considerations, as well as Jackie's urging, encouraged the First Family to relocate from their regular home in the family compound). Many mornings, Jack and two Secret Service agents would walk right through Ted's house to get to the beach. "Jack, you don't call before you're

Near their home on Squaw Island, not far from the Kennedy compound in Hyannis Port, Joan and Ted Kennedy walk with their children, Kara and Ted Jr.
BOSTON GLOBE

Ted Kennedy breaking good news about his candidacy in the Democratic primary for the party's nomination as U.S. Senate candidate to his brother Jack—the back of the golf cart is packed with nieces and nephews. September 3, 1962.

make. Ted won the Democratic nomination by a shockingly huge 67 percent.

As Ted had told reporters in the spring, when he announced that he was running for the Senate, his sisters "may be visiting in the state, and we certainly won't keep them in a closet," but he didn't want to be seen as depending any further on his family. One family member apparently insisted on it anyway. It turned out that, although she said "I am past retirement age," seventy-two-year-old Rose Kennedy was the star on the campaign trail. She would talk to people standing on chairs, answer endless questions about how to raise children, and was photographed in hundreds of pictures putting her arm through the arms of the delighted Massachusetts women eager to meet her.

Although it was never articulated by her, in some respects Joe's stroke had liberated Rose. She seemed to be a late bloomer coming into her own. She had done the famous "Coffee for Kennedy"

through my front door," his sister-in-law huffed in mock insult. "I don't have to, Joansie, I'm the president."

When Ted made his first appearance on *Meet the Press* as a Senate candidate, Jack was relieved that he managed to avoid making a specific stand on aid to education, since it was a sensitive issue in Congress at the moment and one on which the administration was seeking to find compromise. During the day of the televised debate between Ted and Edward McCormack, challenging each other for the Democratic Party nomination, the president was out sailing. He rushed the boat back to shore to make certain he had enough time to watch. He paced nervously up and down a hall, deeply worried about the slightest mistake that Ted might

Rose Kennedy with an admirer at a "Tea with Rose" fundraiser for Ted Kennedy's Senate campaign. September 1962.

events when Jack ran for the House, the Senate, and then the presidency. Now she became genuinely political in her press interviews. She deftly handled a question about public funding to parochial schools by saying she sent her children to both types of schools "so they would get to know all groups of children and they would see that a chauffeur's son or a mechanic's son is sometimes smarter than they are." Rose Kennedy headlined sold-out, jam-packed fund-raisers for her son in auditoriums and halls throughout the Bay State, surprising her audiences by shining a flashlight down the center aisle to a woman at the end of a row, whom she then introduced as "Teddy's pretty, young wife." The blond Joan Kennedy would then rise from her chair briefly to an ovation. Rose was campaigning for Teddy, but she was clearly loving the attention herself. To the whispered epithet of "dynasty," she was quick to draw a comparison to another political Massachusetts family—the Adamses. "They were wonderful," she said, "something to be proud of."

Whether Rose was proud or tentative at the moment she never said, but two days before Teddy garnered the whopping 67 percent victory for his party's nomination for the Senate, Eunice Shriver made history. That day, September 18, excerpts from the September 22 issue of the *Saturday Evening Post* were released to the press, and the world discovered that the president of the United States had a retarded forty-three-year-old sister, Rosemary. "For a long time my family believed that all of us working together could provide my sister with a happy life in our midst," Eunice wrote, adding that Rosemary was now institutionalized. Eunice Shriver also went further than anyone ever had, publicly or privately, to suggest that her sister's condition had been worsened by an experimental lobotomy: "It fills me with sadness to think

this change might not have been necessary if we knew then what we know today."

If all of this was shocking to the world, Eunice Shriver and her honesty became an incredible beacon of hope for the millions of families who had lived in silent confusion and shame about their own children who were mentally retarded or otherwise challenged. It was a difficult revelation for Rose Kennedy, who had always thought this should be kept private. It took her a full year to talk about Rosemary publicly—and then she became an activist for all handicapped and retarded children.

President Kennedy never publicly discussed it. He was proud of Eunice, but he was not really used to women like this. She was determined to make a difference in the area of public policy, even at the price of a personal revelation, yet was not seeking any sort of public credit for it. Jack had to take notice now—Eunice was serious about getting the administration to draft landmark federal legislation on behalf of the mentally retarded and the handicapped.

In the middle of the hubbub over Eunice's astounding revelation and Ted's blitzkrieg Senate campaign, it was announced by the White House that the president was suddenly returning to Washington from Chicago because he "had a bad cold." Waiting for him on the tarmac at Andrews Air Force Base was Attorney General Robert Kennedy. This was no ordinary cold—this was potential nuclear annihilation. The Cuban Missile Crisis had begun.

When her sister-in-law became First Lady, Jean Smith remarked, "Jackie never bombards him with questions, like we do. She approaches him in a leisurely way, knowing that he'll talk about things when he's ready." With the Cuban Missile Crisis, all that changed.

"There was a little squib . . . in the *New York Times*. It said that 'at four o'clock in the afternoon, the President had called up Mrs. Kennedy and they went and walked out in the rose garden,' " recalled Chuck Spalding. "He was sharing with her the possible horror of what might happen." No less a person than the president's military aide, Major General Chester Clifton, later confessed, "JFK turned to his wife for advice whenever a crisis arose . . . he would talk to her about it and she would talk with him. She wouldn't advise his staff, she would advise him—that's why nobody knew about it." The British ambassador remembered having a meeting at the time of the crisis with the president. Since the ambassador was also a discreet personal friend of the president's, the presence and participation of the First Lady in their talks would raise no red flags. "Jackie told me she took notes when Jack and I talked about this," he later recalled.

When the president was about to helicopter away from the White House in the midst of the crisis,

On Sunday, October 21, Jackie Kennedy told the chief usher to cancel the dinner-dance she planned to host for the Maharajah and Maharani of Jaipur because there was "something brewing that might turn out to be a big catastrophe." It was the Cuban Missile Crisis. Instead, she held a small private dinner for them; they are seen here on the lawn with her in the midst of the crisis. October 24, 1962.

Dr. Janet Travell found it strange that the 'copter suddenly lowered, the back door opened, and Jack emerged. Then she noticed a figure with "hair wild in the gale of the rotors" who began racing across the lawn to the president. It was his wife. "She met him almost at the foot of the helicopter steps and she reached up with her arms. They stood motionless in an embrace for many seconds," Travell recorded in her diary entry for Friday, October 19. "Then she returned under the awning and he was away. Perhaps no one else noted that rare demonstration of affection. A few days later in the publicized hours of the Cuban Missile Crisis, I remembered it. I thought of its deep significance—the unbreakable bond of love between them that showed clearest in times of trouble."

That Jackie flatly refused to take the pink tickets necessary for entry for herself and the children to an emergency shelter at a Defense Department installation in rural Virginia was the most tangible proof of her unconditional love for the president. It must have shocked yet heartened him. As Kenny O'Donnell remembered, the First Lady simply "refused to leave him alone in the White House." After this decision, Jack seems to have made his wife a full political partner and confidante, if only in this crisis.

"Maybe it was during the Cuban Missile Crisis when husband and wife meant the most to each other," a *Time* reporter observed. "He would tell her everything that was happening." What she told him, unfortunately, was left unrecorded. It is possible, however, that she offered practical advice based on human psychology. She had carefully observed the Politburo members during the 1961 Vienna meeting with Khrushchev and felt that only Gromyko could be taken at his word. She offered this impulse based only on her keen ability to size up public personas and the people behind them.

One of the twenty-nine engraved silver calendars of October 1962 given by President Kennedy to his top advisers and aides who helped him through the Cuban Missile Crisis, with the thirteen historic days more heavily engraved. This one, inscribed with his wife's initials as well as his, and given to her, was one of only two given to women—the other went to his secretary.

Jackie's "reports," as one senator characterized her letters to the president following her meetings with foreign leaders, were, he said, "full of subtle political observation . . . [that] held back nothing by way of praise or criticism." In all likelihood, Jackie posed to Jack the timeless questions of human motivation and suggested he consider the emotions, rational strategy, and fears of the Soviets as he made decisions. Whatever she said, it seemed to go beyond mere wifely emotional support at a time of crisis. In later acknowledging those he considered to be his most trusted advisers with a symbolic gift as a reminder of the crisis they shared, he included Jackie among the recipients. That he reached out to her in this crisis was an important personal turning point for Jack, a breakthrough of sorts. "If it was earlier in their marriage, I don't think he would have called her then," Chuck Spalding affirmed.

Throughout this time, the most dangerous period of the Kennedy administration and the world at large, Jack depended upon other members of his family. His single most crucial adviser was the attorney general. When photographs from reconnaissance planes proved without a doubt that the Soviet Union was sending ships to Cuba, it was feared that they were carrying offensive materials and missiles. The president established three specific plans of reaction: let the ships through; establish a naval blockade; destroy existing Cuban missile sites and invade the island. It was Bobby Kennedy who vehemently urged against the invasion alternative, advice completely counter to what most military advisers were telling the president. His advice weighed heavily in the president's thinking. It was Bobby, against some formidable senior officials and experts in foreign affairs, who made the case for Slow Track, the blockade of the Soviet ships, as opposed to Fast Track, which called

Bobby Kennedy, standing at far left, was his brother's most crucial adviser during the Cuban Missile Crisis. The president is leaning at right over the table. Cabinet Room, the day after the crisis was resolved. October 29, 1962.

for bombing Cuba and, he feared, potentially setting off retaliation by Khrushchev. It was Bobby who met with the Soviet ambassador and told him blankly, "Agree to remove your missiles from Cuba, unilaterally and unconditionally, within twenty-four hours or we will bomb them." That night the two brothers dined together with Dave Powers. Jack said Powers ate as if it were his last meal. "I'm not so sure it isn't," cracked Powers.

In the midst of his final weeks of campaigning for the United States Senate, Ted consulted by phone with his brother's adviser and speechwriter Ted Sorenson. Throughout the campaign, the White House had been quietly helping the third brother to frame and shape issues of national and international scope. Now, the candidate called and said he was going to speak about Cuba. "Get another topic," Sorenson advised soberly.

Joe Kennedy happened to be staying in the White House at that very time, his second of only three visits there. Jack and Bobby went into the Lincoln Bedroom to say good night to him. They kissed him. Certainly his support, if not his advice on foreign relations, would have been greatly cherished at a moment like this. Earlier in the day, up on the Truman Balcony, Joe—in his wheelchair with Ann Gargan at his side—had watched the president alight from his helicopter on the South Lawn. A wire service photographer noticed the little vignette and snapped a picture via telephoto lens. It was the only picture ever released to the public showing the infamous businessman, in the mansion he had fought so hard to get his family into. The irony was that he was utterly powerless at what would prove to be the most dangerous moment the president faced.

Rather unusually, the president saw his father twice during the crisis. He slipped away, up to Hyannis Port, for some private reflection on the stretch of beach there, and held some meetings with military advisers in the ambassador's living room, which had windows facing the sea. At one point the old man angrily banged his cane to get the attention of his nurse, Rita Dallas. He wanted to see the president. The nurse interrupted the tense meeting with the request. The president said he was busy. She left, and Joe made the same demand. She interrupted the meeting a second time. "When Dad wants something," Jack told his advisers sheepishly, "he wants it." Finally he went up to see his father, who mumbled some sounds. "Thanks, Dad, I'll take care of it," the son replied; "I'll do it your way." When the president addressed the nation, Rose Kennedy watched. Feeling desperately worried about her son, she cried openly—which she rarely did, not even upon Joe's stroke.

When Jack ultimately decided on a blockade it became a waiting game with the Soviets. Even the best intelligence could provide only an educated guess about the possible reaction of the Soviets—including nuclear retaliation. This led to an overwhelming national anxiety—but not panic—with concern that President Kennedy make no missteps. It was precisely the sort of situation that called for cool detachment yet decisive action, necessitating absolute emotional stability. No matter how tough Kennedy was, he was first and foremost a human being. He depended on his wife as a foundation of advice on human behavior, and could discuss the potential consequences of the crisis in a larger, even philosophical context of humanity. In his children, however, he found a personal motivation to safely resolve the Cuban Missile Crisis.

On Monday morning, October 22, the president went into a very early meeting in the Cabinet Room. At one juncture, he took a breather and paced outside on the terrace. He noticed Caroline and her schoolmates playing on the lawn. He gave his special signal to her—two loud claps—that usually evoked an immediate response. This time, however, Caroline was delayed and Jack went back into his meeting. A few minutes later, Caroline ran into the Oval Office. "Where's my daddy?" she asked Mrs. Lincoln. She was told that the president was in a serious meeting and could not be interrupted. "But I *have* to," she whined, just before she darted into the Cabinet Room and blurted out to the room of military and political advisers, "Daddy, I would have come sooner, but Miss Grimes wouldn't let me go."

After his broadcast to the nation on the missile threat, Jack went upstairs to read stories to Caroline. Then he and his wife ate dinner alone together. At one point during the thirteen-day standoff, Powers watched him sadly reading at night to Caroline. "If it weren't for the children, it would be so easy to press the button," Jack said to Dave Powers. "Not just John and Caroline, and not just the children in America, but children all over the world who will suffer and die for the decision I have to make."

Although he rarely expressed his religious convictions, during the crisis Jack did try to go unnoticed to St. Matthew's Church with Dave Powers. In

After posing on the Lincoln bed in their Halloween costumes, left to right, Jean Kennedy Smith, Stevie Smith, Caroline Kennedy, and Jackie Kennedy paid a surprise visit to the Oval Office. Jackie had taken a leather garment bag and cut out arm and eye holes for herself. Right: Although John was too young to go out trick-or-treating with them that day, he did get to try on his cousin's costume as he and his sister posed with their father. October 31, 1962. Below: Halloween was a big deal to the White House kindergarten students, who all came in costume on that special day, complete with ice cream and orange-and-black crepe paper. October 31, 1963.

the last pew of the church, they prayed together. Throughout the crisis, he found the most solitary peace in his Rose Garden. When it was clear that the Soviets were backing down and that there would be no missile launchings, he wrote to his wife's friend Bunny Mellon, the horticulturist who had designed the site for him: "I need not tell you that your garden has been our brightest spot in the somber surroundings of the last few days."

During the crisis, Jack had joked that Caroline could not put her Halloween pumpkin out on the Truman Balcony that year because people passing by might think the menacing carved features were Castro's. Now the annual holiday was celebrated excitedly by the Kennedy children. The president himself helped his children carve one of the many pumpkins that popped up all over the stately mansion.

With Halloween coming just three days after the Cuban Missile Crisis had been resolved, the Kennedys were particularly gleeful that year. Jackie even dressed up—wearing black stockings, black boots, and a black garment bag over herself, with

President Kennedy stops in for a visit at Dorchester with his grandmother Josie Fitzgerald (seated), uncle Tom, and aunt Bunny, after voting in Boston.

BOSTON HERALD

holes cut out for her eyes and mouth. After a visit to the Oval Office, the First Lady took Caroline and her cousin Steve Smith out to the home of friends in Georgetown—everyone wearing masks. Recalled Arthur Schlesinger, "On Halloween evening in 1962, the doorbell rang at my house . . . my fourteen-year-old daughter opened the door to the trick-or-treaters . . . small hobgoblins leaping up and down . . . After a moment a masked mother in the background called out that it was time to go to their next house . . . it was, of course, Jackie."

Watching all the fun from the sidelines was two-year-old John. He was too young to go with them, so the next year he celebrated his first Halloween. Dressed in costumes, he and his sister made their way over to the Oval Office. They asked Mrs. Lincoln if their father would guess it was them; not a chance, she assured them. When they came into

The three Kennedy brothers confer.

people of Massachusetts could make a judgment as to his qualifications and as to whether there are too many Kennedys," the president snapped angrily. He returned to vote on Election Day, visiting both his father and his grandmother and maternal uncle in their homes. On November 6, 1962, Edward Moore Kennedy won his first U.S. Senate election with 54 percent of the vote. Teddy's election—he had just reached the minimum age, having turned thirty that year—was seen as a great victory for the White House. The fact that he actually scored higher in some precincts than had Jack when he ran for the same Senate seat, and that Teddy received over 1 million votes in 1962 while Jack had not even gotten 700,000 in 1958, irked the president not a little bit. Baby Brother was no longer just the jolly fellow who could get people to laugh. Jack quickly realized this.

his office, the president acted frightened by them and told them to go away. John pulled off his mask, followed by his sister. Jack blurted out, "Why it's Sam and Mary!" This drove John crazy. "I'm not Sam!" he yelped.

After the missile crisis, the president flew to his home state—for his first campaign appearance on behalf of Ted. "I want to introduce myself," he said as he opened his speech. "I am Teddy Kennedy's brother!" Jack's usual carefree manner with reporters was not on display when he was asked point-blank at a press conference about there being "too many Kennedys in Washington." The "dynasty question" was a driving issue of the campaign. "The

Ted's election to the U.S. Senate spurred charges of political dynasty. One of the more lighthearted reactions is this cartoon.

Caroline and John Kennedy shared their birthday parties in the White House because their birthdays were only two days apart. In 1962, the party was held in the President's Dining Room in the family quarters. Opposite page: The president stopped by to visit the children, and his sister Eunice Shriver was one of the mothers in attendance, bending toward her daughter, Maria; Jackie helps John cut his cake; Jackie feeds birthday cake to Caroline. This page: Caroline blows out the candles of her cake. Tricycle races in the East Wing corridor, cartoons in the movie theater, and Marine Band music were also part of the day, followed by the opening of the presents. The First Lady listens to Caroline describe one of her gifts as John and cousin Maria Shriver listen in; Caroline's grandmother Janet Auchincloss talks to Caroline in the West Sitting Hall after she has opened the gift from "Grand Mere," an angel costume. November 27, 1962.

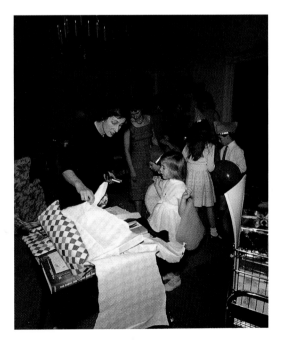

Although John had missed out on trick-or-treating a few weeks earlier, it was made up to him when his mother hosted a large birthday party for both him and his sister, their birth dates being November 25 and November 27, respectively. Caroline and John had twenty-seven of her friends to their joint party, including their Shriver cousins, Eve Fout's daughter, and the kindergarten class. It was a formal affair with linens and china and crystal. Creamed chicken pot pies were served. There was a grab bag. Caroline's and John's grandmother Janet, father Jack, and aunt Eunice were in attendance, as were the other children's mothers and Jackie's secretaries.

Usher John Ficklin oversaw the pandemonium that broke out when Rene Verdon and his pastry chef carried in the two beautiful cakes. Then came the singing of "Happy Birthday"—one round for each child—and blowing out the candles. Next came ice cream. Each child got an animal puppet, and then it was a showing of *Bambi*, Caroline's favorite cartoon, in the movie theater. Outside the theater, there was a tricycle race. As their gifts were brought to them in the hall there, the duo tore through wrapping paper and boxes. A Marine Band combo played children's songs. Then it was time to go, and the children scattered. It wasn't really over yet, however. Some friends came upstairs with the Kennedys and played with the new toys on the floor of the West Sitting Hall. Grandmother Janet Auchincloss brought out her large gift box, and inside Caroline found an angel costume. That night, as Jackie was preparing to put John to bed, Caroline came into the room in her new costume, impersonating an angel. The trio began playing with the pet parakeets. Soon enough, the president heard the noise and joined them.

By November 26—the day between the children's birthdays—Christmas cards and gifts were ready to be mailed. This year, Jackie was sending as a gift to special friends a photograph of her driving a sleigh with the children in it, pulled by Macaroni across the South Lawn. With children in the house, the holiday season was especially lively. Caroline slipped down to see the large tree in the Entrance Hall of the state floor with Clipper, Jackie's German shepherd. Both children anticipated the gingerbread house a kindly pastry chef from New Jersey sent them every year. Caroline was also determined to place her order for the season with Santa Claus.

Jackie felt strongly that too many gifts—especially those bought at stores—would spoil the children and that it was inappropriate to indulge them. She encouraged them to make their gifts for family members, and she was restrained in what she gave her children. (One year, she painted two watercolors for reproduction and public sale as Christmas cards, *Journey of the Magi* [the three kings], and *Glad Tidings* [an angel with horn]. Hallmark manufactured the cards, contributing proceeds to the planned national cultural center.)

This was in marked contrast to the president. Caroline Kennedy told her father that she wished she could talk to Santa Claus about her presents. Without saying anything further to her, he called one of the White House operators. Later that day, Kennedy phoned Caroline to say that she had a special call. He put her through to the operator. Caroline listened for a few moments, then excitedly reeled off her list. Once she hung up, she burst with joy down the hall: "I've just talked to Mrs. Santa Claus. I left a whole list of presents for me and John!"

The Kennedys never spent Christmas Eve or Christmas Day in the White House. As tradition dictated, they joined the extended family clan in Palm Beach, using the Paul home again. In 1962, joined by the Radziwill family, the president's immediate family spent Christmas Eve together. Jackie hated knowing that those who served the president were separated from their families—and that year she encouraged everyone from Secret Service agents to secretaries to bring along family members. That is why Jackie invited Provie and her son Gustavo to spend Christmas Eve with them. Gustavo had become a close friend of John; it was a relationship encouraged by the First Lady. So, as the Bouvier sisters had always traditionally done as children, now Caroline, John, Tony, Tina, and Gustavo would put on a Christmas pageant. Making hats out of balloons, casting the Holy Family and Wise Men, and directing the production was Jackie Kennedy. Caroline, playing the Blessed Mother, took her role quite seriously, baby doll in her lap and blue cape over her head. Gustavo was a Wise Man. Tina was the angel. John and Tony just played around as the shepherds, breaking up the show, laughing and pushing each other, even getting the president down on the floor to play with them. Rose, Joe, Eunice, Jack, Maude Shaw, Provie, Lee, and Stas were the audience. The grand finale had Jackie harnessing the children with red ribbon as the flying reindeer.

On Christmas Day they had dinner with the extended Kennedy family, that year including the Radziwills. Joan Kennedy remembered one typical holiday gathering of the clan:

. . . the whole family gathered for one of those Kennedy living room games, not charades but kind of like a variety show. Some of the family got up and did skits, or jokes. I played some Chopin. Jackie read a poem, a serious one I remember, certainly not Ogden Nash, probably Edna St. Vincent Millay. Jack then decided that he was going to sing! And he said, "Joansie, please accompany me on the piano." I was terrified. He didn't have a great singing voice and he kept changing key. I managed to follow his voice and keep changing keys on the piano. But Jackie knew what I was doing. She came up afterwards to me. "Joan, you are a terrific musician because you made Jack sound great. I guess it's us against them!" she said in reference to the fact that we did poetry and music and the others did skits. "We're different from the rest. We did our own thing." She said this with great heart, and I felt like, in effect, this slightly older sister-in-law was taking me in under her wing.

Jack always put great effort into choosing Jackie's Christmas gifts. By Christmas Eve 1962, he had managed to winnow down his choice to six drawings from the collection of the Wildenstein Gallery in New York. He propped each one on his desk and stood back. He simply could not make a final selection. He called in his sister-in-law Lee to help him. Lee looked at the selections, then piped up, "There is one in London I know Jackie would like."

"That one no doubt is of animals. I am getting tired of seeing animals," he cracked. "Yes, it is," Lee sighed. In the end he had a Renoir wrapped and put under the tree for Jackie.

As 1963 got under way, the president would repeatedly tell his secretary with a broad smile, "Soon you will have three coming over to get candy from your candy dish."

Jackie was pregnant, and Jack was ecstatic.

Scenes from the First Family's Christmas night gathering with Eunice Shriver, Joe and Rose Kennedy, and the Radziwill and Parades families. Opposite page: Jackie watches the Christmas pageant she directed, with John as Shepherd, Caroline as Blessed Mother, and Gustavo Parades as a Wise Man. President Kennedy listens to his niece Tina while her mother, Lee, looks on, and Jackie looks at stockings over the fireplace. After the play, Caroline gives her baby doll to her grandfather Joe, as Eunice looks on. This page: Caroline has some words with her mother while John plays in Jackie's lap. President Kennedy plays on the floor with his nephew Tony and his son. December 25, 1962.

Ted Kennedy in the Oval Office visiting his brother for the first time as a U.S. senator, with other freshman Democratic senators. January 18, 1963.

8

COMING TOGETHER, 1963

I am the President of the United States. When I say I want to go to
Ireland, it means that I'm going to Ireland.
—JOHN F. KENNEDY

He appreciated her gifts and she worshipped him and appreciated
his humor and his kindness, and they really had fun together.
—JANET AUCHINCLOSS

On January 5, 1963, Edward Moore Kennedy was sworn into office as a United States senator from Massachusetts, commencing what would be one of the longest incumbencies in that position. Rose and Joan Kennedy attended his swearing-in ceremony, and were later joined by Eunice and Jean and their husbands for a celebratory feast of chicken salad sandwiches on Boston brown bread in his new office. A crying three-year-old Kara was barred from the ceremony. Six was the minimum age for admittance to the visitors' gallery, even for new senators' daughters.

From the outset, Ted Kennedy determined to stand on his own, even if that meant finding himself in conflict with his brother in the White House. Despite his personal family loyalty, and the obvious fact that Jack had helped Ted rise to the Senate, the young man did not want to be perceived as being the president's puppet—or to, in fact, *be* one. "I didn't want to have people think he was calling the shots on my vote," Ted later recalled. Unlike Bobby, Teddy was also willing to publicly stand against his brother: "We parted company on some votes that I thought might hurt Massachusetts."

On the other hand, Ted got no special help from his brother. Despite the fact that the president would pepper the senator with questions about the views and possible support of legislation he could receive from other senators, when the younger man asked his brother for help, he was told bluntly, "Teddy, those are your problems now." When the new senator complained to his older brother that a pending Defense Department closing of a Springfield, Massachusetts, rifle factory would leave thousands unemployed, the president smilingly replied, "Tough shit!" It was all said with laughter in a humorous spirit, but it was real. "Some pipeline I have into the White House," the senator sarcastically told a friend about his supposed preferential treatment.

Simply because of his being the president's brother, however, the new senator received national, even international, media attention. *Life* magazine did a photo essay on his first week at the new job. A week later,

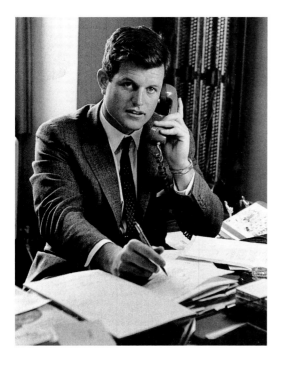

Senator Edward Moore Kennedy at his desk. Circa 1963.

Look magazine did a glamorous spread on the beautiful Joan. This one particularly annoyed the White House: Joan had let it slip that Jack's back condition prevented him from lifting his son and that Jackie sometimes wore wigs. At their new home in Georgetown, the young Kennedys were soon known to be far warmer and more embracing of colleagues than Jack and Jackie had been. Ted was a more natural, open, and warm person than his brother, and even people like the southern conservative racist senator James O. Eastland of Mississippi became his friend. The attention paid to the brother who was fourteen years the president's junior underlined an obvious fact. There was now somebody in the national spotlight who was even more youthful, telegenic, gregarious, and genuinely athletic than Jack Kennedy. After one cocktail party, Ted ran after some of his guests and told them to stay for dinner. "I'm not my brother Jack," he told them. They stayed until three in the morning.

If the president felt any small pang of jealousy, or even wistfulness about his own vanishing youth, he never verbalized it. In fact, it seems that Jack Kennedy knew instinctively that it was healthy to encourage Ted's independence—not only for Ted but also for himself. Jack Kennedy felt none of the need to compete fiercely with Ted that he had felt with his brothers Joe and Bobby, and even somewhat with his father. "By the time I arrived in the Senate and he was President the sense of great age difference had almost disappeared," Ted reflected. "What would never disappear was the fact that he was the older brother and I was the younger." Relinquishing a need to compete was the first of many points of maturation in his family dynamics that the president would experience in 1963.

Even if Ted Kennedy could not expect access to the Cabinet Room merely because of his family connection, he and Joan were occasionally invited to dinner in the private family dining room. In the summer, with both of their wives up at the Cape, Jack Kennedy frequently invited Ted over just to spend time with him. The latter recalled: "[W]hat I did was to stop by on the way home from the Senate and go into the Oval Office by the back door at the end of his working day. Then we'd have a daiquiri, take a swim together, then just sit around and talk about everything. Sure, I'd make him laugh. We'd gossip about the Senate . . . I remember during the summer, when Jackie and the kids were away, the two of us would go upstairs and have dinner alone [on the Truman Balcony] and sometimes spend the whole evening just talking and laughing."

The president and his brother the senator receiving honorary degrees together at Boston College. May 1963.

BOSTON HERALD

Ted's and Jack's deepening relationship ripened more quickly in the coming weeks and months. If Ted's refusal to be used by the administration surprised Jack, perhaps even caused the president briefly to resent such a reaction, it ultimately earned his respect. On a personal level, the natural and easy humor of the new senator from Massachusetts was a godsend for the president. Teddy and Jack loved to top each other with jokes and brutal teasing. Publicly,

both Jack and Ted used humor to diffuse lingering charges that the latter's election was part of some undemocratic dream of dynasty. In one speech, the president remarked that with all of Congress, himself, and the vice president out of the capital that day, he had received a telegraph from his youngest brother: "Everybody's gone. Stop. I have just seized control."

Ted and Joan joined Jack and his family one spring weekend at Camp David, staying in one of

Joan and Ted Kennedy arrive for a weekend at Camp David with Jack and Jackie Kennedy. April 6, 1963.

Ted Kennedy lifting an ambivalent John at the Camp David skeet range. April 7, 1963.

A Camp David cabin guest bedroom.

the modern cottages provided for presidential guests. Having discovered the joys of the Camp David presidential retreat in the Maryland mountains, where the family spent several late-winter weekends before their new country home was done, Jack tried to lure Jackie to go there. Camp David offered not only a swimming pool but riding paths and horse stables, as well as tennis courts and wooded areas for long walks. On the weekend that Ted and Joan visited them at Camp David, there was some skeet shooting as well as a drive and tour of the historic battlefields at nearby Gettysburg, Pennsylvania. Recalled Senator Kennedy: "I remember one of the great treats when I first came to Washington was when Jackie would call up and ask me to join her and my brother in going out around the region to see some of the Civil War sites . . . a wonderful Sunday pastime. We would tour the battlegrounds and my brother and Jackie knew everything about the Civil War."

Jackie's excursions that year would not include any foreign trips. She was increasingly limiting even her private activity. In the early spring, Jackie's obstetrician, John Walsh, who had deliv-

President Kennedy, seated in car at right, with Joan Kennedy and Ted Kennedy (obscured), touring through the Gettysburg, Pennsylvania, battlefields. April 7, 1963.

ered John by cesarean surgery in 1960, advised her to cancel all her official activities in an attempt to remove any stress that might threaten the birth of her new child, due in September. This meant forgoing a trip with the president to Ireland, Italy, and Germany in June 1963, but before Jack left, Jackie would host a private birthday party for him.

Kennedy's annual birthday celebration had become an opportunity to raise money for the Democratic Party; since Franklin Roosevelt's administration, presidential birthdays had always been turned into fund-raising events for charity or party. In 1961, there had been a gargantuan birthday for Jack in the Boston Armory, with a two-ton cake trucked in from a Connecticut bakery and Democratic Party faithful paying nominal ticket prices to fund-raise for the party.

In 1962, Kennedy's birthday had made the news. It was an extravaganza with a touch of vulgarity, perfectly suited for Madison Square Garden, where thousands were in attendance. This was the event at which Marilyn Monroe sang "Happy Birthday, Mr. President" to him before a rather shocked audience in what, he joked, was her "sweet, wholesome way." The First Lady was then in Glen Ora, attending a horse show. The Shrivers, Lawfords, and Robert Kennedys were there, all enjoying the parade of famous performers at the gala. There was a rumor that Jack later hosted a private party that Monroe attended in the family suite at the Carlyle. There was indeed a private party—but Jack's family and about a hundred others were in attendance. It was held at the duplex apartment of fund-raiser Arthur Krim. The only scene made by Monroe that night, however, according to Bill Walton in an oral history released only after his death and Jackie's, was something of a show Monroe did in a window of the penthouse bedroom—for the benefit of roof sharpshooters. As far as other documentation of their relationship, there is little to none. It is generally accepted that Kennedy and Monroe met four times: the birthday; an October 1961 Lawford party in Santa Monica; a New York dinner party in February 1962; and on March 24, 1962, when they were both houseguests at the Palm Springs home of Bing Crosby, the last incident being where they had a reputed assignation. Try as he might, a later biographer, a former *New York Times* investigator, could not establish anything more definitive. However, it is agreed even by those who claim to have known that there were more such encounters that Jack was not in love with Monroe. And although Jackie was said to have expressed disapproval of any exploitation of Monroe, to what degree she was aware of any liaison between her husband and the actress is also a

President Kennedy at the Madison Square Garden celebration of his birthday. Jack Kennedy loved the world of Hollywood and culti-vated personal friendships with many famous performers through brother-in-law Peter Lawford. The feeling was mutual in Hollywood. At the president's 1962 birthday celebration, performers included Mitch Miller, Diana Ross, Henry Fonda, Jimmy Durante, Louis Armstrong, Ed Sullivan, Peter Lawford, Carol Channing, Ann-Margret, Robert Preston, Van Johnson, Shirley MacLaine, Maria Callas, and Jack Benny, who is seen talking to the presi-dent and Eunice Shriver at the private party that followed in Arthur and Mathilde Krim's apartment. Also performing at the private party was Diahann Carroll, who sings and is watched by, at far left, Ethel Kennedy and Pat Lawford, and, at far right, Marilyn Monroe. May 19, 1962.

matter of conjecture. Certainly, if anyone in Jack's family knew further details it was Peter and Pat Lawford, who were close to both individuals. Doris Goodwin, friend and chronicler of the Kennedys, felt that the entire family had a "startling capacity to lead compartmentalized lives." It was in the book written by his second wife, after his death, that the posthumous words of Peter Lawford claim that a real relationship had existed. In a February 24, 1976, interview, however, he said that stories of an affair were "garbage." Later, neither Jackie nor her adult son took the stories seriously. "I wonder

why they didn't add Gracie Allen to the list," she later cracked to friend Roswell Gilpatric.

Perhaps because of the publicity ensuing from the 1962 birthday event, Jack's 1963 birthday was spent with family and those who knew him best. Jackie, Ted Kennedy, Bobby and Ethel Kennedy, Sarge and Eunice Shriver, Lem Billings, Red Fay, Jim Reed, David Niven, Ben and Toni Bradlee, and Toni Bradlee's sister Mary Meyer were among those at his birthday dinner party on the rarely used *Sequoia* (the navy yacht used by Truman but decommissioned as the official presidential yacht

In this previously unpublished photograph of a unique meeting of two figures whose stories would later intertwine are President Kennedy and opera singer Maria Callas. Callas was such a hit that the First Lady, who was not present, heard about it and later invited Callas to come to the White House to perform at the state dinner for Haile Selassie. In her official correspondence with Callas, Jackie assured her, "We would do everything to make it perfect for you." Callas's response is at right.

Milano, July 21, 1963

My dear Madame Kennedy,

I would love to sing for you at the State dinner in
honor of the Emperor Haile Selassie of Ethiopia on
October first, but I am afraid I will be occupied at
that period with recordings. Therefore, if you could
submit to me some other dates, I will be more than
happy to consider them.

As for the accompaniment wouldn't it be wonderful if
we had Leonard Bernstein to accompany me either on
the piano or with a small orchestra and have him
participate. I know him very well and we both admire
each other. Of course, these are just suggestions,
and I am sure these details can be worked out later.

I thank you for having thought of me and, especially
as being an American, I would be more than happy and
would feel deeply honored to sing at the White House.

I thank the President and you for your admiration for
which I am deeply touched, and I look forward to meeting
you as last year at Madison Square Garden you were
not present.

With all my very best wishes,

Sincerely,

Maria Callas

Madame Jacqueline Kennedy
The White House
Washington

Jackie and Ted organized a party for Jack's best friends and close family members on the night of the president's birthday. At the dinner table, Red Fay did his comical rendition of "Hooray for Hollywood." As gifts were given out, Jack shows Jackie a framed picture of himself as a young boy with his pet dog, given him by Lem Billings. Seated at left with their backs to the camera are Lem Billings and actor David Niven. Seated opposite them are Sargent Shriver, Ted Kennedy, and the president. Obscured behind Jackie is Red Fay. Eunice Shriver sits behind her. May 29, 1963.

by Eisenhower). Recalled Reed, "He was amongst all his old friends and amongst his family and he had a wonderful evening. The weather was extremely warm, some thunder showers, but it lasted I'd say until one or two o'clock in the morning . . . Many of the presents given to him were, of course, humorous in nature. There were many toasts . . . Jackie seemed to enjoy it." Humor was also the theme of a party held earlier that day for him by his staff in the West Wing. Led by Pierre Salinger, the office staff had one gag gift after another for him: boxing glove for his congressional battles, a toy JFK in his rocking chair, the new *Air Force One* that he wanted—a toy plane—and a box with a sign that read COMPLAINTS IGNORED. There was also a toy space capsule with an attached

greeting for a "good trip" from his likely Republican opponent in 1964, Barry Goldwater.

Two weeks later, President Kennedy had what could only be described as an emotional turning point in his life. "Those were the three happiest days of my life," he would later tell a friend of the time he spent in Ireland.

He had been to Ireland once before, and had been left with a hurtful memory. Now he wanted to go there again. "Ireland?" asked aide Kenny O'Donnell as they charted the schedule for his visit to Germany, England, and Italy. "There's no reason for you to go to Ireland. It would be a waste of time. It wouldn't do you much good politically. . . . If you go to Ireland, people will say it's just a pleasure trip."

The president's staff threw him a surprise party for his 1963 birthday. He received gag gifts, including a toy JFK in a rocking chair, a sign that said COMPLAINTS IGNORED, and, from Jackie, a basket of "authentic antique White House lawn." The finale came when his press secretary, Pierre Salinger, gave the president a cold speech to read. With good timing and serious demeanor, Kennedy delivered a humorous spoof about the Kennedy family based on the Gettysburg Address. May 29, 1963.

The president's large, hooded gray eyes did not blink. "That's exactly what I want, a pleasure trip to Ireland." There were several domestic trips to get through before Europe—including one on June 6 to Texas, where, on a podium in El Paso with Governor John Connally, he was presented with two .45 Colt revolvers—but planning for Ireland absolutely preoccupied him. He researched his paternal and maternal lines, he studied the impact of Irish immigration on American history, he pored through even more Irish poetry and literature. "He's getting so Irish," cracked Dave Pow-

ers, "he'll be speaking with a brogue." He even opened the trip to his staff members of Irish ancestry.

Jack touched down in the land of his ancestors on June 26, having earlier that same day delivered his famous speech at the Berlin Wall. Staying in Dublin at the American ambassador's home, he joked that he would support the Democratic candidate for president in 1968 who would promise to name him as the next ambassador to Ireland.

He got up early the next morning, especially eager. He was going to be seeing his family, in a small thatched-roof cottage with a dirt floor in the kitchen, in the tiny village of Dunganstown. He helicoptered from Dublin to the New Ross County wharf. His great-grandfather Patrick had left for America from that very wharf. "He carried nothing with him except two things—a strong religious faith and a strong desire for liberty," Jack told the ecstatic crowds, then pointed toward a nearby fertilizer plant. "If he had not left New Ross, I would be working today over there." Local children broke out into a folk song, "The Boys of Wexford." The choir director, a nun, handed Jack a printed page of the lyrics, which he kept as a treasure, and he joined in the singing. "We are proud of the fact that one of our race, you, Mr. President, has been chosen to lead the great American freedom-loving people," declared the mayor as he gave Jack an engraved silver goblet.

Then, to the delight of the farm families along the way, the presidential motorcade twisted through winding country roads and narrow town streets on its way to the Kennedy farmhouse. People cried openly as he passed them, seeing him as one of them, an emigrant descendant who had captured the greatest honor of the American dream. Evelyn Lincoln observed, "He felt he had come home. All the cares of the world had suddenly

President Kennedy riding through the streets of New Ross County on his way to his family's ancestral cottage in the town of Dunganstown. June 27, 1963.

gone from his shoulders. The more fuss they made over him, the more he beamed."

The moment it came together for him was when the chubby, red-cheeked Mary Kennedy Ryan, his third cousin, her two daughters Mary Anne and Josephine, and another cousin, Frank Kennedy, hugged him just outside the family homestead in Dunganstown. With him were not only his sisters Jean and Eunice but also his sister-in-law Lee Radziwill: despite her Polish title, her British residence, and her French surname, she was half Irish. Black turf sent warmth from the fireplace as it had when his great-grandfather had lived there. "The fire feels good," he told Mary.

Advance people had not conjured up this woman. Jack knew her. He had searched out the

Jean Kennedy Smith, Mary Anne and Josephine Ryan (daughters of Mary Ryan), Jack Kennedy, Eunice Shriver, and Mary Ryan, in the Dunganstown family home. June 27, 1963.

Jack Kennedy and his cousin Mary Ryan (her grandfather Patrick Kennedy was the great-grandfather of the president). At the tea table Mrs. Ryan set for his party in front of the family home. June 27, 1963.

Kennedy home during his first trip there, in 1947. After figuring out their relationship, she had invited him in—along with his startled English friend Pamela Churchill. He took snapshots of Mary and her then-little children, as well as several other local children to whom he could claim kin. In the previous few weeks, Mary had had the task of sorting out Kennedys. "You haven't shown your face here in twenty years!" she had shouted while wagging a finger at a relative who was not included in the final choice. "You won't be hurrying out of here," Mary warned aides who looked at their wristwatches. She had Jack plant a tree to remember the visit. Cousin Jim Kennedy offered a glass of Irish whiskey. Jack took it and quickly handed it over to Powers, who happily guzzled it and gave the glass back to him. A local presented a sheepskin

rug to be placed by Jackie's bed—for twins. Outside, now before cameras, Mary offered a spread of smoked salmon, scones and homemade butter, tongue sandwiches, a "great cake" of frosted fruitcake, and a full tea service on two long wooden tables covered with homespun tablecloths: "We want to drink a cup of tea to all the Kennedys who went and those who stayed," said Jack.

Jack shocked his sisters with his sudden fullfaced kiss of Mary Ryan—quite unlike him. He said his good-byes and headed out in the roaring motorcade. He went on to address the Irish Parliament and take part in other official duties. In Cork—where Jackie's maternal ancestors had come from—he introduced an American monsignor as the "pastor of a poor, humble flock in Palm Beach, Florida" and got his usual laughs. "The outpouring of love was really overwhelming," said Jean Smith of the trip. Noted Evelyn Lincoln, "It was difficult for the president to say good-bye."

Dunganstown, however, moved him most. It was to Dave Powers that Jack Kennedy finally revealed the events of his first visit to the humble Kennedy cottage. Pam Churchill—later Harriman—was a good friend, but when she had jokingly remarked of his ancestral home, "God, it looked like Tobacco Road!" it cut him. He remembered the incident with as much hurt sixteen years later. "I felt like kicking her out of the car," he said. "For me, the visit to that cottage was filled with music."

Kennedy bought wool sweaters for Jackie and the children, but for him, the most precious gift was the silver goblet presented to him at New Ross. It seemed to be a tactile reminder, a touchstone of his very self, his roots. He cherished small souvenirs—an Irish poem he scribbled on dinner place cards, a postcard of the Kennedy cottage he placed in his dresser mirror. "I imagine that he was never easier, happier, more involved and detached,

At the Shannon Airport, with his sister Eunice, about to depart Ireland, Kennedy told the story of an Irishman from the same county as the Kennedys who had emigrated to America and had himself photographed in front of the White House, then sent the picture to the home folks saying it was his new summer home. "I hope you will all come and see us," Jack concluded. "This is not the land of my birth, but it is the land for which I hold the greatest affection and I certainly will come back in the springtime." June 29, 1963.

more complexly himself," offered Schlesinger of Kennedy's trip to Ireland.

As he returned, Kennedy was hitting his stride. In June 1963, he had an astounding 82 percent approval rating in a Gallup poll, beating even FDR and Ike. This is not to say he was universally popular. Many patriotic and right-wing groups like the John Birch Society, the Christian Crusaders, the Circuit Riders, the Liberty Lobbyists, and the White Citizens Council continued to hate him not only because of his Catholicism but also because they felt he was soft on communism since he sought a test ban treaty with the Soviets rather than their annihilation. Personally, he seemed more genuinely happy. He was no longer in severe physical pain, his back troubles reduced greatly by

new treatment. Nor did he seem to have a need for regular mistresses anymore.

Most of all, with such a public celebration of his ethnic roots, he seemed genuinely relaxed. Irishmen like Powers and Fay had always known his love of his heritage—his always wanting to hear funny stories of the Boston Irish, celebrating St. Patrick's Day in the office in some way, reading Irish literature, memorizing Irish poetry, listening to Irish records, and asking friends to sing Irish songs. But now the nation, his WASP friends, and everyone worldwide had witnessed his full embrace of who he was. There were the inevitable attacks. Senator Goldwater charged that Kennedy had ignored his duties to visit his "native" land. Columnist Drew Pearson said the trip had been a waste of federal funds. "That was one column nobody in the White House gave a damn about," said one adviser. Usually sensitive to any criticism, Jack certainly didn't care. He even practiced speaking Gaelic with the Irish nanny who took care of Ted's children, asking her to correct him if he made a mistake.

Jack made Jackie, rather than his mother or his siblings, his primary outlet for a full expression of emotions about Ireland. He asked her to get jacket buttons for him that carried the insignia of the Irish American brigade that had fought in the Civil War. Jackie, realizing the significance of the silver goblet, asked that the florist keep it filled with flowers and in his office on a table where he could always see it. She reflected on what the trip had meant to him: "It wasn't just a sentimental journey. Ireland meant much more . . . he had always been moved by its poetry and literature because it told of the tragedy and the desperate courage which he knew lay just under the surface of Irish life. The people of Ireland had faced famine and disease, and had fought against oppression, and died for independence . . . They dreamed and sang and wrote and thought and were gay in the face of all their burdens."

Although he would continue his nocturnal activities when he was apart from Jackie, after Ireland Jack seemed to be opening up to her more. Overriding everything else of importance to him was the imminent addition of a new child to his family. In his absence, the First Lady had made no public appearances but had also focused on their family. She took the children for an impromptu blimp ride—terrifying the Secret Service—and hosted a picnic for them and their friends on the South Lawn. June 1963 found her just as relaxed as he was, especially with the arrival of her best friend, former boarding school roommate and bridesmaid Nancy Tuckerman, who moved down from New York to become Jackie's social secretary. "Tucky" instinctively knew Jackie's personal quirks, habits, and limitations, and was privy to her confidences and outrageous sense of humor.

For both the Kennedys, their closest bond and joint happiness was in their children. Sometimes the children influenced their father in ways they did not realize. In May, Caroline had visited Arlington Cemetery with her best friend, Agatha Pozen. Her chatter about it was so excited that Jack decided to make his first visit. After walking through the Custis-Lee Mansion there, he took in the view of the capital city from its east porch, beneath him an elegantly sloping greensward, the rows of white tombstones flanking this green panel on either side. "I could stay here forever," he told the friend who had accompanied him.

Summer meant Hyannis Port for the family, and that is where Jackie worked and waited for her baby's birth. Jack was first reunited with his wife, after his return from Europe on the Fourth of July. For the first time, seemingly unconcerned, he did

Jackie held a lawn picnic for her children and their friends. Her close friend and new social secretary, Nancy Tuckerman, sits with Jackie and Caroline on the South Lawn looking at the end-of-year picture of the White House kindergarten group. Caroline fetches some food for her friends from the picnic basket. June 7, 1963.

not yell at the photographers to halt their work as he and Jackie embraced.

Visitors to the Kennedy compound in the summer of 1963 would have, as author Laurence Leamer suggested, "a sense that they were in the mist of an explosion of life." On Independence Day, Ethel had given birth to her eighth child, Christopher. Not only was the First Lady pregnant, but Eunice arrived that weekend with the news that she was expecting as well. She was also in the midst of planning her forthcoming "camp" project of sports activities and competitive games she scheduled for later that month, for mentally retarded and disabled children on her own property in Maryland. That Fourth of July weekend, Eunice enjoyed watching the Navy Department films that had been made of the Irish trip, which Jack insisted everyone see in the movie theater in his father's basement. After attempting to cajole them into watching it all again, he found himself looking at the movies alone.

Eunice had other things on her mind. Before she went to Ireland with her brother, she had also continued her unrelenting mission. In preparation for Jack's first message to Congress on the issues of mental retardation and illness, that past February she had painstakingly worked over the words. In May, she formally addressed the Women's Committee of the President's Commission on Employment of the Handicapped with vigorous criticism of the federal government for not having employed even one mentally retarded person among the two hundred thousand handicapped who had been hired.

For the first time, the president and his wife embrace without inhibition in front of a photographer. July 4, 1963.

Independence Day at Squaw Island, on the oceanfront where the president was renting his home. Jackie sits among the children. With her are Stevie Smith, Bobby Kennedy Jr., and her son John. July 4, 1963.

She made the point vigorously with her brother seated near her. He would hire the first such person to work at the White House.

Eunice would be seeing less of her brother that summer. In 1962, the John Kennedys had rented the modern, split-level suburban-type home of family friend Morton Downey on Squaw Island, about a mile away from the extended family. In 1963, they rented Brambletyde, a weathered, more traditional Cape Cod–style house on the island. Jackie so liked it that she and her husband made overtures to purchase it—until an outrageously unreasonable price was put before the president.

Still, not only was the rented home on Squaw Island easier for the Secret Service to protect, it seemed to afford Jackie the privacy she needed. Although she made time apart from what Ted Kennedy called "the larger, rambunctious family," he also recalled how, when a head of state was scheduled to visit, Jackie took the various State Department suggestions for an official gift as a matter of discussion to the extended family table. "In all of us going through the ideas, Jackie led the discussions. It was engaging. She permitted everyone to offer their creative ideas," the senator later recalled.

Jack wanted to do anything to limit stress on his wife. Knowing her history of difficult pregnancies and childbirth, said his friend Jim Reed, "President Kennedy was extremely solicitous of Jackie and very careful in making certain that everything

Caroline naps while the pregnant First Lady reads. August 4, 1963.

was all right." One Saturday morning, Jackie felt some discomfort and Jack tried to contact her doctor. Unable to do so for over an hour, he became angry. "I just hope," he told Walsh, "that if you do go off for a walk for any period of time that you always tell someone where you are, how you can be reached immediately in case I do have to get in touch with you."

Other than his worries about Jackie, the sunny weekends of July passed peacefully for Jack. Every weekend he took at least one of his favorite yacht cruises, surrounded by the family as they lunched, tickling Caroline, relaxing with different house-guests—Lem Billings, Red Fay and his wife, Chuck Spalding, Jim Reed, and David Ormsby-Gore. He increasingly enjoyed the companionship of brother-in-law Steve Smith. Smith had so success-fully run Ted's campaign that he was now in New York laying the financial tracks for Jack's 1964 reelection campaign, but spending nearly all of the week in Washington, working closely with the Democratic National Committee.

Whether the weekends were beginning or end-

The president sunning on his yacht Honey Fitz. *Steve Smith is at left; Eunice Shriver, in sun hat, is at right. July 28, 1963.*

ing, the president always first came to kiss his father on the head as the old man sat on the porch to watch the helicopter either arrive or leave. In the early summer, he would charge up to his dad with a shout of "Let's go find Mother!" but by the end of July, Rose Kennedy was back in Europe. Despite the hovering presence of Ann Gargan, Joe seemed more isolated, almost forgotten. He was a mysterious and, because of his twisted features and his ability only to moan noises or shout "No," a frightening figure for the smallest of his twenty grandchildren. They had to be coaxed up to him for a hug and kiss.

The first weekend in August had come to a close. The president had spent it in Hyannis Port, with Red and Anita Fay and their daughter, Sally, as houseguests. Fay recalled one intimate vignette of the weekend, being called by Jack into his bed-room to chat, as the president and his wife lay affectionately with each other, lingering in bed.

Jack and Jackie finishing lunch as Peter Lawford suntans. August 4, 1963.

The president talking to his father about the noise made by the presidential helicopter. The front porch of Joe Kennedy's house. July 4, 1963.

The president then returned to Washington as usual on Monday morning, but made sure he was in regular touch with the Cape. He was determined to be with Jackie when the baby was born. Remembering that he had been in Europe when their stillborn daughter, Arabella, was delivered, he had told a friend with great guilt, "I'm never there when she needs me."

On August 7, Jackie was getting ready to take Caroline to ride her pony at the stable in nearby

Maria Shriver making a funny face with cousin Caroline watching. Aboard the Honey Fitz. *July 28, 1963.*

The president tickles his daughter as Maria Shriver and Stas Radziwill look on. July 28, 1963.

Osterville, where Macaroni was housed. She was due in five weeks, but felt some slight labor pain. She called for Dr. Walsh but asked that Jack not be bothered since it was probably a false alarm. Walsh rushed Jackie to the hospital set up for just such a possibility, at nearby Otis Air Force Base on Cape Cod, accompanied by the Secret Service agents who worked out of a temporary trailer several dozen yards away from the Kennedys' Squaw Island home. In Washington, at 11:40 A.M., Secret Service agent Jerry Behn seemed tense to Mrs. Lincoln when he came up to her desk to inform her that Mrs. Kennedy had gone to Otis but that she did not want the president to be told. Evelyn went ahead and told the president. Knowing that

Walsh would be with Jackie, he called Dr. Travell, who gave him the details. Preparations for an emergency cesarean delivery had begun. "Jackie will be all right," she told him. "How about the baby?" he asked. "Fifty-fifty," she replied. "I'm coming up as fast as I can." he snapped.

At 11:53 he took off from the White House in the helicopter to Andrews Air Force Base. At 12:10 a Jet Star plane left Andrews and arrived at Otis at 1:25. "He just kept sitting and staring out of the window," remembered Jackie's press secretary, Pam Turnure, who went up with him and Nancy Tuckerman. "[O]bviously his thoughts were completely with her, and it was a very quiet trip—getting there as soon as possible—rushing to the hospital."

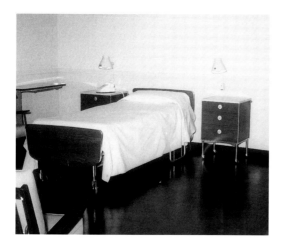

Jackie Kennedy's room at Otis Air Force Base Hospital, where she gave birth by emergency cesarean. Jack Kennedy rushes in to see his wife within three hours of her having given birth.

NEW BEDFORD STANDARD TIMES (RIGHT)

Jack immediately went to see Jackie in her room. She had given birth to a son while he was en route from Washington to Boston. Named Patrick Bouvier, he weighed four pounds, ten ounces. He was having problems breathing and had been placed in an incubator. Dr. Walsh contacted a pediatric specialist from Boston's Children's Hospital who was whisked to the Boston airport by car and then to Otis by presidential helicopter. It was immediately decided to rush little Patrick to Children's Hospital. The tiny infant was carefully carried in his Plexiglas incubator and taken by helicopter ambulance to Boston, followed by another helicopter that carried the president. Jackie never saw Patrick.

Leaving the hospital briefly, the president went to a suite at the Boston Ritz-Carlton Hotel. He summoned Mrs. Lincoln, who recalled, "There sat the President on the bed, without his coat . . . He

was staring into space." He dictated a short note and sent a check to the family of a Boston policeman who had been killed in the line of duty. He returned to the hospital.

The next morning, August 8, Jack helicoptered back to his wife's side at Otis. Whatever conversation transpired between them was never disclosed, but she still did not know the real condition of the baby. The president then went immediately back to Patrick in Boston. The premature child, suffering from a lung condition involving the hyaline membrane, was fighting for his life and had been placed in a special room with reduced air pressure to ease his hard breathing and the stress on his little heart. Jack asked for a heart specialist from New York, sending a Jet Star to fetch him. When Patrick briefly rallied, the elated father called his wife with the good news. It was not to last. Meanwhile, Ted Kennedy visited Jackie at Otis. Jean Smith, Janet

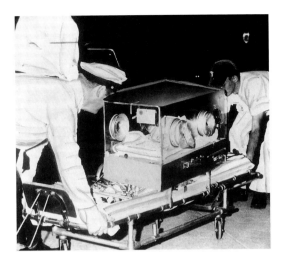

Patrick Kennedy being transported in an incubator to Boston Children's Hospital, via helicopter.

Auchincloss, Pat Lawford—all rallied around the couple, supporting and visiting them, helping in any way they could. "Oh, nothing must happen to Patrick because I just can't bear to think of the effect it might have on Jackie," the president told his mother-in-law.

At nine that night, Bobby Kennedy was at his brother's side, and they both drove out to be with Patrick, now moved to Harvard's School of Public Health. Bobby's presence heartened Evelyn Lincoln; despite the staff and press corps surrounding him, the president "had seemed completely alone." He spent the night in the hospital, holding his son's little hand through an opening in the breathing chamber. He spoke to Patrick, urging the infant to hang on. That night the president was given an empty hospital room to stay in. He didn't really sleep, but rather roamed the halls. When he spied a small child who was covered with severe burns, he forgot his own heartache and sat down to write the child's mother. At two in the morning, an alerted Dave Powers woke Jack. "Every means

known to medical science was used in an attempt to save the child's life," remembered Cardinal Cushing. The baby died at 4:04 A.M., August 9, after thirty-six hours of life. "He put up quite a fight," said Jack. "He was a beautiful baby." Jack quickly asked Powers to go outside the room and call Ted with the news. "He didn't want anyone to see him crying," recalled Powers.

At that moment, something finally broke in Jack Kennedy. For the first time, he let the floodgates of his emotions open uninhibitedly to many people. He could no longer just hold it in. Pierre Salinger watched his boss "weeping in an adjacent boiler room" by the intensive care unit. Mrs. Lincoln recalled, "I was with him at the hospital when he was holding Patrick's hand and the nurse said, 'He's gone.' And tears came into his eyes. I had never seen tears in his eyes before." It was a shock to Dave Powers as well—who had never seen Jack weep: "He just cried and cried and cried." The next morning, after returning to the hospital to thank the doctors and staff, Kennedy went back to his wife. Jacqueline Kennedy—who later regretted that she revealed the fact—admitted that he wept when telling her the news. This tragedy, after his father's stroke, after his own hope of conquering his crushing back pain, after the sentimental trip to Ireland, this one event seemed to be the most important turning point in the emotional change that occurred in John F. Kennedy during his presidency. "I am convinced," said Mrs. Lincoln, "this was one of the hardest blows the president experienced . . . he looked at this little boy and wished with all his heart there was some way to give him a chance to live . . . It wasn't so much grief for his own son, but for a potential that would never be realized."

The funeral was held on August 10 in Cardinal Cushing's private chapel in his Boston residence.

Jack sat alone in the front pew as Cushing said the Mass of the Holy Angels. The Auchinclosses, Little Janet and Jamie, a visiting Lee Radziwill, and all the Kennedy siblings and their spouses attended the mass. Afterward, Jack and the cardinal were alone in the chapel. Jack began sobbing again and put his arm around the tiny coffin. "Jack, you better go along. Death isn't the end, but the beginning," the cardinal told him. "He wouldn't take his hands off that coffin," he later recalled. "I was afraid he'd carry it right out with him." Jack put into Patrick's coffin a St. Christopher's medal that he had been given by Jackie on the occasion of their wedding. The baby was buried at Holyhood Cemetery, in the family plot, in Brookline, Massachusetts. After this ceremony, Jack again cried, not wanting to leave him. "It's awful lonely here,"

Jack Kennedy and his mother-in-law, Janet Auchincloss, on the way to Patrick's funeral.

ASSOCIATED PRESS

he said. "Come on, Jack, let's go," Cushing admonished. "God is good."

When Jack returned to Jackie, she told him, "There's just one thing I couldn't stand. If I ever lost you." He nodded, "I know, I know." In telling her about the funeral mass, he cried again in her arms.

Nancy Tuckerman and Pam Turnure stayed with Jackie in the small, makeshift military hospital as she recuperated for four more days. She firmly told the doctors, "I will be back next year. I will have another child." Some years later, when Schlesinger

stated that Kennedy "kept his family small," Jacqueline corrected him, and in the process illustrated just how much they had considered Arabella and Patrick as their children, despite their short lives: "He never wanted them all crowded together like Bobby and Ethel—so some children in the middle were miserable and the parents harassed. But he always wanted a baby coming along when its predecessor was growing up—that is why he was so glad when he learned that I was having Patrick. But he wished for five children. Before we were married he said that. And he had four children in seven years."

After several days back in Washington, the president returned to Otis to pick up Jackie on August 14, bringing Caroline and John. Jack and Jackie emerged from the building holding hands, then were driven to *Marine One* for the short helicopter ride to Squaw Island. The mood in the helicopter was somber. Caroline fully comprehended the loss of the baby and was agitated. Only her father was able to calm her. When she arrived at the house, her mood and that of her little brother suddenly lifted with a surprise the president had arranged. Several weeks earlier he had accepted an Irish wolfhound puppy—Caroline named him Wolfie—from an Irish admirer named Kennedy. Impulsively, Jack had now followed up on another offer

Jack Kennedy escorts his wife out of Otis Air Force Base Hospital. They were joined on the short helicopter ride to their Hyannis Port home by John, playing with his toy airplanes, and Caroline, who sits on her equally somber father's lap. At their house, Jackie and the children were surprised by the president, who had secretly had the White House puppies and two new dogs brought up from Washington. Still, Caroline remained saddened, fully cognizant of the loss of her brother. August 14, 1963.

NEW BEDFORD STANDARD TIMES (UPPER LEFT)

without his family's knowledge—it was what he called a "sad-looking" cocker spaniel, which arrived from Dublin. He named the dog Shannon. Not only were the two new Irish dogs there, and the regular menagerie of Clipper, Charlie, Pushinka, but so were two of the four puppies—Streaker, Blackie, White Tips, and Butterfly—that had recently been born to Pushinka, fathered by Charlie. The other two were given away to children who won essay-writing contests.

Summer was not over. Indeed, for this family summertime didn't end on Labor Day weekend as it did for most Americans—it went until the end of September. And to the clan of growing toddlers and young adolescents summer was a veritable summer camp. They were divided into two groups by age, with a printed daily schedule that began at 9:30 A.M. and ended with dinner at six. Group II organized at Bobby Kennedy's house to begin their day of riding horses, swimming, lunch, naps, baseball, and walks. The smaller children had kickball, throwing and running games, and bike rides. Special day activities meant sailing, fishing, speedboat

As the president arrives for the weekend at Hyannis Port, he and his helicopter are rushed by children—Bobby Shriver, Sydney and Victoria Lawford, and Caroline (partially obscured). August 25, 1963.

Robert Kennedy holds up his son David for the camera. Ethel Kennedy and Jean Smith are at left, the president in the center, behind his brother, his hands on his head. August 3, 1963.

rides, *Marlin* cruises, or a trip to the nearby Storyland amusement park. Earlier that July, in fact, Jackie had essentially given up her own birthday celebration to the children. Caroline's "gift" to her mother was to host a party for her cousins, and Jackie had her secretary, Mary Gallagher, blowing up balloons and creating intricate games for them, with the First Lady's birthday cake to be enjoyed by the children. The party was typical of many for the children that summer—hot dogs, hamburgers, a visit from the jingling ice-cream truck.

Jack particularly relished the audacity of some of his nephews. When he spotted Bobby Shriver mugging on television, Jack shot up and shouted into the phone at Eunice, "He's the biggest publicity hound we've got around here!" The effect of having an uncle who was the president was not lost on them. "We were all, every one of us, raised to be president," Chris Lawford later said. "The presi-

Smith, Lawford, Shriver, and Kennedy cousins play piñata on the lawn. The eldest grandchild, Kathleen, stands in the background at right with her mother. August 31, 1963.

President Kennedy drives an assortment of nephews and nieces on his golf cart past his father's home.

Caroline Kennedy, taught by her mother, had no hesitation with her grandfather because of his paralyzed condition. John, holding his father's hand, was more uncertain. August 25, 1963, and August 4, 1963.

Jack Kennedy watches his nieces Courtney Kennedy (far left), Maria Shriver (partially obscured), and Sydney Lawford, and daughter Caroline, ride their ponies at a nearby stable. August 31, 1963.

dency is in our system, and we can't get it out." The children adored their uncle the president, and every time he arrived at the Cape in his helicopter they all ran out to greet him, "In 'forty-three, they went to sea!" the older ones repeated for him in a rhyming poem about the *PT-109*. "Thirteen men and Kennedy! To seek the blazing enemy . . ."

Before Jackie gave birth to Patrick, she had taken her children daily to the nearby Osterville stables, where Joe Kennedy had often gone riding with his grandchildren. Here they could ride what were now three ponies owned by the president's children, all gifts of LBJ—Macaroni, Tex, and Leprechaun. After Jackie lost the baby, however, it was Jack who brought Caroline and her cousins Maria Shriver and Sydney Lawford to ride their ponies here. Caroline's "boyfriend," Stevie Smith, was her

closest pal in the White House, but the girls were her summer companions.

The president's focus, however, remained fixed on his wife. "He did so much to protect Mrs. Kennedy at that time," Turnure later recalled. Bill Walton concurred, and noted something new about the couple. "She hung on to him and he held her in his arms—something nobody ever saw at any other time because they were very private people." Jackie, however, also tried to buck him up. "He felt the loss of the baby in the house as much as I did," she said. Most frequently he resorted to humor, trying to make her laugh. "See that smile on her face?" he told a friend after having been successful. "I put it there." When she was hurt that Adlai Stevenson did not write to her after the loss, Jack immediately asked Schlesinger to get Stevenson to write. He spoke of their life together beyond the presidency, saying he wanted to be ambassador to Italy because "Jackie would like it." During his returns to the White House for work during the week, he always saw to it that a simple bouquet of freshly cut flowers from the Rose Garden was made up for him to take to her himself. "Each time he have been sometimes very painful for Jackie, he really adored her," Schlesinger later observed. "They were extremely close and affectionate after the death of the baby." The greatest change was simply that Jack had learned to open up so completely to Jackie. "[U]p to then . . . they never wanted to . . . show their innermost feelings for one

DOUBLE TROUBLE

John Kennedy, in a wet dress of his mother's, climbs on a sailboat—aptly named for him.

wanted to take her something that would let her know he had been thinking about her," said Mrs. Lincoln, "and to share with her something of his life in Washington."

While there are suggestions that he still carried on, there were no longer ongoing relationships with other women. "[W]hatever vagaries must another . . . for the first time . . . what [they] felt for one another became apparent to the world, and this was something that people . . . had never known," Pam Turnure recalled. "Suddenly it was all in the open, and the President's real devotion to Mrs. Kennedy . . . was a new side that had never been seen so microscopically before."

John Kennedy uses the binoculars aboard the Honey Fitz to watch his cousin and aunt, Timmy and Eunice Shriver, swim in the ocean. The president once watched Eunice swim without fear of nearby sharks—and then the predators left. He cracked, "See, Eunie, even the sharks are afraid of you!" August 31, 1963.

Jackie's depression remained, however, and her husband now gently tried to prompt her out of it. "Jackie," he told her, "we must not create an atmosphere of sadness in the White House because this would not be good for anyone—not for the country and not for the work we have to do." Her mother thought that the president's remark made a "profound impression" on Jackie. Somewhat glibly, Janet Auchincloss commented that Jackie "kept her chin up and went on." While it was true that her daughter was following proper Janet's rule to behave without emotion in front of others following the tragedy, it was also true that the young woman had slumped into one of her severe depressions.

Before coming to Newport on September 12, where the couple would celebrate their tenth anniversary at the site of their wedding reception, Jack called art dealers to suggest a selection of antiquities, including jewelry, and paintings from which Jackie could choose her gift. He was also planning a more long-term surprise for her. Secretly, he was taking French lessons from Jacqueline Hirsch, who taught Caroline and her classmates. She told him it would be about a year before he could speak the language fluently. "I bet I do it in six months," he quipped. He also asked

A somber Jackie Kennedy, three weeks after Patrick's death. August 31, 1963.

the gardener to fix a bouquet of fall flowers from the Rose Garden. For her part, Jackie presented Jack with an astounding piece of handicraft: she had put together intricate albums tracing the important moments of his administration and simultaneously tracing the development and blossoming of his Rose Garden. She also gave him a St. Christopher's medal to replace the one he'd placed in Patrick's coffin.

Jack carried his bouquet to Jackie when he arrived at Hammersmith for the small dinner her mother was hosting for them. One guest noted how loving the couple was toward each other—despite the presence of others: "They are the most remote and independent people we know, and so when their emotions do surface it is especially moving." There was a lot of laughter. Yusha Auchincloss made a toast, saying Jack's and Jackie's marriage had been a good thing for him—because otherwise he'd never have had a chance to get into the White House. Jack stood up in response, saying, "Because of Jackie, I got to live in the two finest American houses—the White House *and* Hammersmith Farm." Among the expensive ancient Roman sculpture, antique Greek bracelets, framed French engravings, and paintings he offered her as her gift,

In a candid moment, Jackie Kennedy hugs her husband as he arrives for their tenth wedding anniversary party, at the lawn entrance to Hammersmith Farm. September 13, 1963.

Jack kept needling her with the comment "Now, you can only keep one; you have to choose." As Janet remembered, "I think perhaps she kept two."

Janet Auchinloss reflected several months later on the couple at the time of their anniversary: "They'd certainly been through as much as people can go through together in ten years . . . all their strains and stresses, which any sensitive people have in a marriage, had eased to a point where they were terribly close to each other . . . in those rare moments when one could be alone with them on a quiet evening when there weren't a million pressures pending—they were very, very, very close to each other and understood each other wonderfully."

That weekend in Newport, the couple went for a cruise and hit the golf course. This time, after riding about the links in a cart together, Jackie accepted his challenge and tried hitting the golf

Jack and Jackie Kennedy alone together in a golf cart the day after their tenth wedding anniversary. The First Lady is wearing the president's leather jacket. September 14, 1963.

ball—but only hacked it, much to her husband's delight. She had always enjoyed trying to make him laugh, and it seemed to be a well-needed light moment. It was just as quickly gone. Jackie remained depressed.

One person seemed to understand this better than anyone else—her sister, Lee. When Lee had lost a child through miscarriage during Jack's Senate years, he had also been shaken. Liz Carpenter was one of several people lunching with him at the time: "He came in and very somberly stated that she had lost her child. He was clearly very upset, very moved." Lee had flown over for Patrick's funeral and to comfort her sister. At Hammersmith, Jackie received a phone call from Lee, who had returned to Europe after Patrick's funeral and was calling from the yacht of Greek shipping tycoon Aristotle Onassis. Lee urged Jackie to come join her as a complete break from the tragedy. Joe, Rose, and Jack Kennedy were acquaintances of Onassis.

Jack urged Jackie to accept the invitation—contrary to the persistent belief that it was otherwise. Most of the president's staff, especially Salinger and O'Donnell, urged against the trip with warnings of inevitably negative press—the First Lady had already been attacked in the press for her sybaritic Mediterranean jaunts, and was even picketed for vacationing in Italy. An incident underlining this took place in the Oval Office between the

"IT'S BEEN TEN YEARS JACK - WHEN ARE WE GOING TO SETTLE DOWN?"

A cartoon commenting on the many separations of Jack and Jackie Kennedy as their tenth wedding anniversary neared: "It's been ten years Jack—when are we going to settle down?"

president and Pam Turnure, who voiced her strong disapproval of the proposed trip. Jack replied, "Well, I think it will be good for Jackie, and that's what counts." Now O'Donnell weighed in, telling Jack, "You know, you have an election year coming up, and it may not look right to have this sort of trip." To this, the president snapped back, "We will cross that bridge when we come to it, and that's final. I want her to go on the trip. It will be good for her, and she has been looking forward to it."

Before she had gone to Newport, Jackie had joined Jack's clan on September 7 for Joe Kennedy's seventy-fourth birthday party, at his Hyannis Port home. It was the first time the president had seen his mother for months; he'd advised her not to return from Europe for Patrick's funeral. The president's mother had attended balls, a wedding, and concerts in Paris, Copenhagen, and Berlin (she told the press that the Berlin Wall's splitting up of families was "tragic and heartbreaking") hooking up for a time with her friend, heiress Mary Lasker. Before she had left, in May, she gave a series of ten lectures with slide shows of her life, family, and the famous people she had come to know. Billed as "An Evening with Rose Kennedy," it raised funds for Catholic women's charities. She exhorted the mothers of teenage girls, "Please, please tell them that to be sophisticated, to show that you've been places, you don't have to drink. The girl that does will lose her

Joe Kennedy's birthday dinner party. The patriarch sat at one end of the table, while his son sat at the other. In the second picture, from left to right: Jackie Kennedy (obscured), Bobby Kennedy, Jean Kennedy Smith (back to camera), Ethel Kennedy, Sargent Shriver, Joan Kennedy, Pat Lawford, Jack Kennedy, Rose Kennedy, Eunice Shriver, Steve Smith, Loretta Connelly (Joe's sister), Ted Kennedy. September 7, 1963.

Joe and Rose Kennedy with all their grandchildren. September 7, 1963.

figure and her face." Like Jack, Rose enjoyed public speaking and public attention.

Rose and her son the president were the only two family members at Joe's birthday party who refused to wear funny paper hats. After dinner, the grandchildren were invited in to wish him greetings, kiss him, and pose for a picture. First, however, Ethel Kennedy had a word with them: "Everything we have, we owe to Grandpa. Everything! So when you go in to see him, remember that every toy, every pet, the house we live in, everything, we owe to Grandpa." After the children left there was the usual family gag—often a song parody about the day's event with witty and biting lyrics. Joan Kennedy played the piano and everyone sang "Happy Birthday" to Joe. Then there were joke gifts, and finally Sargent Shriver and Jean Smith held up a presidential flag with a saying—HE'S ALWAYS IN THE BUSHES! It was an inside family joke—one of Joe's famous quotes that always cracked them up but fell flat for those outside the clan.

By now, the Kennedys had learned to integrate their debilitated father into new family routines.

Before she left for any of her trips, Jackie usually left a funny note for him in his room, as she had before going to Italy the summer before: "We will see you soon when we get home & bring you some marvelous present . . . Please put the picture of Jack & me & Caroline & John right by your favorite chair where Eunice will see it—& nail it down so she can't take it away & put Timmy there instead." In fact, it was both Eunice and Jackie who acknowledged honestly Joe's condition. "[S]he could be even more natural in a way than the President could be," said Pam Turnure of Jackie. "It pained the President to see him. . . ."

Jack Kennedy managed his way through coping with Joe. During Joe's third and final visit to the White House, that previous May, Jack called him "first class" for getting his favorite crabs sent from

Pat Lawford, Lem Billings, Ethel Kennedy, Bobby Kennedy, Eunice Shriver, and Ted Kennedy sing to their father—to Jack's delight. When Joe responds with a laugh, they all applaud. Jackie is sitting at the near end of the sofa. September 7, 1963.

HE'S ALWAYS IN THE BUSHES! reads the joke flag presented to Joe, as his children Jack, Eunice, and Jean laugh. September 7, 1963.

the famous Miami restaurant Joe's Stone Crabs. Of course, both Jack and Joe knew that the old man was no longer making such arrangements, but it was an appreciation from father to son. His brothers and sisters now followed Jack's habit of kissing Joe on the forehead before he or they left a room. He could also still show anger—if the cocktail hour was too long, or if he thought Jack was not working hard enough. His moans and the thrashing of his still-strong left arm let them know he knew what was going on. Now, however, he could also listen to and be calmed by his son. When some flat champagne was served one night, he began shaking angrily and sputtering. "Dad, you've done it again. I'm willing to challenge anybody that there's nobody else tonight in Palm Beach drinking Dom Perignon champagne that is flat." Suddenly, Joe relaxed and smiled.

In October, while Jackie was in Europe, the president made a midmonth trip to Boston. At Hyannis Port, he and his father breakfasted together, went out on a *Marlin* cruise, and lunched. Then it was time for Jack to go. "I miss him," Jack admitted to his father's driver. He waved good-bye to Joe and boarded the helicopter. It didn't move. Joe suddenly seemed worried to his nurse. Joe hadn't seen that Jack had come back out of the helicopter door. The president touched Joe's shoulders with a "Look who's here!" This time, he not only kissed his father, he also put his arms around him. As he left, Jack told the nurse, "Take good care of Dad till I get back." As he went into the helicopter, the president's eyes welled up.

On that same Boston trip, on October 19, the president attended a Democratic fund-raiser with Ted. The two were by now teasing each other from podiums in public. "I am independent," Ted cracked. "I've been helping him for a number of years. I think it's time he stood on his own two feet." Jack began wistfully, saying his days of campaigning would soon be over—"But Teddy is around, and,

President Kennedy bids farewell to his father on the front porch of his Hyannis Port home.

Jack and Ted Kennedy joked at one another's expense at a Boston fund-raiser. October 1963.

therefore, these dinners can go on indefinitely." In the audience was Jackie's sixteen-year-old half brother, Jamie, who had taken time off from boarding school to be there. Jack was his hero. Jack had family on his mind constantly during the trip, even making a private visit to Patrick's grave.

Meanwhile, in Greece and Turkey, the Bouvier sisters were yachting, swimming, and touring. On Lesbos, they saw the remains of the Palace of Minos; on Crete, the ruins of the Palace of Knossos; in Istanbul, the Blue Mosque. Then they were in Morocco at the invitation of King Hassan—drinking camel's milk, visiting the Marrakesh bazaar, eating honeyed dates, and joining the Thousand and One Nights festival, in honor of the fortieth day of life of the king's son. Jackie and Lee teased each other as they always did. While being served "endless glasses of mint tea," the First Lady announced to the king's harem that Lee had "a lovely voice and would now proceed to sing." Then, Lee recalled, "Jackie forced me to sing 'In an Old Dutch Garden Where the Tulips Grow' . . . It was one moment of Jackie's humor I didn't share."

Still, the trip was a "greater separation" from Jack than Jackie had anticipated. They tried to keep in touch by phone—but the connection was often lost and the time difference made it difficult. Others would see cables, so, Jackie seemingly courted her husband by handwritten love letters from Greece, some of which ran ten pages long. In one she expressed what was a sad realization for her: she could really relax on such trips, but with the constant responsibility of his office, he never really could. She wanted to somehow relieve that burden in any way she could, even if that meant sharing the weight of his work. His reaction to her proposal, upon her return, was unambiguous. He no longer wanted to travel around stag, to go about without his wife. He was tentative about asking Jackie, for he knew she might respond as her history suggested she would, but he wanted

The Bouvier sisters examine jewelry antiquities in Heraclion, Crete. October 8, 1963.

For the October birthday of Nancy Tuckerman, Jackie's best friend, former roommate at Miss Porter's School in Farmington, Connecticut, bridesmaid, and now social secretary, the First Lady planned a surprise party in the White House movie theater. After a surprised Nancy Tuckerman walked into the theater, she was greeted by a laughing Jackie. Nancy Hough, on the curator's staff, did a perfect Jackie Kennedy impersonation and often did so on the business phone, scaring employees with fantastic orders. Jackie had curator Jim Ketchum play the French decorator Boudin as he "restored" the theater with Hough parodying Jackie—with the real one sitting right beside her (top). The greatest shock of the day had been entirely Jackie's making. She had forced the usually staid chief usher, Mr. West, to wear one of her bouffant wigs and one of Maude Shaw's white uniforms—and a sign around his neck that said MISS WARD, the name of the housemother at Farmington. There was cake and punch, enjoyed by Jackie, Tuckerman, West, and Pam Turnure (press secretary), and finally the First Lady corraled all of the guests present to sing a chorus of the school song, "Farmington, we sing to thee . . ." Electrician Traphes Bryant observed that the Tuckerman birthday party was what convinced him that "Jackie had recovered from the death of her baby." October 24, 1963.

Jackie Kennedy is greeted by her husband and children as she arrives home from Europe. October 17, 1963.

them to begin traveling together publicly as a couple.

Upon her return on October 17, recalled Dave Powers, "She had ideas bubbling about everything . . . [asking] excited questions about the Nuclear Test Ban Treaty signing ceremony. She said she was really sad to have missed it . . . She felt it was the most important step he took for nuclear disarmament, that it was an important extension of peace to the Soviets and that he could trust them, if they proved their trust. . . . 'I'll never be away again at such important moments of accomplishment. Everyone needs to have support

and pride from those they love when they have accomplished something great.' "

It was thinking along these lines that led to her eager response to agree to accompany him, even on political trips. She accepted instantly the first offer, the first political trip of the 1964 campaign, a swing through Texas—Houston, Fort Worth, Dallas, Austin. She even suggested that she would go with him to the Army-Navy game two weeks later, and would spend part of their next summer out west, in Montana. "We'll just campaign," she enthusiastically told him. "I'll campaign with you anywhere you want."

Another woman in his family had already done

President Kennedy hands his sister Eunice Shriver the pen he used to sign the first federal legislation on behalf of the mentally handicapped, which she spurred. October 31, 1963.

her part for President Kennedy's legacy. On October 31, 1963, President Kennedy signed a bill authorizing $329 million for research and treatment of mental retardation, and the building of community health centers to help cope with the condition. Eunice had done it—she had shepherded through the first federal legislation on behalf of the mentally retarded. It had to have been one of the proudest family moments for Jack as he handed her the pen he used to sign the bill.

Jack had become even closer to Eunice while Jackie was gone. She had previously served as substitute First Lady for state events honoring the presidents of Afghanistan and Yugoslavia, and at the welcoming ceremony for the queen of Holland. Now, on October 11, he had asked her to be host-

ess for the arrival ceremony of Irish president Sean Lemass, whom they had met in Ireland, while Jean—who had also been with them—presided over the state dinner. Lemass was given full honors, as if he represented a nation as important to the United States as Saudi Arabia—including a twenty-one-gun salute and a large motorcade through the capital. After the dinner, Jack and Eunice really relaxed. He invited friends upstairs to the private quarters, and as Ted began singing some of the favorite old sentimental Irish songs, Jim Reed took in the scene, watching his old friend. "The President had the sweetest and saddest kind of look on his face," recalled Reed. "He was standing by himself, leaning against the doorway, and just seemed transported into a world of imagination." Eunice watched him, too. She whispered to Lemass, asking him to get some recordings of authentic native music for her; it would be her Christmas gift to Jack, recalling the days they had shared together four months earlier.

So much had changed for Jack: his father's illness, his youngest brother's rise, his sister's victory. His newborn son had died. He had reclaimed his heritage. By autumn that year, he was even able to ease off the Novocain injections because he had built up his back muscles with the exercises created for him by Dr. Hans Kraus of New York. His back pain had eased. "I wish I could have known you years ago," he told Kraus.

The most fundamental change, however, was obvious even to his wife. In the next few months she would recall, "I know my husband was devoted to me. I know he was proud of me. It took a very long time for us to work everything out, but we did, and we were about to have a real life together."

October 1963

9

THE LAST OF TIMES, 1963

The poignancy of men dying young haunted him.
—JACQUELINE KENNEDY

You've got to live every day like it is your last day on earth—and it damn well may be!
—JOHN F. KENNEDY

Ever since she learned in the winter of 1962 that Gladys Tartiere would not extend the lease at Glen Ora past the winter of 1963, Jackie had been looking for a permanent home in horse country. Paul Fout found the land for her, and Jackie began drawing her own rough floor plans of how she wanted the rooms to flow. It was her first experiment at armchair architecture. The house she designed had fifteen rooms on one floor, one side being a wall of sliding glass doors measuring thirty-two feet and overlooking a flagstone patio where the children had a swing set—and a bomb shelter. She named the house Wexford, in honor of the Irish county where the Kennedy family originated. The site was located up a long, muddy hill, with a view of the Blue Ridge Mountains, just outside the small town of Atoka, Virginia. It was far more isolated than Glen Ora had been. Again, a sign warned the curious that this was well-guarded private property. "It's the only house Jack and I ever built together, and I designed it all myself," she explained. "I don't want it to be exploited and photographed all over the place just because it was ours." In planning it, Jackie spent considerable effort and time—and money.

The day after Jackie's October 24 surprise birthday party for Nancy Tuckerman, the family made their first weekend trip to Wexford. Jack didn't like it. He would try it again the next time he was home for an entire weekend. They returned there on November 10, this time with Ben and Toni Bradlee. Although Jack still liked Camp David much more, he had a truly relaxing weekend with his friends and family. It was a modern house; although Jackie was placing antiques throughout its rooms, it could not escape the look of a classic 1960s ranch house—which it was. The land mattered more to Jackie. There were woods for the children to ramble in and explore, a sloping hill perfect for sleds in the winter, and a vast clearing for Macaroni to meander and Sardar to jump. Eunice Shriver complained that one could "hardly travel on the road when it rains," but the isolation of it was what appealed to the First Lady—despite the outrageous costs. The early November weekend, however, had been fun for Jack: he read the paper lazily, he talked to his chil-

Jackie Kennedy, her children, and Maude Shaw walk up the hill to their new weekend home, Wexford. October 26, 1963.

dren a lot, he laughed when Macaroni tried to chew on his head. He seemed to be so relaxed that weekend that he could endure Jackie's new house, at least for a while. If Jack was sometimes difficult to deal with as a spouse, Jackie was a challenge as a wife with her own compulsions. By the middle of November 1963, however, it was obvious to anyone close to them who recalled that period how strongly rooted in a realistic love the Kennedy marriage really had become. Now more than ever, he took tremendous delight in indulging her taste for

luxury. Before leaving for Texas, for example, he went to great lengths in the midst of his work to find the perfect fur coverlet for Jackie's 1963 Christmas gift. Endless examples were brought to him in the Oval Office, but on inspection he rejected all of them, insisting none was just right for her. He had experts called, and finally asked a close friend of the couple to help him. He was now paying the sort of detailed attention to her gifts that she did to his.

And Jackie had come to not only tolerate

President and Mrs. Kennedy's bedroom at Wexford. May 22, 1963.

The family living room at Wexford. In the dining room, Jackie had hung some amusing erotic Indian art on the walls along with other, more innocuous scenes. May 22, 1963.

Jackie jumping on her horse Bit O'Irish at Wexford. November 10, 1963.

but embrace her public role beside her husband. This was expressed in her telling J. B. West to now instruct the staff to refer to her as "the First Lady."

The morning after they got back to the White House from Wexford, Jack Kennedy impulsively decided to take his son along to Arlington National Cemetery for his speech and wreath-laying on Veteran's Day, November 11, 1963. Jackie remained at Wexford, and Jack took the children back to Washington. Having to be the sole responsible parent for his children had become one of the greatest possible joys for the president. They had even continued their nightly swimming sessions,

Jack Kennedy talks to John, on his bike, while Caroline tries out the new swing set. November 10, 1963.

The Kennedys on the grass next to their new home, with their dog Clipper. Toni Bradlee is at far left; the man at right is unidentified. November 10, 1963.

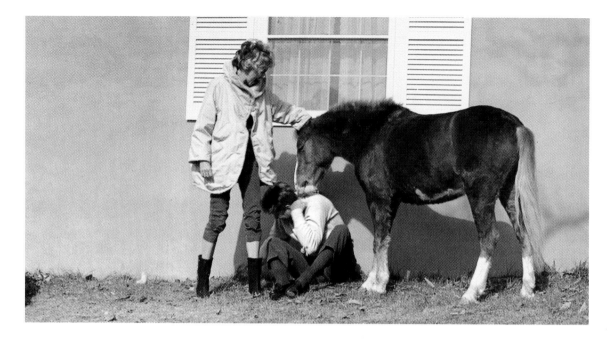

Kennedy shouted to the photographer, "You are about to see the president be eaten by a horse." Toni Bradlee pets Macaroni. November 10, 1963.

Caroline and John ramble through the woods adjoining Wexford. November 10, 1963.

which they had begun in October, when Jackie was in Greece.

During the Arlington ceremony the president became concerned that his son would become fidgety and asked that he be brought to him as the event broke up. John boldly marched up to his father, his hands behind his back, oblivious of the adoring crowds behind rope lines. Both laughed, and John clasped his father's legs in affection. He further amused Jack by walking backward, with his hands behind his back, impersonating his father, who was attempting to remain somber. Most onlookers enjoyed it, too, although *Time* sourly reported that "a good, firm nanny might well be employed to keep a 2½-year-old out of solemn ceremonies." The president and one of his military aides then took the boy by his hands and swung him over the steps as he let out childish yelps of glee. In the car, Jack gave him a little push—and John pushed him back. "I'm going to tell Miss Shaw on you," the father told the son. "I'm going to tell Mrs. Lincoln on you!" the son replied to the father. As they were leaving the cemetery, Jack told Con-

The president carrying his son by the arm down the steps at Arlington National Cemetery. November 11, 1963.

gressman Hale Boggs something he had said the previous spring after a visit there: "This is one of the really beautiful places on earth. I could stay here forever." He echoed this to Secretary of Defense Robert McNamara: "This is one of the really beautiful places on earth. I think, maybe, someday this is where I'd like to be."

The time he had spent with his children during their mother's absence the month before seems to have not only been a joy to him, but intensified his desire to play with and tease them. Jack's increasing insistence on integrating his children into official public ceremonies continued. Jackie seemed less resistant to it as well—not necessarily because she approved, but because she realized she was defeated. While she was away, Jack had directly crossed her orders. Not only did he let a photographer take pictures of the children—he invited him in. In this case, it was Cowles Publications photographer Stanley Tretick, Jackie's cagey nemesis, whom the president made his partner in crime. Many—but not all—of the photographs were

One of the ghostly images taken of the president and his son, walking the West Wing colonnade at night. October 1963.

From the South Portico, the four Kennedys watch the Black Watch Highlanders perform. November 13, 1963.

being printed for the *Look* edition that came out the week after Thanksgiving. Jackie would later say they were among the most beautiful she had ever seen of her children. She would gratefully thank Tretick.

Days after he had taken John to Arlington, Jack now insisted to Jackie that Caroline be allowed to separate from her schoolmates and watch the colorful lawn performance of the Black Watch, Royal Highland Regiment, with her family. Mother, father, daughter, and son sat tightly together against the November chill as they listened from the South Portico balcony to the melancholic strains of bagpipers. Caroline precariously bal-

anced herself on the arm of her father's chair and held her arm tightly around his neck.

Later, in early evening, the children came back to see their father after they'd put on their pajamas. This time, he romped and rolled and tickled them on the floor. They jumped and tackled him. Suddenly, his secretary came into the Oval Office. "What would the people think," she asked, "if they saw the president of the United States down on the floor?"

"After all," he replied, "I am also a father."

Before they went back to the residence, they all came out on the walkway overlooking the Rose Garden. John chased Shannon, one of the dogs.

The president and his two children in profile. November 13, 1963.

Caroline looked up into the sky and began reciting, "Star light, star bright . . ." as she saw the first star of the night. Jack told her to repeat the lines for her mother.

On November 20, the Kennedys hosted their annual Judiciary Reception. That evening was also the birthday of Bobby Kennedy, and both he and his wife were at the White House, making a stop upstairs with Jack and Jackie before heading home for a party Ethel Kennedy was hosting for her husband. Jack and Jackie would miss Ted's and Joan's wedding anniversary dinner two days later, on November 22. Later that evening, Jack spoke to Eunice as well as to Peter Lawford, while Jackie read notes from

both her mother and mother-in-law, both encouraging her to have a good time in Texas.

The next morning, as they prepared to leave, Jack was enraged when he discovered that his military aide had not provided him with precise weather conditions. "He was furious," Evelyn Lincoln recalled. "He really raved and ranted." Jack phoned the naval office himself and "lit into" the man who answered the phone. All of this rare display of cursing and anger was because of Jackie. He wanted everything to be absolutely perfect for her; he didn't want one thing to cause her discomfort, and they had been told that the weather was to be colder in Texas. Now, the president immediately called Provie Parades and told her that the First Lady's wardrobe should be lighter than the wool suits and other heavier clothes that had been packed. It was too late; the luggage had been sent ahead to the plane. It took him a while to cool down.

Jack had said good-bye to Caroline earlier that morning, and she was still in school when he left. She was somewhat distracted by the excitement that the next day promised: she was to have her first sleep-over, at the house of her best friend, Agatha Pozen. Still, she had carefully chosen her clothes that morning—just for her father. Although it was raining, the president had said of his son, "I want him with me." John was in all his glory while sitting on board the helicopter with his father as they waited for Jackie. The president began teasing John with little kicks to the boy's foot. "Don't, Daddy," he reprimanded. Jack kept doing it. Finally, John was insistent: "Don't!" When they arrived at Andrews Air Force Base, John said, "I want to come!" His father told him firmly, "You can't!" The little boy cried until his Secret Service agent, Bob Foster, managed to distract him with tales of Jasper the Jet as *Air Force One* took off for Texas.

There were many people who told President Kennedy or his aides not to go to Dallas. On October 23, Adlai Stevenson had been heckled and hit with a protest sign and warned Arthur Schlesinger that the president might provoke the same reaction. On October 3, Senator William Fulbright told Kennedy several times, "Dallas is a very dangerous place. I wouldn't go there. Don't you go." Governor John Connally—who would, with his wife, Nellie,

be accompanying the Kennedys and Johnsons in Texas—felt that the stop in the city should be reconsidered since its residents were "too emotional." Pierre Salinger received a letter from a woman resident of the city. "Don't let the President come down here," it said. "I'm worried about him. I think something terrible will happen to him." A newspaper editor in the state capital declared, "He will not get through this without something happening to him." Indeed, nasty jokes, quips, and riddles were known to be circulating in the city about the Vatican, the Kennedy marriage, even the First Lady's water-skiing. One popular question that circulated: Which Kennedy do you hate the most—Bobby, Jack, Teddy, or Jackie? As early as 1961, at a White House reception for publishers, the hostility was evident. The editor of the *Dallas News*, Ted Dealey, had openly insulted Kennedy by declaring that he was so soft on the Soviets that "many people in Texas and the Southwest think that you are riding Caroline's tricycle." As the president arrived in Dallas there were five thousand handbills circulating with his face on them over the caption "Wanted for Treason."

The Kennedys' first stop, in San Antonio on the afternoon of Thursday, November 21, proved to be a roaring success. It was the same that night in Houston, and the next morning outside the Fort Worth hotel where they had spent the night and appeared at a fund-raiser breakfast. Through the tumult, Jack remained sensitive to family matters. At a space research lab in San Antonio, he asked whether an experimental oxygen chamber that he was being shown would help premature babies. After Jackie gave a Houston speech in Spanish, Jack pulled aside a spectator to ask if his wife had spoken the language well: of course she had, the president was told. He proudly reported this to her,

President and Mrs. Kennedy greet well-wishers over a fence. Love Field, Dallas. November 22, 1963.

and she was touched by his gesture. He constantly checked to make certain she was comfortable and enjoying herself—so much so, she said, she promised to campaign with him in California two weeks later. Negative signs (BAN THE BROTHERS, said one) were outweighed by the positive (JACKIE, COME WATER-SKI IN TEXAS!).

After the Fort Worth breakfast event, the Kennedys briefly returned to their hotel suite.

While in the room, they looked at the morning edition of the *Dallas News*. At first glance it seemed friendly, with the heading WELCOME MR. KENNEDY TO DALLAS, but there was something grim about it. On closer examination, one noticed its threatening, funereal black border. The copy went on to menacingly question the president about acquiescing to Communists. Jack showed Jackie, telling her, "We're heading into nut country today. . . . Last night would have been a hell of a night to assassinate a president."

An hour and twenty-five minutes later, the Kennedys landed at Love Field in Dallas and were greeting enthusiastic crowds from behind the cyclone fence on the tarmac. They entered the blue limousine, the bubbletop down at Jack's direction (" . . . if you're going out to see the people, then they should be able to see you"), and began their motorcade through the streets of Dallas.

Thirty-five minutes after the motorcade began, as the Kennedy car proceeded onto Houston Street from Main Street, bullets rang out and Jack Kennedy was shot with Jackie beside him. Her husband's shattered cerebellum was literally all over her lap and legs. She cried out, "My God! They've killed Jack! They've killed my husband!" In shock, she climbed onto the back of the car, either to escape the bullets or to help a Secret Service agent into the car—she could not remember any of it. When she later saw the famous Zapruder film of the moment of the assassination, Jackie told William Manchester, none of the scene was familiar. They rushed to Parkland Memorial Hospital, but when the car pulled into the emergency room lot, Jackie refused to let go of Jack. She

The motorcade through Dallas. November 22, 1963.

didn't want anyone to see his head, and only after some coaxing, and after she covered his wound with a Secret Service agent's jacket, did she let go. She knew instantly that he was dead. She left the car and burst into the emergency room as soon as Jack was lifted to a gurney. Their car sat in the hot sun, a crushed bouquet of red roses on the backseat, stained by blood.

Endless delays were probably to be expected, considering the panic and confusion that broke out among the medical staff of Parkland Memorial Hospital, the frantic Secret Service—who had lost their man—and the stunned friends and staff who all crammed into the airless cubicles, hallways, and rooms as each second more and more of them absorbed the magnitude of what had just happened. By the time several of the president's middle-aged aides were struggling to move the heavy bronze coffin of their fallen leader up the stairs into *Air Force One*, the reality had sunk in. Before takeoff, Lyndon Johnson was sworn in as president. Many people gently suggested that Jackie change out of her stained suit and into a white one laid out for her. She refused.

•   •   •

The presidential limousine pulled under a sign that says EMERGENCY ONLY. Parkland Memorial Hospital, Dallas. November 22, 1963.

The president's coffin being carried onto Air Force One. Opposite: The widowed First Lady follows right behind her husband, still wearing her bloodstained suit. November 22, 1963.

In Washington, Janet Auchincloss had just returned home from the Chevy Chase Club after a game of golf when she got a phone call from Nancy Tuckerman, who was working in the White House East Wing. Joan Kennedy was having her hair done at Elizabeth Arden's in Washington, getting ready for her anniversary dinner that night. Pat Lawford had heard the news at home in Santa Monica, was taking no calls, and was getting ready to fly to Washington with Peter. Jean Smith was simply strolling in New York when she heard the horrible news on the street from a screaming woman. She wanted to be alone and walked all the way home lost in her own thoughts. Rose Kennedy heard the assassination news flash on the television. She went out for a long lone walk on the beach, where both she and Jack so often sought balance within themselves.

Sargent Shriver was with his pregnant wife,

Eunice, and their four-year-old son, Timmy, at the Hotel Lafayette. Sarge got the first call, saying Jack had been shot, but Eunice thought her brother had survived so much that he would survive again. Then the second call came and they sped to the White House. Steve Smith, already at work on the 1964 campaign, was having a business lunch in New York at La Caravelle. Teddy Kennedy was at the moment enjoying the traditional honor of presiding over the Senate in the vice president's chair on the rostrum. Bobby Kennedy got a phone call at home from J. Edgar Hoover. He turned and told Ethel.

The young were in school or playing. Jamie Auchincloss was in boarding school in New England; Kara and Teddy Kennedy Jr. were playing with their cousins Caroline and John. David Kennedy, on being quickly picked up from school by a family friend, played with a toy telephone, then bluntly asked, "Jack's hurt. Why did somebody shoot him?"

The word traveled rapidly across the world: Bobby called the Radziwills in London—Stas had first heard rumblings of something wrong while he was in his club. Yusha Auchincloss made quick plans to fly to Washington from the Middle East. All of the extended family now flocked to the capital, to the mansion, to the nuclear family.

Only the eldery and infirm seemed to be kept out of touch with the tragedy. Joe Kennedy would have the news kept from him for the rest of the day and night, until Ted and Eunice could personally tell him the next morning. Josephine Fitzgerald, now nearly a century old and quite fragile, was never told that her grandson had been killed. She died several months later.

By nightfall, Bobby had been helicoptered to Andrews Air Force Base to be there when *Air Force One*, carrying Jackie and the coffin, arrived. From there he would ride in the ambulance with them as they went to Bethesda Naval Hospital for the autopsy and embalming. Coming to comfort Jackie were Nancy Tuckerman, Ethel, Jean, and Jackie's mother and her stepfather. It was then, from her mother, that Jackie learned the disruptive ordeal that Caroline and John had been through in the last half day.

Caroline was supposed to have had her first sleep-over at her friend Agatha Pozen's house. Agatha's mother was driving her, trailed by a Secret Service car. Mrs. Pozen had the car radio tuned to the classical music station, when suddenly there was a news emergency. She quickly snapped off the radio as she drove, panicked that Caroline had heard the news. When she made a stop, the Secret Service agent in the car behind her ran out and practically snatched Caroline. The little girl started to cry. She was reassured that her mother wanted her at home. She was raced home by the driver and found herself in the Yellow Oval Room with a group of people who usually did not gather like this: her grandmother Janet, her aunt Jean down from New York, her mother's secretary. John and Maude Shaw were a familiar comfort. An order had come through from the Secret Service on the airplane to immediately take Caroline and John to their grandmother's house. Now, the bewildered and increasingly suspicious Caroline and the blissfully playful John were rushed out with overnight clothes frantically thrown into bags by Maude Shaw.

Hearing this, Jackie became visibly annoyed. She wanted her children and Maude Shaw right back in their rooms in the White House. Another car rushed them from the Auchincloss home in Georgetown to the White House. After recounting this ordeal, Janet said she "asked Jackie whether she wanted me or Miss Shaw or anyone to tell the children about their father's death. She thought for a minute and then she said, 'I think Miss Shaw should do exactly what she feels she should do. She will have to judge how much the children have seen or heard or whether they are wondering. She will just have to use her own judgment.' When Janet Auchincloss telephoned this decision to Maude Shaw, the elderly woman was determined to keep fighting with herself not to cry: Caroline was standing right there. As she read to the girl, after putting John to sleep, Shaw's eyes welled with tears and Caroline asked what was wrong. The nanny explained that Caroline's father had gone to heaven to be with a lonely Patrick, but now both would look down on the others from heaven as guardian angels.

"I am going to walk behind the casket," Jackie declared at Bethesda Hospital while the funeral plans were being organized by Sargent Shriver.

Nancy Tuckerman went back to the White House, where friends and staff were frantically working to hang crepe, fix a catafalque, and make other arrangements. Searching for the perfect wooden cross, Sarge finally provided the German one that hung in his bedroom. They finished their work at 4:10 A.M. At 4:20, President Kennedy's flag-draped coffin was carried through the north entrance of the White House. Bobby and Ethel Kennedy and Jean Smith followed it, behind Jackie, who was still dressed in her stained pink suit.

They entered the East Room, where the coffin was laid to rest. Nancy recalled that there were some prayers—"very short, maybe three minutes—a few prayers from the priest when she came in with the Attorney General and the rest of the family." Now, for the first time, Jackie broke down, sobbing, her knees buckling, kissing the bunting beneath her husband's casket. Bobby then took her down the hall toward the elevator. Butler Nelson Pierce was standing in the usher's room, the door of which opened to the elevator hall on the state floor, and he recalled, "As she came around the corner from the hall to the elevator, our eyes met and there was a rapport there just for an instant. She was crying very hard at the moment, but there was that rapport and I knew no words were necessary."

Although Jackie could not really sleep, even with a sedative, she wanted to know that family was around her. "Before we left," Janet Auchincloss later remembered of her departure from Bethesda Naval Hospital, "I asked Jackie what I could do, and she asked me if I would spend the night at the White House." Things had not always been easy between this mother and daughter, but the usually stoic Janet reflected, "This touched me very much." In the early morning hours of November 23, Jackie had her mother and stepfather rest in

Still in the suit she was wearing at the moment of the president's assassination, Jackie Kennedy returns with her husband to the White House in the early morning hours. November 23, 1963.

the president's four-poster blue bed—they sped from the hospital to their Georgetown home to fetch their toothbrushes. The hard mattress, there for Jack's back condition, made it impossible for them to sleep. Jean stayed in the Queen's Bedroom. Bobby Kennedy went to sleep for a few hours in the Lincoln Bedroom. There he finally broke down and sobbed, crying out, "Why, God?"

By daybreak, Bobby was visiting with the children and Jackie, who sat on her bed in a robe. John told his uncle that a "bad man" had killed his father. Caroline added, "Daddy was too big for his coffin." Into that coffin, Jackie's children placed letters for their father, while Jackie left a bracelet from Lee,

The president is borne to a catafalque in the East Room. Among the family members present are Hugh and Janet Auchincloss, Ethel Kennedy, Jean Smith, and Robert Kennedy. Jackie Kennedy stands at center. November 23, 1963.

scrimshaw he had liked, some cuff links she had given her husband as a gift, and the St. Christopher's medal she'd given him on their recent tenth anniversary. She took a lock of his hair. It was something she had done at her father's funeral. Bobby placed in the coffin a lock of his own hair, his *PT-109* tie clip, and rosary beads his wife had once given him.

The president lay in state at the U.S. Capitol on Sunday, November 24. The funeral mass and burial were scheduled for Monday, November 25, John's third birthday. By then, Ted, Eunice, and Rose Kennedy had come down from Hyannis Port, and Lee and Stas had flown to Washington. From her bedroom on Saturday, Jackie handwrote reams of lists of people to be invited and contacted, as well as instructions for the funeral. Her mangerial skills were utilized to their greatest capacity. She remembered that the president had spoken of the Irish drill cadets of the Military College at the Curragh at a Dublin ceremony for leaders killed in the Irish Independence rebellion of 1916. She had the Irish ambassador called and asked to fly the cadets over immediately for the funeral. She wanted the Catholic mass to be held in St. Matthew's, which they had considered their home church. In the cortege, the riderless horse was her own Sardar. She decided that Jack would be buried at Arlington Cemetery, not in Boston, and she was driven across the Potomac to inspect the gravesite, on a gentle slope that rolled away from the pillared Custis-Lee Mansion—a site she first noticed in 1941 and which Jack had just commented on a week or so before. "It was extraordinary," thought one of her secretaries; "she always knew exactly what she wanted." She chose her husband's picture and wrote the prayer beneath it for the mass card. Remembering the last day she, Jack, and the children had been together in public, she asked the Black Watch Regiment of bagpipers, drummers, marchers, and Highland dancers to return.

For Jackie, the night before the funeral and burial, there came a sign of support from a confidante that she later recalled meant the most to her. As she went to her bed that night, Jackie found a handwritten letter written and placed there by Lee. Somehow it said exactly what the widow needed to help her carry on. It was addressed to "Jacks" and was signed "Pekes," their childhood nicknames for each other.

Perhaps some people were surprised to see the two children in matching blue coats walking through the North Portico onto the steps that Monday morning, but Jackie wanted both of her children with her at their father's funeral. Jackie, as she had determined, walked behind the caisson carrying the coffin. Flanking her were the president's two brothers. Right behind the three of them, a line of supportive family members fanned out—Steve Smith, Sargent Shriver, Jamie Auchincloss, and Clint Hill, the Secret Service agent who had run up onto the car to help Jackie in Dallas.

Ted Kennedy later reflected on how important Jackie's conduct during the walk to the church and the funeral was to the rest of the extended families: "I think we had extraordinary respect for her inner strength and fortitude at the time of that walk beside her, and for her presence in the church. She was an extraordinarily powerful example . . . for the family. While others were sort of trying to find themselves, to put this whole tragedy into some kind of context, she was a pillar of strength and resilience. It helped all the rest of us to sort of carry on."

Caroline and John followed in a car, but they would be the center of attention at the funeral. John made noises and played with his flag in the church. Although his salute in front of the church became iconic, he comprehended nothing of the loss; despite being told that his father had gone away, John would ask for his father several times over the next few weeks and months. Caroline had saluted her father's

Jackie Kennedy in the Entrance Hall of the White House with her children, about to walk out and drive to the U.S. Capitol Building, where the president lay in state. November 24, 1963.

Flanked by Robert and Ted Kennedy, and followed by Jamie Auchincloss, Sargent Shriver, Steve Smith, and a Secret Service agent, Jackie Kennedy led the walking procession to St. Matthew's Church for the president's funeral. November 25, 1963.

coffin at the Capitol service—in fact, the day before her brother did.

The children did not come to the burial service, but every other member of Jack's and Jackie's extended families did—along with George Thomas, Mrs. Parades, and Mrs. Lincoln. Jackie had invited every member of the household staff to join the family and friends at a private mass on Saturday in the

East Room. She also invited household staff to the funeral, where they intermingled with the heads of state. Cardinal Cushing said the burial rites, Jackie was given the folded flag from the coffin, Bobby escorted her away. President Kennedy was buried.

Back at the White House, there was a reception. Senator Kennedy escorted the likes of General de Gaulle and Prince Philip to meet privately with

Caroline Kennedy being driven with her brother in a car to their father's funeral. She sometimes held the hand of a Secret Service agent through the car window. November 25, 1963.

On his third birthday, John Kennedy is led to a pew after having been led away briefly during the funeral when he was talking out loud. November 25, 1963.

Caroline Kennedy saluted her father the day before her brother did so. November 24, 1963.

ASSOCIATED PRESS

Outside St. Matthew's Church, following the funeral, left to right, Ted Kennedy, Peter Lawford, Steve Smith, Lee Radziwill, Pat Lawford, Robert Kennedy, and Eunice Shriver. Caroline Kennedy (partially obscured), Rose Kennedy, and Jackie Kennedy are in front. November 25, 1963.

The extended family stands for the burial service of the president in Arlington Cemetery. Among those in the picture, left to right, are Sydney Lawford, Pat Lawford, Eunice Shriver, Rose Kennedy, Peter Lawford, Robert Kennedy, Jackie Kennedy, Evelyn Lincoln, Ted Kennedy, Stas Radziwill, Lem Billings, Steve Smith, Yusha Auchincloss, George Thomas, Providencia Parades, Bobby Kennedy Jr., Joan Kennedy, unidentified Kennedy niece, Bobby Shriver, Sargent Shriver, and Timmy Shriver. Also in the crowd are Franklin Roosevelt Jr., Mamie Eisenhower, Senator Hubert Humphrey, and President Johnson. November 25, 1963.

Jackie in the Yellow Oval Room. They then came down and joined the growing reception in the State Dining Room. A photographer who captured de Gaulle and Prince Philip talking also caught Joan Kennedy in the frame. Meanwhile, Jackie came down into the Red Room and stood with the senator to receive foreign delegates. When Soviet Deputy Premier Mikoyan approached, Jackie seized the moment to make a political statement related to what others did not realize had been a bonding time for her marriage. "Please tell Mr. Chairman President that I know he and my husband worked for a peaceful world," she said in an oblique reference to the Cuban Missile Crisis, "and now he and you must carry on my husband's work." As Jackie returned upstairs, an impromptu

The late president is saluted at his burial service in Arlington Cemetery. November 25, 1963.

French president Charles de Gaulle confers with Prince Philip of England at the State Dining Room reception following the funeral. Joan Kennedy is at right. November 25, 1963.

At the White House reception following the funeral, Ted Kennedy and Jackie Kennedy greet the Soviet delegation. At that moment, the widowed First Lady broached the subject of nuclear missile reduction. November 25, 1963.

Ted Kennedy and Eunice Shriver look over the State Dining Room during the funeral reception. November 25, 1963.

family receiving line in the State Dining Room formed of Bobby, Jean, Teddy, and Ethel. Eunice and Teddy tried to identify the dignitaries.

Among family and the closest of friends, Jackie hosted an impromptu third birthday party for her son. She suggested that they sing Jack's favorite song, "Heart of My Hearts." When they did, Bobby Kennedy fled the room. Occasionally, she silently watched news footage of the day's funeral on television as if it were not she on the screen, according to one witness. To friends like Ari Onassis, who had come in from Hamburg, Germany, she recounted the assassination again in great detail. She had done this first for Bobby, and then for Nancy and the others at Bethesda. She had been confiding it to many people. On some level, she was still in shock while trying to rationally think ahead of the imme-

diate plans that needed to be made. Her greatest concern was where she and the children would live when they left the White House. Former ambassador Averell Harriman instantly offered his Georgetown home for their use.

The wake began to dissipate. Jackie's Bouvier cousin John Davis was identified downstairs and permitted up. He had just arrived from Italy and had missed the funeral. Janet's sister Winnifred D'Olier was there. Amid this imposing crowd of wealth and power sat a timid young woman who, invited by Jackie, had been driven and flown there by Irish authorities. Lee recognized her from the trip to Ireland and brought her over to an astonished Jackie. It was Jack's young cousin Mary Anne, the daughter of Mary Ryan, whom he had met in Ireland. "Mrs. Kennedy gave her a rosary

Although an impromptu adult party was held for John Kennedy's third birthday following the state reception on November 25, the First Lady held one last children's birthday party for him and his sister ten days later. December 5, 1963.

that he had on him, and she also gave the dog tag that he had. He had two of them . . . she sent one of them home to my mother," recalled Mary Anne's sister Josephine.

Two days later, Bobby wrote a note to his son Joe: "You are the oldest of all the male grandchildren. You have a special and particular responsibility now which I know you will fulfill. Remember all the things that Jack started—be kind to others that are less fortunate than we—and love our country."

Three days later, Jackie went to Hyannis Port for the Thanksgiving holiday. She was unable to share the day with Jack's extended family. She stayed alone in the Squaw Island house, refusing even a plate of turkey and trimmings.

Despite her grief, life went on for Jackie. In between making requests to President Johnson to rename Cape Canaveral to Cape Kennedy, and continue efforts on behalf of The National Cultural Center and Pennsylvania Avenue redevelopment, and giving a history-shaping interview with journalist Teddy White, she began packing. She gave out items of the president's to his staff—to George Thomas, who so helped Jack with his back, she gave his rocking chair. She penned recommendations for Secret Service agents and a sympathy letter to the widow of the Dallas police officer who was also fatally shot by the

Moving crates with the First Family's personal objects in the basement of either the White House or the Old Executive Office Building.

The day they left the White House, Caroline and John Kennedy were brought to a staff room, where Christmas gifts for them had been sent from the public; they were permitted to choose one each for themselves. December 6, 1963.

assassin—Lee Harvey Oswald. As far as a reason for the assassination, Jackie insisted she didn't care—all that mattered was that her husband was gone.

In guiding Lady Bird Johnson through the house, she said, " . . . some of the happiest years of my marriage have been spent here." When Jackie cleaned out the Oval Office desk, she discovered

that Jack had clipped two newspaper stories and kept them close by, in his drawer. Both were about her India trip, one noting how she had "even out-done President Eisenhower as a drawing card," the other quoting her on how she wished her husband had been with her.

In the evenings, she penned personal letters of

Caroline Kennedy's kindergarten class continued to meet at the White House until the end of the 1963 term. On December 16, she performed in a Christmas show with them in the movie theater. Her mother was in attendance.

thanks to world leaders and close friends. To Nikita Khrushchev, she handwrote on the first of December, the Sunday after Thanksgiving, an extraordinary letter, illustrating further her convictions about nuclear war:

I would like to thank you for sending Mr. Mikoyan as your representative to my husband's funeral. He looked so upset when he came through the line and I was very moved. I tried to give him a message for you that day— but as it was such a terrible day for me, I do not know if my words came out as I meant them to . . . You and he [Jack] *were adversaries, but you were allied in a determination that the world should not be blown up. You respected each other and could deal with each other . . . President Johnson will make every effort to establish the same relationship with you. The danger that troubled my husband was that war might not be started so much by the big men as by the little ones. While big men know the needs for self-control and restraint—little men are sometimes moved more by fear and pride. If only in the future the big men can continue to make the little ones sit down and talk, before they start to fight . . .*

As Jackie's letters flowed out across the world, gifts were flying in from around the globe. It was Christmastime in the White House. While the Kennedy family possessions were being nailed into wooden crates and stored on the basement level of the Old Executive Office Building, several floors up Nancy Tuckerman was already overseeing the gargantuan task of responding to what seemed like endless millions of cards and letters—and Christmas gifts for the children. Caroline was deeply saddened. There was, as one witness described it, a "haunted" look in her eyes. Maude Shaw took her and John down to the mail room: their mother was permitting them each to have a toy. President Johnson had the kindergarten class continue meeting in the Solarium through the end of the school term, right around Christmas, some two weeks after the three Kennedys had moved out. At that year's Christmas pageant, however, there was no mistaking that Caroline was the saddest among her classmates. Her mother joined the other parents to watch. John was delighted with his new toy airplane.

On December 6, Jackie was packed. She went to the phone room and thanked all the operators. Then she asked to see staff members—every one of them. "The day that she left," remembered Nelson Pierce, "the ushers all went up and had their picture taken in the West Hall with her . . . She had all the staff people up at that time—the carpenters, the maids, the butlers—everyone in the house was invited up to say good-bye to her and it was so wonderful seeing her smile—to be able to smile." Caroline was in school for at least a half hour more, but John was there, bowing and shaking hands and making the whole staff laugh.

Jack and Jackie had together redesigned the Presidential Medal of Freedom and made the award ceremony into an important event. Now, President Johnson would be presenting the awards for 1963. Jackie wanted to see the ceremony—but without the audience's seeing her. She would slip in when everyone else was in place, and watch the ceremony from behind a screen. As she waited to be called down to the East Room, she chatted with one of her favorite housepainters, Joe Karitas. Joe had been the one who patiently painted and *repainted* the family rooms over for her until they were just the shade she wanted. "I told her how much I enjoyed working with her," Joe recalled, "and she invited me to come to see her at the house and bring my wife. She said, 'I'll be very lonely. You've worked with me and I think so much of you. I'd like to have you come and see me.' "

After attending the East Room ceremony, but slipping away before its conclusion, Jackie Kennedy met her children on the ground floor with Maude Shaw and the three dogs the children had decided to keep—Shannon, Clipper, and Wolf. They walked out of the residence into the West Wing. They passed by Jack's Rose Garden without stopping, got into their car, and left the White House that was no longer their home.

Jackie Kennedy shakes hands with some of the maintenance workers in the private quarters of the White House on the morning of her departure. John says good-bye to the kitchen staff. December 6, 1963.

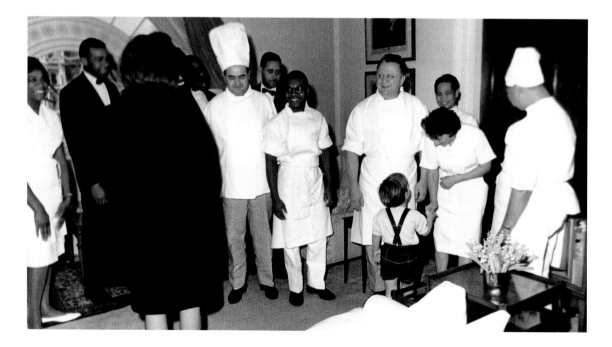

Maude Shaw bids farewell to a household staff member, followed by John Kennedy holding his flag, and Jackie Kennedy holding her daughter Caroline's hand, as they all walk through the Rose Garden and toward their car, leaving the White House. December 6, 1963.

Twenty-six years after they left the White House, Caroline, John, and Jackie Kennedy posed beneath a picture of the president at the library bearing his name. 1989.

EPILOGUE

*S*ince 1963, Sargent and Eunice Shriver's advocacy for individuals with mental retardation has included development of the National Institute for Child Health and Human Development, establishment of national standards and testing for individuals with mental retardation, national public awareness campaigns, changes in civil service regulations to employ persons with mental retardation based on functions, establishment of research centers at major medical schools across the United States, creation of the worldwide Special Olympics movement, and creation and implementation of the Community of Caring concept to reduce mental retardation among babies of teenagers. Their son Mark serves in the Maryland House of Delegates. Ted and Joan Kennedy divorced in 1981. Edward M. Kennedy has been reelected to his U.S. Senate seat seven times since his assumption of that position in the special election of 1962. Joan Kennedy has written about teaching piano to children, and has performed as a classical pianist in concert. Ted's and Joan's son Patrick serves in the U.S. Congress. Pat Lawford divorced Peter Lawford in 1966; he died in 1984. After being elected to the United States Senate seat from New York in 1964 and running for the Democratic presidential nomination in 1968, Bobby Kennedy was assassinated that same year. His son Joseph served as a U.S. congressman, and his daughter Kathleen serves as lieutenant governor of Maryland. Steve Smith died in 1990. Jean Kennedy Smith founded Very Special Arts for the mentally disabled in 1974 and was named U.S. ambassador to Ireland by President Clinton in 1993. Joe Kennedy died in 1968. Rose Kennedy died in 1995, at the age of 104. Rosemary Kennedy is still a resident at St. Coletta's home in Wisconsin.

Jackie Kennedy married Aristotle Onassis in 1968. He died in 1975. That year the former First Lady returned to work after twenty-two years, employed as an editor in book publishing. She died of cancer in May 1994. John Kennedy was founder and executive editor of the political magazine *George*. He died in a plane crash in 1999. Caroline Kennedy married in 1986, earned an L.L.D. from Columbia University, co-authored two books, and has three children. John and Caroline's mother managed to raise them with a proportionate sense of themselves as human beings—despite their being the famous children of a famous president. With his trademark wry humor, John Kennedy cracked to this author at a *George* event, "The first time I went to therapy, I lay down on the couch and the doctor started telling *me* about *my* childhood!" Perhaps apocryphal, the remark nevertheless illustrated his ability to separate the absurd from the meaningful.

A February 1996 Marist Poll found that 31 percent of those polled said John F. Kennedy was the president they most admired.

A NOTE ON SOURCES

The photographs and other illustrations guided the narrative of both the nuclear and extended Kennedy families. Although it is the first book of its kind to focus on the integrated story of this famous family between the years 1961 and 1963 exclusively, it is a synthesized one, drawn from accounts of the numerous individuals within the families. While its intent was to be the first personal biography of President Kennedy as told through the evolution, conflicts, and resolutions of his family dynamics and relationships, underlined by new analysis by the author, its sources and information are derivative.

In 1995 and 1996 I personally conducted interviews with friends and relatives of Jacqueline Kennedy Onassis for the oral history biography I wrote of her, *As We Remember Her* (1997). There was a tremendous amount of original material that had to go unused from that project and much of it has finally been used here. Among those individuals I interviewed at that time are two of the principle figures in this book, Senator Edward M. Kennedy and Eunice Kennedy Shriver, the brother and sister of President Kennedy. Their observations and words are fully utilized here as they were not able to be in *As We Remember Her*, and they are thanked again. I also wish to thank Jamie Auchincloss, and Mimi Cecil, his and Mrs. Onassis's Lee cousin, who both provided personal photographs at that time.

Hundreds of newspaper and magazine articles and dozens of books about President Kennedy, Jacqueline Kennedy, and the other members of the extended family were read and have become part of the general, institutional background of information for this work. It would be impossible to list each one individually and, perhaps, unnecessary given the fact that the text here is probably secondary to the illustrations (as much as a "word" person hates to realize and admit). Thus, a selected bibliography is provided, listing those sources from which many quotations were taken and which were the most frequently consulted sources for factual information.

SELECTED BIBLIOGRAPHY

Adler, Bill, ed. *More Kennedy Wit*. New York: Bantam Books, 1965.

Andrews, Jay David. *Young Kennedys*. New York: Avon Books, 1998.

Anthony, Carl Sferrazza. *America's First Families: An Inside View of 200 Years of Private Life in the White House*. New York: A Lisa Drew Book/Touchstone/Simon & Schuster, 2000.

——. *As We Remember Her: Jacqueline Kennedy Onassis in the Words of Her Friends and Family*. New York: HarperCollins, 1997.

——. *First Ladies: The Saga of the Presidents' Wives and Their Power, 1961–1990, Volume 2*. New York: William Morrow, 1991.

Baldrige, Letitia. *Of Diamonds and Diplomats*. Boston: Houghton, Mifflin, 1968.

Bishop, Jim. *A Day in the Life of President Kennedy*. New York: Random House, 1964.

Boller, Paul. F. *Presidential Anecdotes*. New York: Oxford University Press, 1981.

Bradford, Sarah. *America's Queen*. New York: Viking Penguin, 2000.

Bradlee, Benjamin C. *Coversations With Kennedy*. New York: W.W. Norton, 1975.

Brogan, Hugh. *Kennedy*. London: Longman, 1996.

Brogan, Hugh, and Charles Mosley. *American Presidential Families*. New York: Macmillan, 1993.

Brown, Gene, ed. *The Kennedys: A New York Times Profile*. New York: Arno Press, 1980.

Bryant, Traphes. *Dog Days at the White House*. New York: Macmillan, 1975.

Burns, James MacGregor. *John Kennedy: A Political Profile*. New York: Harcourt, Brace, 1959.

Cameron, Gail. *Rose*. New York: Berkeley Medallion Books, 1971.

Cannon, Poppy, and Patricia Brooks. *The Presidents' Cookbook*. New York: Bonanza Books, 1969.

Clymer, Adams. *Edward M. Kennedy*. New York: William Morrow, 1999.

Collier, Peter, and David Horowitz. *The Kennedys*, New York: Warner Books, 1984.

Curtis, Charlotte. *First Lady*. New York: Pyramid Publications, 1962.

Davis, John H. *The Bouviers*. Washington, D.C.: National Press Books, 1993.

DeGregorio, William A. *The Complete Book of U.S. Presidents*. New York: Barricade Books, 1993.

Dickerson, Nancy. *Among Those Present*. New York: Random House, 1976.

Druitt, Michael. *John F. Kennedy, Jr: A Life in the Spotlight*. Kansas City: Andrews McMeel Publishing, 1996.

Durbin, Louise. *Inaugural Cavalcade*. New York: Dodd, Mead, 1971.

Edwards, Susan. *The White House Kids*. New York: Avon Books, 1999.

Egoscue, Pete. *Pain Free: A Revolutionary Method for Stopping Chronic Pain*. New York: Bantam Books, 1998.

Epstein, Dan. *Twentieth Century Pop Culture*. London: Carlton Books Limited, 1999.

Faber, Harold. *The Kennedy Years*. New York: The Viking Press, 1964.

Fay, Paul B. *The Pleasure of His Company*. New York: Harper and Row, 1966.

Fuller, Edmund, and David E. Green. *God in the White House*. New York: Crown Publishers, 1968.

Gallagher, Mary. *My Life With Jacqueline Kennedy*. New York: David MacKay Company, Inc., 1969.

Goodwin, Doris Kearns. *The Fitzgeralds and the Kennedys*. New York: Simon & Schuster, 1987.

Harding, Warren G., and J. Mark Stewart. *Mere Mortals*. Worthington, OH: Renaissance Publications, 1992.

Heller, David and Deane. *Jacqueline Kennedy*. Derby, CT: Monarch Books, Inc., 1961.

Hellman, John. *The Kennedy Obsession: The American Myth of JFK*. New York: Columbia University Press, 1997.

Hersh, Seymour M. *The Dark Side of Camelot*. Boston: Little, Brown, 1997.

Higham, Charles. *Rose: The Life and Times of Rose Fitzgerald Kennedy*. New York: Pocket Books, 1995.

Hunt, Conover. *Dealy Plaza: National Historic Landmark*. Dallas, TX: Sixth Floor Museum, 1997.

Kellerman, Barbara. *All the President's Kin*. New York: The Free Press, 1981.

Kelly, Nile. *Presidential Pets*. New York: Abbeville Press, 1992.

Kennedy, Rose Fitzgerald. *Times to Remember*. Garden City, New York: Doubleday, 1974.

Kessler, Ronald. *The Sins of the Father: Joseph P. Kennedy and the Dynasty He Founded*. New York: Time Warner Books, 1996.

Kunhardt, Philip B., Jr., ed. *Life In Camelot: The Kennedy Years*. Boston: Little Brown, 1988.

Leamer, Laurence. *The Kennedy Women: The Saga of an American Family*. New York: Villard Books, 1994.

Lieberson, Goddard, *As We Remember Him: John F. Kennedy*. New York: Macmillan, 1965.

Lincoln, Evelyn. *My Twelve Years with John F. Kennedy*. New York: David MacKay Company, 1965.

MacMahon, Edward, and Leonard Curry, *Medical Cover-Ups in the White House*. Washington, D.C.: Farragut Publishing, 1987.

MacNeil, Robert. Ed. *The Way We Were*. New York: Carroll Graf Publishers, 1988.

Manchester, William, *The Death of a President*. New York: Harper & Row, 1967.

——. *One Brief Shining Moment*. Boston: Little, Brown, 1983.

——. *Portrait of a President*. Boston: Little, Brown, 1962.

Martin, Ralph. G., *A Hero for Our Time: An Intimate Story of the Kennedy Years*. New York: Fawcett, 1988.

Matthews, Jim, publisher. *The Complete Kennedy Saga:* Hollywood: Special Publications, Inc., 1963.

Michaelis, David. *The Best of Friends*. New York: William Morrow, 1983.

Mills, Judie. *Robert Kennedy*. Brookfield, CT: The Milbrook Press, 1998.

Mitchell, Arthur. *JFK and His Irish Heritage*. Dublin, Ireland: Moytura Press, 1993.

O'Donnell, Kenneth P., David F. Powers, and Joe McCarthy. *"Johnny We Hardly Knew Ye": Memories of John Fitzgerald Kennedy*. Boston: Little, Brown, 1972.

Packard, Jerrold M. *American Monarchy*. New York: Delacourt Press, 1983.

Pessen, Edward. *The Log Cabin Myth*. New Haven: Yale University Press, 1984.

Reeves, Richard. *President Kennedy*. New York: Touchstone/Simon & Schuster, 1993.

Reeves, Thomas. *A Question of Character*. Rocklin, CA: Prima Publishing, 1997.

Rowan, Roy and Bruce Janice. *First Dogs*. Chapel Hill, NC: Algonquin Books, 1997.

Salinger, Pierre. *With Kennedy*. New York: Doubleday, 1966.

Schaaf, Dick. *RFK*. New York: New American Library, 1967.

Schlesinger, Arthur M., Jr. *Robert Kennedy and His Times*. New York: Ballantine Books, 1978.

——. *A Thousand Days*. New York: Fawcett Premier, 1965.

Sciacca, Tony. *Kennedy and His Women:* New York: Manor Books, 1976.

Seale, William. *The White House Garden*. Washington, D.C.: White House Historical Association, 1996.

Shaw, Maude. *White House Nannie*. New York: New American Library, 1965.

Smith, Amanda, ed. *Hostage to Fortune: The Letters of Joseph P. Kennedy*. New York: Viking Press, 2001.

Sorenson, Theodore C. *Kennedy*. New York: Harper & Row, 1965.

Stoughton, Cecil, Chester V. Clifton, and Hugh Snidey. *The Memories*. New York: Norton, 1973.

Strausbaugh, John. *Alone With the President*. New York: Blast Books, 1993.

Sullivan, George. *Presidents at Play*. New York: Walker and Company, 1995.

TerHorst, J. F., and Col. Ralph Albertazzie, *Flying White House*. New York: Coward, McCann, Geoghegan, 1979.

Thayer, Mary van Rensselear. *Jacqueline Kennedy: The White House Years*. Boston: Little, Brown, 1967.

Thomas, Helen. *Dateline: White House*. New York: MacMillan, 1975.

Verdon, Rene. *The White House Chef Cookbook*. New York: Doubleday, 1967.

West, J. B. *Upstairs at the White House*. New York: Coward, McCann and Geoghegan, Inc., 1973.

Whalen, Richard J. *The Founding Father: The Story of Joseph P. Kennedy*. New York: New American Library, 1964.

Youngblood, Rufus W. *Twenty Years in the Secret Service*. New York: Simon and Schuster, 1973.

Oral Histories from the John F. Kennedy Library

Since the 1980s, oral histories that relate stories of the White House and pre–White House years of President Kennedy and his family members have been consulted. These include:

Alsop, Joseph

Arata, Lawrence

Auchincloss, Janet

Avery, Issac

Baldrige, Letitia

Barboza, Joanne

Behn, Gerald

Billings, LeMoyne

Boring, Floyd

Bruce, Preston

Bryant, Traphes

Burke, Kenneth

Burkley, George

Burns, J. M.

Cavanaugh, Rev. John

Crafts, Edward

Cramer, Robert

Cushing, Richard Cardinal

Davens, Edward

DeValera, Eamon

Douglas-Home, William
Doyle, Patrick
Fox, Sanford
Gallagher, Edward
Gilpatric, Roswell
Grennan, Josephine
Halle, Kay
Heffernan, Roy
Hennessey, Louella
Highley, David
Hirsch, Jacqueline
Holness, Wilma
Hopkins, William
Horton, Ralph
Huber, Oscar
Hurley, Francis
Jacobsen, Ben
Karitas, Joseph
Kennedy, Robert
Kennedy, Rose
Kilpatric, Carroll
Knebel, Fletcher
Knebel, Laura Berquist
Kroch, Arthur
Lawford, Peter
LeMass, Sean
Lempart, Helen
Lincoln, Evelyn
Luce, Henry
McCormack, Edward
McDonald, Torbert
McHugh, Godfrey
Marshall, Burke
Minihan, Andrew
Morgan, Edward
Morrissey, Francis X.
Mulkern, Patrick
O'Donnell, Kenny

O'Ferrall, Frank
Pierce, Nelson
Powers, Dave
Powers, Johnny
Reinhardt, G.
Reston, James
Roberts, Chalmer
Roberts, Charles
Salinger, Pierre
Schlesinger, Marion
Shaw, Maude
Shepard, Tazewell
Shriver, Eunice
Shriver, Sargent
Smathers, George
Sorenson, Theodore
Spalding, Charles
Stedman, Donald
Sutton, Billy
Thomas, George
Thaxton, Cordenia
Travell, Janet
Tretick, Stanley
Tubridgy, Dorothy
Tuckerman, Nancy
Turnure, Pamela
Walton, William
West, James Bernard
Williams, Irwin

Clipping Files

The Washington Star Collection, Jacqueline Kennedy and Kennedy family clippings, 1960–1963, Washingtoniana Collection, Martin Luther King Library, Washington, D.C.

Jacqueline Kennedy clippings, 1960–1963, John F. Kennedy Library, Boston, Massachusetts.

PHOTOGRAPHY CREDITS

ACKNOWLEDGMENTS

The rich institutional knowledge and photographic memory of James Hill, archivist in the John F. Kennedy Library's audio-visual department, made this book possible. In the last two weeks of August 2000, Jim worked with me, day by day, hour by hour, in helping to find the items I searched for as I went through some 60,000 images. Without him, this book could never have happened. Alan Goodrich, chief of the division, was away at the time, but upon his return he also, with his treasury of knowledge, helped in finding and identifying stray items I needed. These people are living proof that, beyond the tasks required of them as federal employees, they carry with them an astounding archive in their minds and in and of themselves are rich resources. June Payne and Maura Fitzgerald were, as always, friends as well as the professionals that they are in the research room at the Kennedy Library. As such, over the years, they have been of tremendous help in guiding me to the most helpful of the oral histories at the library. Of course, the White House photographers, although "just doing their job" as government employees, must also be thanked for their work: the late Abbie Rowe, Cecil Stoughton, and Robert Knudsen.

I also want to thank Max Kennedy for his granting me permission to review and use items from the Robert F. Kennedy Collection in the audio-visual department. Melody Miller, a friend, was as always a great help. She was able to identify many Kennedy family members and friends in the pictures. Yusha Auchincloss, also a friend, was as helpful as ever in providing accurate family information. Shea Van Horne provided an important last-minute photograph. Special appreciation is given to Benno Graziani for his permission to use one of his personal photographs and his transatlantic expedition of it. Without Laila Shereen and Steven Keller aiding me in compiling the bibliography on the last day of writing, and their nightly excursions to the Las Venus Lounge to check in on me, this book would never have been completed. I also wish to thank Nancé Hackscaylo for all of the help she was willing to offer at the lounge in the summer of 2000. I would also like to thank my editor Lisa Drew, assistant editor Jake Klisivitch, production editor Edith Baltazar, copy editor Ravin Gustafson, agent Lisa Bankoff of ICM, her assistant Patrick Price, and my friends and family.

Finally, I thank the late John Kennedy, my former boss at *George* magazine, who shared several amusing anecdotes, quotes, and stories in response to my historically curious inquiries, gently asked. I also thank the late Jacqueline Onassis, who provided copious notes and recollections in response to my inquiries about her White House tenure for the preparation of my two-volume book *First Ladies*.

INDEX